Raceball

HOW THE MAJOR LEAGUES COLONIZED THE BLACK AND LATIN GAME

Rob Ruck

Beacon Press Boston

Beacon Press
25 Beacon Street
Boston, Massachusetts 02108-2892
www.beacon.org

Beacon Press books
are published under the auspices of
the Unitarian Universalist Association of Congregations.

14 13 12 11   8 7 6 5 4 3 2 1

This book is printed on acid-free paper that meets the uncoated paper
ANSI/NISO specifications for permanence as revised in 1992.

Text design by Jody Hanson at Wilsted & Taylor Publishing Services

Library of Congress Cataloging-in-Publication Data

Ruck, Rob.
Raceball : how the major leagues colonized the black and Latin game / Rob Ruck.
p. cm.
Includes bibliographical references and index.
ISBN 978-0-8070-4805-4 (hardcover : alk. paper)
1. Baseball—Social aspects—United States. 2. Discrimination in sports—United
States—History. 3. Baseball—United States—History. 4. Major League Baseball
(Organization)—History. 5. African American baseball players. 6. Hispanic
American baseball players. 7. United States—Social conditions. 8. Latin
America—Social conditions. 9. Caribbean Area—Social conditions. I. Title.
GV867.64.R83 2010

796.357'64—dc22   2010037079

For Maggie

CONTENTS

INTRODUCTION

Thousands of cameras flashed inside a packed Yankee Stadium as New York left-hander C. C. Sabathia rocked back and, with the relaxed delivery that had carried him to the Cy Young Award two years before, prepared to throw the first pitch of the 2009 World Series. Shortstop Jimmy Rollins, leading off for the Philadelphia Phillies, stared back at the Yankees' portly ace. The matchup between these two men marked only the second time that the World Series had begun with an African American on the mound and at the plate. There was just as remarkable a backstory to the moment. Born less than two years apart in racially diverse East Bay communities in California, Sabathia and Rollins had taken startlingly parallel paths to Yankee Stadium that October evening. Neither man would have been there if not for RBI— Reviving Baseball in Inner Cities, a twenty-two-year-old program designed to stem the hemorrhaging of baseball in black America. Sabathia, who has called the dwindling number of African Americans in baseball a crisis, says that the game saved his life. "It took me off the streets . . . kept me focused."[1]

As cameras recorded that first pitch, Rollins, trying to bunt his way on, pushed the ball down the first baseline, right at the Yankees' Mark Teixeira, who tagged him out before he reached the bag. Teixeira, the descendant of Portuguese and Italian immigrants, tossed the ball to second baseman Robinson Cano, who grew up in San Pedro de Macorís, the Caribbean town best known for churning out major league ballplayers. Cano rifled it to Derek Jeter, the son of a biracial couple from Michigan, who relayed it to Alex Rodriguez, a Dominican American who had been so torn between which country to play for in the inaugural 2006 World Baseball Classic that he ended up not playing at all.

While the ball ricocheted around the infield, Johnny Damon, an army brat of Thai, Croatian, and Irish heritage; Dominican Melky Cabrera; and Nick Swisher, a second-generation major leaguer from West Virginia repositioned themselves in the outfield. Puerto Rico's Jorge Posada, one of four Yankees seeking a fourth championship ring, settled back into his crouch behind home plate while Panamanian Mariano Rivera and Dominican Pedro Martínez watched from opposite dugouts. The two pitchers, both destined for the Hall of Fame, switched effortlessly from Spanish to English as they joked with teammates from Puerto Rico, Venezuela, Panama, Mexico, the Dominican Republic, and the United States. Meanwhile, Yankees designated hitter Hideki Matsui, one of two Asians in the Series, worked on his Teddy Roosevelt imitation. Talking softly but carrying a big bat, the player whom Japanese fans call Godzilla would earn Most Valuable Player honors at the Series' end.

Sabathia, the recipient of the largest contract ever paid to a pitcher in the history of baseball, and Rollins, the 2007 National League MVP, were not the only African Americans on the field. Slugger Ryan Howard had powered the defending champion Phillies into the postseason, and shortstop Jeter captained the Yankees as he burnished his own Hall of Fame credentials. The moment was one reminiscent of the United Colors of Benetton advertising campaign, with players of mixed-race and non-European ancestry accounting for almost two-thirds of the starting lineups.

But the array of African Americans, Latinos, and Asians on the field masked a profound irony—African Americans, who had once fought to integrate baseball, have largely left the game. The share of black ballplayers in the major leagues has plunged by two-thirds since its historic high in the late 1970s. And although Major League Baseball's workforce has a new international complexion, its globalization has come at the expense of baseball beyond U.S. borders, especially at the game's withering grass roots.[2] Power remains concentrated in the hands of white owners and front-office personnel. Few African Americans and Hispanic or Latino Americans can be found among the ranks of managers, general managers, and owners. More than half a century after baseball's integration, these positions remain largely white preserves.

Nowhere is the demographic reversal of who plays baseball more evident than in the Caribbean. While African Americans are disappearing from baseball, Latin Americans have stormed major league diamonds in record numbers. African Americans now hold fewer than one-tenth of all big-league roster spots, while Latinos fill more than a quarter of them and make up about half of those in the minor leagues. In the first decade of the twenty-first century, Latinos dominated All-Star lineups, swept individual awards with stunning regularity, and even powered the Boston Red Sox to their first World Series titles since 1918.

David Ortiz and Manny Ramirez were the toast of New England in 2004 as they led the Red Sox's comeback from a three-games-to-none deficit to beat the New York Yankees in the American League Championship Series and go on to win the World Series. Dominicans and Bostonians alike relished their victory over the Yankees. It had not been that way in 1918, the last time the Red Sox had captured the World Series, when the *yanquis* were occupying the Dominican Republic. U.S. Marines had invaded in 1916, a year after seizing Haiti. American troops stayed for eight years on the Dominican side of Hispaniola, longer in Haiti, and returned again in 1965.

It was baseball's Yankees who came to the DR in 2009, when a dozen of the team's Latin players and coaches, including senior vice president Felipe Lopez, visited the presidential palace in Santo Domingo to meet with President Leonel Fernández. The celebration continued that evening: Mariano Rivera, who was on the mound when the Series ended, threw out the ceremonial first pitch to open a Dominican League playoff game at the 16,500-seat Estadio Quisqueya. It was an appropriate salute to the Caribbean nation in the forefront of the Pan-American pastime. It also reflected how much the New York Yankees, a team slow to cross the color line, had adopted Latin players. Their playoff roster included ten Latinos—40 percent of the team—but only three African Americans. Dominicans alone outnumbered their black teammates.

The visit to Santo Domingo was part of a months-long, multinational victory lap that began with the traditional ticker-tape parade up Broadway through the Canyon of Heroes to City Hall. And though they brought their World Series trophy to a few local venues as well as Santo Domingo and then across the Pacific to Japan and China, there was no comparable display in black America. The club did not have a black cohort of players to match its Latin contingent. Nor could its three African American players carry the World Series trophy back to some representative black community in the United States where baseball still resonated. Baseball has become unhinged from daily life in black America, and what few black ballplayers remain are no longer as deeply rooted in black neighborhoods as Latino players are in theirs. Despite what baseball once meant to black America, African Americans currently matter less in baseball than at any time in the last fifty years.

The Latin wave, on the other hand, has yet to crest. The Dominican Republic alone contributed as many players to baseball's final four playoff teams in 2009 as the entire African American community, even though the United States' 38 million African Americans outnumber Dominicans four to one. Overall, playoff rosters had twice as many Latinos and Hispanic Americans as African Americans. The disparities are even greater across the major and minor leagues. Although an increasing number of players, like U.S. citizens overall, have multiracial identities, these trends are stark and undeniable.[3] African Americans, of course, have not abandoned sport. The starting lineups in the 2010 National Football League and National Basketball Association championships were at least 70 percent African American. By contrast with the paltry number of black baseball players, African Americans constitute two-thirds of all players in the NFL and three-quarters of the NBA.[4]

Meanwhile, the spectacular trajectory of Latinos in baseball has been marred by controversy. Salsa and merengue may reverberate in locker rooms and in the stands from San Diego to the Bronx, and the impact of Latin players might be at an historic high, but so are the problems and tensions they face. The Latin brand in baseball has been badly buffeted in recent years.

Notable Latin stars have plummeted from grace. The 2009 season began with Alex Rodriguez, the most highly paid player in baseball history, confessing that he had taken performance-enhancing drugs earlier in his career. Later that season, similar admissions ensnared both David Ortiz, the exuberant home-run-hitting icon embraced throughout Red Sox Nation as "Big Papi," and his former teammate, Manny Ramirez, perhaps the game's most feared hitter. Sammy Sosa, whose 1998 home-run-hitting duel with Mark McGwire revived baseball after the 1994 lockout resulted in cancellation of that year's World Series, has been tainted, too. A decade ago, Sosa and McGwire seemed certain to be inducted into the Hall of Fame; now, neither will likely reach Cooperstown.

Signs of discord between Latino and black players have also surfaced. In 2007, Gary Sheffield, a veteran African American player with over five hundred home runs, brought simmering black-Latin tensions in baseball to a boil when he accused teams of favoring Latinos because they were easier to control than black players. "You're going to see more black faces, but there ain't no English going to be coming out," he told GQ magazine. Latinos, he implied, did not stand up for themselves and had unfairly usurped the place of African Americans of equal playing ability.[5] "[It's about] being able to tell [Latin players] what to do—being able to control them," the former New York Yankee claimed. African Americans, he argued, demanded more respect. "Where I'm from, you can't control us . . . So if you're equally good as this Latin player, guess who's going to get sent home?"

Latin ballplayers protested the charge. Atlanta Braves coach Eddie Pérez, a native of Venezuela, said: "I don't think we're taking anybody's food off the table. We're just putting food on the table for us." Latin players made lots of money, he contended, because they were good and played hard. And, in a backhand slap at Sheffield, he added: "You don't hear too many Latin players talk a lot of trash."[6]

Nobody has accused Los Angeles Angels outfielder Torii Hunter, 2009 recipient of the Branch Rickey Award for community service, of talking trash. But he became embroiled in a similar squabble on the eve of the 2010 season when he made the following contention: "People see dark faces out there, and the perception is that they're African-American. They're not us. They're impostors." Like Sheffield, he said that financial disparities between African American and Latino players were driving blacks out of baseball. "As African-American players, we have a theory that baseball can go get an imitator and pass them off as us," he said. "It's like they had to get some kind of dark faces, so they go to the Dominican or Venezuela because you can get them cheaper. It's like, 'Why should I get this kid from the South Side of Chicago and have [agent] Scott Boras represent him and pay him $5 million when you can get a Dominican guy for a bag of chips?' . . . I'm telling you, it's sad."[7]

Sadder still, baseball throughout the Caribbean has been wracked by political passions and global recession. In Venezuela, a few major league organizations have curtailed operations because they fear President Hugo

Chávez's militant populism and a deteriorating social climate in which players have been assaulted or kidnapped. Winter leagues elsewhere in the region have struggled at the gate, with the Puerto Rican league suspending play for a season. Nor have the region's teams met expectations in the World Baseball Classic. The Dominican Republic has yet to advance past the semifinals. In the 2009 Classic, the Netherlands humbled the DR, not once but twice. The Netherlands! Japan won the inaugural games and triumphed again in 2009. Meanwhile, growing numbers of the Caribbean's best players leave their own leagues and head for the United States.

More serious issues than defeats in international competition plague baseball in the islands. The grass roots of the game have been scorched as major league organizations and "agents" known as *buscones* corral players at younger and younger ages. These kids are usually dirt-poor, enthralled by the game, and incredibly vulnerable. For every one of them who reaches the majors, hundreds fall by the wayside and have little to fall back upon. The emergence of the *buscones*, who number over one thousand in the Dominican Republic, has altered patterns of player procurement and encouraged widespread and unscrupulous manipulation of youth by those seeking to profit from their athletic talents. As Dominican scandals involving steroids and age violations splashed across the U.S. sporting pages, fans questioned Caribbean baseball's ethical moorings.

At times it seems as if everybody is trying to game the system, one that Major League Baseball has controlled and profited from since its belated and hesitant integration over sixty years ago. Though MLB is currently attempting to bring order and transparency to the player-procurement system, it has been complicit in that system's worst abuses. It ignored these problems as they festered and only adopted a reformer's posture after its image and the lives of many young men were damaged.

The histories of African Americans and Latinos in baseball have been inextricably linked for over a century, first by their mutual exclusion from the major leagues, then by integration. For major league baseball, no moment was more transformative than Jackie Robinson's arrival in 1947. African Americans and Latinos have since reshaped the game. Together, they have provided the sport with its most iconic figures, won far more than their share of individual honors, and been at the core of almost every championship team since 1947, with the exception of the New York Yankees of the 1950s and '60s. Integration also gave license to Major League Baseball to proclaim that it had overcome the six-decade-long color line that had disfigured the "national pastime." Robinson's triumph was offered as proof of the United States' capacity to resolve its historic racial contradictions.

But the symbolism of integrated and increasingly international play tells only part of the story. Major League Baseball's drive for profit and control—not its desire to rectify historic wrongs—led it to accept integration. That same lust to maximize revenues and exert dominion over players and rivals has shaped its actions in regard to black America and the Caribbean ever since.

The history of African Americans and Latinos in baseball has traditionally been portrayed as a tale of their shameful segregation and redemptive integration. Segregation was certainly shameful, especially for a sport so heavily invested in its own rhetoric of democracy and American exceptionalism. But for African Americans and Latinos, integration was also painful. Although long overdue and a catalyst to social change, integration cost black and Caribbean societies control over their own sporting lives. It changed the meaning of sport, and not usually for the better. While channeling black and Latino athletes into major league baseball, integration did little for the communities they left behind. On the contrary, it actively destroyed or weakened institutions in the black community and the Caribbean.

With the launching of the World Baseball Classic in 2006 and the appearance of an astonishing array of nationalities and races in the World Series, major league baseball seems to have become what it has long proclaimed it was: a global game played on a level playing field for men of all races and nations. But it's not as democratic and progressive as it claims to be. Nor has it ever been. Today more than ever, Major League Baseball sets the parameters for African Americans and Latinos in baseball. The major leagues, not black America or the Caribbean, benefit the most from their participation. By imposing its imperial will on black America and the Caribbean, MLB has achieved unprecedented prosperity, but gutted the game at the grass roots along the way. Baseball has never been stronger as a business, never weaker as a game. It didn't have to be that way.

CHAPTER ONE

The Gospel of Baseball

Baseball's future as an international game, one free of racial constraint, could scarcely have been imagined in the early 1900s. But there it was, on display in Havana, Cuba. That was not the case in the United States, where the backlash to Reconstruction had forced African Americans out of major league baseball by the 1890s. Racial divisions in the United States grew even fiercer during the new century; by comparison, Cuba became a showcase for multiracial, international play. Cuba was no racial utopia, but the Liga Cubana was an anomaly, the only place in the world where the best professional ballplayers of all nations and colors competed with and against each other. The island game approximated the idealized vision of baseball often evoked but rarely attained in the United States. It offered Cubans the fullest realization yet of what José Martí, the architect of their independence struggle, had hoped to achieve: a nation for all.

Baseball had already taken on a mythic cast in both the United States and Cuba by the twentieth century. The game's proponents in the States gushed about its progressive, democratizing effects. "I see great things in baseball," Walt Whitman wrote in 1889. "It's our game—the American game." Whitman compared baseball to the U.S. Constitution, arguing that it was "just as important in the sum total of our historic life."[1] For Mark Twain, baseball was "the very symbol, the outward and visible expression of the drive and push and rush and struggle of the raging, tearing, booming nineteenth century." During World War I, National League president and former Pennsylvania governor John Tener declared that "baseball is the very watchword of democracy." Nothing under heaven, he pronounced, had such a leveling influence. "Neither the public school nor the church can approach it. Baseball is unique."[2]

Such sentiments resonated with Cubans, for whom baseball had become a symbol of "American" modernity and democracy as they sought to end Spanish colonial rule. Despite the rise of Jim Crow and a spate of lynchings in the United States during the 1890s, Cubans had taken to their northern neighbor's national pastime with fervor. It would become part of their struggle for independence.

During the second half of the nineteenth century, upheaval and conflict roiled the island. By the end of the Ten Years' War, an unsuccessful prelude to Cuban independence that lasted from 1868 to 1878, the island was more dependent on the United States' economy than it was on Spain's. By the time Cuban slavery whimpered into oblivion in 1886, almost all of Cuba's sugar and tobacco was bound for U.S. ports. Thousands of U.S. ships, in turn, arrived annually in Havana Harbor.[3]

As Cuba's economy and infrastructure became tied to the United States, Spanish influence became ever more problematic. Colonialism blocked Cubans from controlling their island's resources and impeded economic modernization. When insurgency erupted in 1895, Spain dug in, refusing to relinquish one of its last New World possessions. It garrisoned several hundred thousand troops there, far more than it had ever deployed to suppress rebellions elsewhere in its empire. The fighting, economic uncertainty, and Spanish repression convinced many Cubans to flee, at least temporarily, to the United States, where they joined thousands of their compatriots already living abroad as students, workers, and merchants. Sizable Cuban enclaves developed in Key West, Tampa, New Orleans, Philadelphia, and New York City. Other Cubans left for Venezuela, Mexico, and the Dominican Republic.

Baseball was on the rise in the United States during the heights of the Cuban diaspora. Although the game was initially played primarily in the Northeast, during the Civil War men from all parts of the country had been exposed to baseball in the military, where it was played during lulls between battles. When peace came, they returned home and formed teams in hundreds of towns and cities. The rules varied greatly. How many innings to a game, whether a batter was out if he was "soused" (hit by a thrown ball when he was between bases), and other conventions of play differed from town to town.

Players occasionally pocketed a few dollars or received jobs to play, but the game was considered an amateur activity until the creation of the first professional ball club, the Cincinnati Red Stockings, in 1869. After an early effort to form a professional league fell apart, the National League emerged in 1876. Its 1903 alliance with the rival American League laid the foundation of Major League Baseball. Organized baseball, as it is often called, has attempted to exert a monopoly over the professional game and its players ever since. By the early 1900s, with a strong professional league in place and baseball played on sandlots across the land, the ever more culturally cohesive United States had its national pastime.

So, too, would Cuba. Cubans living in the United States could not help but be affected by their host nation's embrace of the game. Many expats played on college, sandlot, and factory teams and brought baseball back to the island in their newly acquired cultural baggage. In 1864 a student named Nemesio Guilló carried a ball and bat home to Cuba from Spring Hill College in Mobile, Alabama. Four years later, Guilló became a co-founder of the Habana Base Ball Club. Within a decade, Cubans who had studied at Fordham College formed Almendares, which would become Cuba's other legendary club and Habana's eternal rival.[4] These men didn't just bring home a new game; they evangelized for what historian Louis A. Pérez Jr. called "a paradigm of progress."[5]

The experience of Cuban expatriates and the growing U.S. presence on the island had prompted a reexamination of what being Cuban meant. The United States offered a fresh, dynamic, and democratic model of the future unlike that of stagnant Spain. Baseball, as part of this embrace of many things American, became common ground for independence-minded Cubans and their North American neighbors. It did not take long before Cubans made baseball into their own game.

Baseball in Cuba was similar to the game then being played in the United States in that the professionals had yet to completely take over. Although professional baseball—loosely defined—appeared in Cuba by

1878, most teams were organized by social clubs strictly segregated by race and class. Amateurism has often been an ambiguous concept in sport, suffused with class distinctions and used by elites to keep the riffraff out of their recreations. In Cuba, the social clubs also blocked Afro-Cubans from membership. Slavery's abolition in 1886 and Cuban independence in 1902 would do little to change this.

For club members, baseball was part of a social ethos. There was a sense of refinement and decorum at games, where female fans sat close by the field in the shade of the *glorieta*, a trellised pavilion or gazebo with a zinc roof, and dined and danced with players afterward. Such a genteel version of baseball displayed status, but only better-off whites could join. Even if club members might have tolerated Afro-Cubans or those from humble backgrounds on their playing fields, they were unwilling to accept them afterward at their dinners and dances.

Those who watched from the stands were a scruffier mix. For despite baseball's elite origins—a function of the better-off having the leisure time to play—the masses had quickly adopted the game. Neither finding a place to play nor access to equipment—usually homemade gear scraped together by the players—was an obstacle.

As more and more déclassé Cubans embraced baseball, its commercialization quickened. Cubans formed their first league, the Liga General de Base Ball de la Isla de Cuba, in 1878, only two years after the creation of the National League in the United States. Its inaugural campaign was more of a championship series than a season of play. Habana, Almendares, and a team from the city of Matanzas met in a brief tournament of games played on Sundays and holidays and the players on the winning squad—Habana—received silver medals as their rewards. No blacks played for any of the clubs.

Amateur clubs proliferated in the capital city of Havana as well as in the provinces; even free Afro-Cubans formed teams of their own. Soon, companies sponsoring teams began hiring men for their ball-playing abilities. Players blithely jumped clubs for greater inducements, and a few professionals were imported from the United States. By the mid-1890s, some teams were salaried while others operated as cooperatives, sharing the proceeds, if there were any. Promoters sold concessions, a sporting press developed, and the Cuban rum company Bacardi sponsored play.

Most Cubans, ineligible to participate in the private social club teams, gravitated to semipro and professional baseball organized by factories, sugar mills, and entrepreneurs. So did the fans, who saw players who were more like themselves in socioeconomic background and appearance.

As violence ebbed in the 1880s and many émigrés returned home, baseball's hold on island culture tightened. More than two hundred Cuban clubs took to baseball diamonds by the 1890s, most of them self-organized, noncommercial ventures. In the provinces, baseball was played mostly during the *tiempo muerto* in the summer, when the sugarcane crops required minimal attention. Merchant ship crews played during layovers in port while Bethlehem Steel and the Pennsylvania Steel Company, both of which had mining operations on the island, fielded teams made up of their foreign-born workers. Cuban teams steamed to Key West and points north to play, while North American clubs like the Hop Bitters from Rochester, New York, and the Athletics from Philadelphia visited the island.

Spain, however, remained in charge on the island, where baseball and the United States were seen by many Cubans as the antithesis of bullfighting and the mother country. José Martí dismissed bullfighting, and by inference Spain, as "intimately linked with our colonial past." Wenceslao Gálvez y Delmonte, an early advocate of baseball, viewed bullfighting with equal scorn, calling it "a barbaric spectacle."[6] Baseball, in stark contrast, was idealized as a sport in which all distinctions of class, race, even gender (due to its popularity among women spectators) could be set aside, where mobility and freedom prevailed. The game brought the humble and the highly born together and was, as Benjamin de Cespedes, a physician and author, called it in 1899, "a rehearsal for democracy."[7]

But the Spanish were unwilling to allow these rehearsals to take place. Their colonial representatives in Havana had temporarily banned the game in 1869 and again in 1873. Further, they refused to allow teams to adopt names too redolent of resistance to colonial rule, and dissolved at least one club for fomenting anti-Spanish militancy. A team in Havana was not allowed to call itself Yara, because authorities thought the name invoked *El Grito de Yara* (the Cry of Yara), the proclamation that ignited rebellion in 1868. Another club drew their wrath for calling itself Anacaona, after the Taína Indian chieftain who died opposing the Spanish conquest of Hispaniola. In 1881, overwrought officials disbanded a team in Cardenas because they feared its practices were schooling players in insurrectionary tactics.

Spanish officials warily monitored the first United States club to visit. The Hop Bitters, whose purpose was to promote the products of their sponsor, a patent medicine company, arrived in Cuba soon after the end of the Ten Years' War. When manager Frank Bancroft tried to distribute U.S. flags with HOP BITTERS printed on them, he was picked up for interrogation. The colonial authorities released Bancroft only after he agreed to desist from handing out the flags, which they feared might spur rebellion.[8]

Far from embracing baseball as a diversion from politics, a form of *pan y circo* like the gladiator competitions of ancient Rome, Spanish authorities saw the game as inciting resistance. Although baseball offered a safer way of expressing one's opposition to Spain than overt politicking, it was deemed too subversive to be allowed when hostilities resumed. After the Cuban War for Independence commenced in February 1895, Spanish authorities again banned the game across the island. They knew that many *independentistas* had tied baseball to their movement in rhetoric and deed. Émigrés in Key West and Caracas used ball games to raise money and rally support for the fight against Spain. On the island, players and former players picked up arms and held leadership positions in rebel ranks. Among the most prominent was Emilio Sabourín, who had played and managed for the Habana Base Ball Club and helped establish professional baseball on the island. The Spanish apprehended Sabourín, then deported him to El Castillo del Hacha in Ceuta, Spain's North African penal colony, where he died of pneumonia.

Frustratingly for the Spanish, the more they railed against baseball and its proponents, the more they elevated the game's political profile. "Baseball," historian Louis A. Pérez Jr. argues, "had become identified with the cause of *Cuba Libre*, fully integrated into the mystique and the metaphysics of national liberation."[9] Playing baseball had itself become an act of defiance to Spanish rule.

Rebellion came to a head in 1898. Soon after the mysterious explosion aboard the USS *Maine* in Havana Harbor in February, the United States entered the war. Its navy quickly smashed the Spanish fleet in the Philippines, while Teddy Roosevelt's Rough Riders subdued Spanish forces in

Cuba and Puerto Rico. But the end of Spain's reign did not mean Cuba was free; the United States was unwilling to allow a truly independent republic to emerge so close to its shores, especially one where many U.S. businesses operated.

The United States compromised Cuba's independence from birth by insisting that its constitution include the infamous Platt Amendment, which made Cuba a virtual protectorate and gave the United States the right to intervene to maintain internal order and supervise the republic's foreign affairs. The United States used this rationale to send the Marines back in between 1906 and 1909, in 1912, and again between 1917 and 1922. All the while, U.S. occupation forces sought to impose their own rigidly segregated notions of race on the island. Some Cubans wondered if they had traded one master for another.

Cubans wrestled with U.S. occupation forces over how racially inclusive and egalitarian postcolonial Cuba would be. During three wars and thirty years of struggle, historian Alejandro de la Fuente writes, "Cubans of all colors and social origins had created a formidable cross-racial coalition and forged a nationalist revolutionary ideology that claimed all Cubans were equal members of the nation, regardless of race or social status."[10] Baseball could fulfill that vision. According to Louis Pérez, "Baseball offered the possibility of national integration of all Cubans, of all classes, black and white, young and old, men and women." Even women found legitimacy at the ballpark, and thus a way to enter the public sphere though sporting crowds. Unlike at bullfighting matches, women were welcomed at games.[11]

The Liberation Army, which had featured Afro-Cuban leaders, had great cachet after Spain's defeat. For these fighters, racial equality was an article of faith. But the U.S. Army, not the Liberation Army, now ruled the island, and occupation authorities sneered at the thought of Cubans, especially black Cubans, governing themselves. When possible, the United States blocked social change on the island. They were joined in these efforts by some of the Cuban elite, which had been pro-Spanish due to their fear of the Liberation Army's black leadership and the specter of a black republic.

Conflict over race inevitably spilled onto the ball field, where disputes over the inclusion of black players and professionalism came to a head in

1900. There were too many good black players in the semipro and sugar leagues (the latter run by the sugarcane factories) and too much potential profit to be made in selling the game to maintain these de facto restrictions. For most fans and players, professional baseball proved far more popular than amateur ball. A more racially inclusive, professional, and commercial brand of baseball won out with the creation of a new league. The Liga Cubana included one all-black club, named San Francisco, and three racially mixed squads: Habana, Almendarista, and Cubano. Augustín "Tintí" Molina and José Poyo directed Cubano. Molina, a key figure in Cuban baseball, would later bring Negro League players from the U.S. to the island. Poyo's father had been José Martí's secretary in Tampa and Key West, where he organized ball clubs to raise money and enthusiasm for the independence struggle. For some of the men involved with the league, baseball continued to hold political meanings tied to notions of a new, independent Cuba. Others looked at it as business.

Those who could not accept playing baseball with darker-skinned and less-affluent Cubans sought refuge in the amateur baseball world still controlled by social clubs. This sector of baseball would survive until the 1959 revolution and mean much to its players and fans, but its development lagged that of the pro game.

The U.S. occupation spread baseball even more. In an ironic turnabout from Spanish rule, the U.S. banned bullfighting but looked favorably on baseball. Even as some Cubans, unwilling to substitute the United States for Spain, fought the North Americans in the mountains, others played against them on baseball diamonds. When North American ballplayers arrived in Havana, they found plenty of eager opponents.

•   •   •

By World War I, Havana had become the baseball world's hub. The port on Cuba's northwestern coast had been the Caribbean basin's most important city since the sixteenth century, when it was settled as San Cristóbal de la Habana. Once a colonial trading post situated near maritime routes central to the Gulf of Mexico, it now facilitated the traffic of people, product, and ideas across a network of Atlantic ports. In these cities, the most dynamic parts of North America and the Caribbean, baseball had penetrated most quickly and most deeply. As far north as New York City, as far south as Caracas, in Tampa, Key West, and by rail to Mexico City, Pittsburgh, Chicago, and California, this sporting world included a have-glove, will-travel motley crew of Cubans, African Americans, assorted Latin Americans, and white U.S. citizens. These men traveled by steamer and railroad, and played ball for a living. In the United States, they performed in the interracial zones of cities full of black and tan cabarets, sandlot ball, and immigrants living cheek by jowl.

Greater Havana was home to a quarter of a million people by the turn of the century, a significant share of the island's overall population of 1.5 million. Like most port cities, it was a mix of people from its own hinterland and faraway places. The end of hostilities and the expansion of U.S. investments in Cuba attracted new waves of immigrants from Europe and the Caribbean. More than two hundred thousand Spaniards and tens of thousands of Canary Islanders, Chinese, Dominicans, Panamanians, Haitians, Puerto Ricans, and Jamaicans arrived on the island to set up shop, build railroads, and cut cane. Havana doubled in size to half a million people by 1925 as Cuba's already diverse racial spectrum became ever more multihued.

The Spaniards, mostly from Galicia and Asturias, brought soccer with them, and their sport rivaled baseball in some neighborhoods during the 1920s and 1930s. But most of these immigrants gravitated to baseball diamonds, not soccer pitches. It became their way of becoming Cuban. The names of Cuban ballplayers, as Roberto González Echevarría, Sterling Professor of Hispanic and Comparative Literature at Yale, observes, reflected their varied origins: Almeida and Pascual from Galicia, Marsans from Catalonia, Marrero and Guerra from the Canary Islands. Black Cubans like Dihigo and Méndez had the surnames of their families' former Castilian slave owners, while Leroux and Taylor denoted Haiti and Jamaica.[12]

• • •

The U.S. military was not the only foreign force occupying Cuba at war's end. An army of North American investors and businessmen stormed the island as soon as the struggle for independence came to its conflicted resolution. Professional ballplayers—especially black ones—were not far behind, arriving on steamers from Key West.

While U.S. corporations increasingly monopolized Cuba's lucrative sugar industry and seized control of the island's infrastructure, the invading ballplayers faced stiffer resistance. Cubans, not North Americans, controlled the island's nascent baseball industry and set the terms of engagement.

Most importantly, Cubans had cultivated the market and owned the venues. They had built Havana's ballparks—Almendares, Oriental, La Boulanger, and later La Tropical—and determined who played there. Cubans promoted the games, brought crowds to the stands, and set the conditions in which major leaguers, Negro Leaguers, and Cubans played. The major leaguers and Negro Leaguers received top compensation, especially in contests highlighting the clash of *Norteamericanos contra Cubanos*, but the gringos could not dictate terms to Cuban promoters and opponents. Of course, when Cuban teams ventured to the United States, they reversed roles and relied on promoters like Negro National League founder Rube Foster and Irish American booking agent Nat Strong, who controlled access to venues in the Midwest and Northeast.

Cuban promoters and visiting teams and ballplayers occasionally haggled over terms and cussed each other out if they felt the other party was trying to take unfair advantage. The foreigners fought for more money while the Cubans castigated those who evinced more interest in drinking and whoring than baseball. But it was a win-win situation for both parties. Havana was a profitable winter market with terrific weather and a cosmopolitan ambience—the city was known, after all, as the Paris of the Caribbean. Ballplayers and owners alike in the early twentieth century needed to make a living in the winter. The only protests came from Major League Baseball higher-ups who objected after Cuban teams started regularly beating visiting major league clubs. They feared a loss of prestige and the devaluation of their brand of baseball in the marketplace. Negro Leaguers did not share such anxieties. For them, Cuba was a place to play ball; happily, it was also a place with far fewer racial restrictions than the U.S.

Cuba had never had a higher profile in the United States than at the turn of the century. The Cuban independence struggle had aroused popular passions there, fueled by early yellow-press campaigns to sell papers via anti-Spanish tirades. Strong sentiment backed U.S. intervention. In the flush of victory, U.S. ambassador to Great Britain John Hay wrote his friend Teddy Roosevelt that it had been a "splendid little war from start to finish."[13] After it ended in a quick and overwhelming victory for U.S. forces, baseball fans in the States could follow Cuban baseball on the pages of the sporting press.

U.S. teams heading to Cuba became unofficial missionaries of American cultural imperialism at a time when the nation was extending its empire. Almost a century before the rest of the world wanted to "Be like Mike," wear Air Jordans, and soar through the air, American athletes were spreading soft power abroad.

For some, U.S. influence in Cuba was part of the "white man's burden" to civilize darker-skinned races. The Reverend E. P. Herrick wrote of preparing "the children of the Antilles" for "the duties and responsibilities of citizenship." His coreligionist, Howard Grose, declared: "What a distance they must be lifted, if they are to reach a real Christian civilization."[14] Baseball, its boosters argued, would spread American culture and values around the globe. Everybody but African Americans, who had been pushed out of the majors in the United States by then, were deemed to be worthy of its civilizing effects. Even Afro-Cubans might benefit, as long as they stayed in Cuba or stuck to the Negro Leagues when in the United States.[15]

A. G. Spalding, the former player turned owner and sporting goods magnate, had sold baseball gear in Cuba even before the war. One of the first to recognize the commercial advantages in baseball's globalization, Spalding had taken two teams on an around-the-world tour in 1888. In 1906 he began publishing his *Spalding Guide* in Spanish, with rules, photos, and narratives of the game's development in the Caribbean. Cuba quickly became baseball's—and Spalding's—best foreign market. Though no Americans had played during the 1900 Cuban professional season (it was held during the summer, when it conflicted with the major league season in the United States), North American ball clubs soon began arriving after the World Series each season, ready to play and to profit.

The Cuban X-Giants, an African American team, visited Havana for the first time in 1900 and played a series of exhibitions against Cuban teams. The practice of African American ballplayers calling themselves and their teams "Cuban" dated back many years. It reflected the cachet that Cuba had acquired in North American baseball circles and the more tolerant attitude that white Americans had regarding Cubans than they had toward African Americans. Modern historians have argued that these black teams called themselves Cuban in order to be more racially acceptable in white venues. If so, their efforts met with mixed success. While sometimes able to pass themselves off as dark-skinned foreigners bringing a touch of the exotic to town, a club calling themselves the Cuban Giants had not fooled Irish fans in New York City during the summer of 1886. A mob, irate over the effort to deceive them, chased the Cuban Giants off the field in Williamsburg. Elsewhere, sportswriters ripped them with nasty racial invective for trying to pass as Cubans. In Havana, of course, the Cuban X-Giants made no pretense of being anybody but who they were, and played against integrated Cuban teams.

The number of teams in the Cuban League varied annually and its season was shorter than in the United States, but crowds frequently surpassed ten thousand fans at a time when major league clubs often drew far fewer to games. A cohort of promoters—men like Abel Linares, Tintí Molina, and Alejandro Pompez—helped build Cuban baseball and craft its relations with North America. Those relations were becoming especially strong with the burgeoning network of black teams that would give rise to the Negro Leagues in the U.S. Cuban teams began barnstorming through the United States during the summer, while African American ballplayers, including the Negro National League's Rube Foster, arrived on the island each winter. Foster, who also pitched for a Cuban team called Fe, was part of a sporting cross-fertilization that brought the best of the black and Latino baseball world together.

• • •

A 1906 revolt against the Cuban government caused the U.S. military to return and occupy Cuba through 1909. Baseball during the occupation inevitably took on political overtones. Cuba's 1907 pro season featured more gringos than ever before, including several white major leaguers and African Americans who would later win election to the Hall of Fame. When Almendares, with its mostly Cuban lineup, beat Fe, a team

José de la Caridad Méndez
(National Baseball Hall of Fame Library, Cooperstown, NY). Date: unknown. José de la Caridad Méndez, who became a Cuban icon in 1908 after shutting out the Cincinnati Reds for twenty-five consecutive innings during winter play, also led the Kansas City Monarchs to victory in the first Negro League World Series, in 1924.

composed mostly of black Americans, the press ridiculed the losers as *los intervencionistas* and fans hailed the game as a victory by Cuba over the United States. Promoters, meanwhile, cheered the large box-office gate it attracted. There was money to be made in casting sport as a *yanqui-cubano* conflict.[16]

These victories over North Americans and the feats of Cubans in them became part of the island's political mythology. Each season brought new heroes. Some, like ballplayers José de la Caridad Méndez, Adolfo Luque, Cristóbal Torriente, and Martín Dihigo, became idols whose stories would be told and retold, refined and embellished, as they were passed down from parents to children.

There was no bigger Cuban icon in sport than José de la Caridad Méndez. The son of an artisan, he was born in the town of Cárdenas in Matanzas province in 1887, a year after slavery's abolition. Like many in Matanzas, Méndez was Afro-Cuban. Though trained as a carpenter and able to play the clarinet and guitar, he was a baseball prodigy who began playing with adults when he was thirteen years old. Slender and short, he threw several different pitches with speed and exceptional control.[17]

After premiering in the Cuban League in early 1908, Méndez imprinted himself on Cuban consciousness after a spell of sensational pitching that fall. The Cincinnati Reds and the Brooklyn Royal Giants, a black team, had come to Havana to play against each other as well as against Habana and Almendares. Though any number of Cuban and black Americans excelled in the "American season," as the late-fall multinational exhibitions were dubbed, Méndez captured his compatriots' imagination more than any Cuban athlete yet.

He did it by shutting out the Cincinnati Reds for twenty-five consecutive innings. Méndez began his feat by no-hitting the Reds into the ninth inning in their first encounter before surrendering an infield single. A few days later, he appeared in relief and blanked Cincinnati for another seven innings. He then shut them out again, running his streak of scoreless pitching to twenty-five innings. After a home-and-away series with semipros from Key West, Méndez had posted forty-five scoreless innings. His place in Cuban baseball lore was inviolable from that moment. That he triumphed against North Americans at a moment when the United States was reoccupying Cuba suffused his accomplishments with patriotic energy. Baseball, with its level playing field, was the one arena where Cubans could compete with the United States and win.

Méndez's deification ran counter to the vicious attacks on black rights, including the suppression of Afro-Cuban religious practices, mounted by the U.S. military and elements of the Cuban elite during the occupation. But while Méndez was triumphant on the ball field, a virulent scientific racism was beginning to win out throughout Europe, the United States, and Latin America. Fierce debates raged on the island over immigration policies designed to "whiten" Cuba by encouraging European immigration while discouraging entry of those from darker-skinned places.

But there was no mistaking the African origins of Cuba's greatest sporting hero. One of his early nicknames, "Congo," reflected the dark hue of his skin and his African heritage. Méndez's name, de la Caridad, signified that he had been entrusted at birth to the Virgen de la Caridad del Cobre, Cuba's patron saint. *La Virgen*, Roberto González Echevarría notes, also represented the Afro Cuban *orisha* (deity) Ochún, a powerful Yoruba god. Méndez, González Echevarría concludes, became "the very embodiment of the Cuban nation" and its struggle for independence.[18] That Cuba's paladin was Afro-Cuban reinforced the centrality of Afro-Cubans and racial egalitarianism in that struggle. After beating the Americans at their own game, Mendez was no longer Congo but *El Diamante Negro* (the Black Diamond). Still, the triumphs of Afro-Cuban Méndez were not enough to stop the massacre of Partido Independiente de Color activists and other Afro-Cubans in 1912.[19] Nor did they correct other forms of discrimination.[20]

With all-native squads beating teams made up of American professionals and Méndez's emergence as the island's most popular player, the game's appeal as a symbol of the new Cuba strengthened. Egalitarianism on the playing field meshed with the 1901 Cuban constitutional convention that had adopted universal male suffrage despite resistance from Cuban elites and the U.S. occupation government. Universal suffrage, historian Alejandro de la Fuente observes, was rare in societies with significant numbers of blacks. Cuba also desegregated public education; as with professional baseball, Cuba anticipated comparable civil rights changes in the United States by more than half a century. Indeed, while the United States was sliding backward on race relations in the wake of the infamous 1896 *Plessy v. Ferguson* Supreme Court decision, with its noxious notion of "separate but equal," many Cubans were determined to move forward.[21]

Cubans surpassed the United States on the ball field too. Major league teams lost more frequently than they won in Cuba before World War I. The Detroit Tigers, minus Sam Crawford and Ty Cobb, lost eight of twelve games to Cuban teams in 1909; the 1910 pennant-winning Philadelphia Athletics dropped six of ten a year later. Granted, the visiting major league clubs sometimes lacked key players, and the psychological stakes were higher for the Cubans, especially with U.S. troops occupying the island. Still, losing rankled owners and American League president Ban Johnson banned league teams from barnstorming Cuba as intact squads. "We want no makeshift club calling themselves the Athletics to go to Cuba to be beaten by colored teams," he rationalized.[22] Losing to Cubans was not meant to be part of the white man's burden.

But the lure of profit kept all sorts of U.S. teams coming to Cuba. Negro League, major league, and independent teams arrived each winter until World War I interrupted. Virtually every Negro Leaguer who would be elected to the Hall of Fame—Rube Foster, John Henry Lloyd, Oscar Charleston, Pete Hill, Smokey Joe Williams, Willie Foster, Cool Papa Bell, Satchel Paige, Josh Gibson, Buck Leonard, Judy Johnson, Monte Irvin, and Ray Dandridge—and many a major leaguer who would join them in Cooperstown—including John McGraw, Walter Johnson, Ty Cobb, Babe Ruth, and Christy Mathewson—played or managed on the island. They competed with and against the best Cubans and Latino players, such as future Hall of Famers Martín Dihigo, Cristóbal Torriente, and Méndez. For several decades, no other place on earth boasted such a diverse and talented collection of ballplayers.

These winter exchanges exposed Major League Baseball figures like Frank Bancroft, who took the first American team to Cuba, and John Mc-Graw, the pugnacious Hall of Fame manager, to the caliber of Cuban play as well as the money to be made there. Despite his earlier rough handling at the hands of Spanish interrogators for distributing American flags emblazoned with a sponsor's name, Bancroft returned to the island in 1910 with the Philadelphia Athletics. He spoke so highly of infielder Rafael Almeida and other Cuban ballplayers he encountered that the Cincinnati Reds signed Almeida and his teammate, outfielder Armando Marsans. The team launched a preemptive strike on those stateside who might have challenged these two players' racial heritage by stressing their privileged-class background and Spanish and Portuguese lineage. The Reds described them as "pure Spaniards, without a trace of colored blood." A *Cincinnati Enquirer* journalist called the two "descendants of a noble Spanish race, with no ignoble African blood to place a blot or spot on their escutcheons. Permit me to introduce two of the purest bars of Castilian soap that ever floated to these shores."[23]

Manager John McGraw had tried to sign a Cuban player on a trip in 1899. He began taking the New York Giants to Cuba each winter before World War I and found Havana so agreeable that he started to winter there whenever possible. In 1919, he and the Giants' new owner, Charles Stoneham, bought part-interest in Oriental Park, which sat in the town of Marianao on Havana's western edge. Oriental Park had hosted the infamous 1915 prizefight during which African American boxer Jack Johnson lost (or perhaps threw) the heavyweight title to Jess Willard. Often used for horseracing, it was suitable for baseball too. McGraw, a feisty competitor known as Little Napoleon, cared little about race or nationality when confronted with a ballplayer who could help his squad or wallet. In 1901 he had tried to pass off Charlie Grant, a light-skinned African American, as a Native American named Chief Tokahoma and have him play for the Giants. But the exuberance of black fans blew Grant's cover.[24] In Cuba, such racial deception was unnecessary.

●　●　●

Baseball, which had played such a strong role gluing together resistance to Spain, now tied Havana to the provinces and Cuba to a larger world. As teams traveled around the island as well as to Tampa, Key West, Mexico's Yucatán Peninsula, and points beyond, Cuban baseball blossomed. So did Cuban music and dance, which, like baseball, were infused with Afro-Cuban culture and became the island's emissaries to the outside world. And as Cuban baseball spread abroad, it carried its multiracial makeup with it.

Although the United States invaded Caribbean basin countries on more than a score of occasions in the early twentieth century, it was not chiefly responsible for spreading baseball throughout the region. Cubans, not U.S. Marines, brought baseball to the Dominican Republic, Venezuela, Puerto Rico, and the Yucatán. Pedro Julio Santana, an early chronicler of baseball in the Dominican Republic, reflected on Cuba's role in bringing baseball to his country. "It is much the same as that which happened with Christianity," Santana mused as he stood in Santo Domingo's colonial zone looking down at La Catedral Primada de América, the first Catholic cathedral in the western hemisphere. "Jesus could be compared to the North Americans, but the apostles were the ones that spread the faith, and the apostles of baseball were the Cubans. They went out into the world to preach the gospel of baseball."[25]

Cuban refugees introduced baseball in the Dominican Republic, first to San Pedro de Macorís in 1886, then to La Vega and Santo Domingo. In Caracas, Venezuela, Emilio Cramer and other Cuban expats organized a league after Cramer opened a cigarette factory there in the 1890s. Cramer formed an all-star ball club, which he named Carlos Manuel de Céspedes, after the planter who freed his slaves and called for the rebellion that ignited the Ten Years' War in 1868. The team staged games to raise money for the rebellion. Cubans also carried their game into Mexico, where baseball took hold in Yucatán's state capital of Mérida around 1890. In each of these cases, the Cubans spreading baseball abroad had been part of the exodus from Cuba due to fallout from the war for independence.[26]

Because Cubans, not North Americans, initiated baseball in these regions, it was played on a racially inclusive basis from its beginnings. Unlike in the United States, race was not a bar to Dominicans, Venezuelans, or Puerto Ricans playing baseball. Baseball among Cuba's disciples also began to take on a nationalistic cast. Dominicans, for example, did not see themselves as playing the U.S. game or even the Cuban game, but the Dominican game. They, like Cubans, appropriated baseball and quickly made it their own.

Dominicans, Nicaraguans, and others in the Caribbean basin shared more than baseball. Most had been occupied at one time or another by the U.S. military. During the U.S. occupation that stretched from 1916 to 1924, some Dominicans—like the Cubans before them—played baseball against U.S. troops while their countrymen fought the *yanquis* in the mountains. Juan Bosch watched these contests as a young boy growing up in the Cibao, the verdant valley in the northern part of the Dominican Republic. Bosch, who became the country's first democratically elected president after dictator Rafael Trujillo's assassination in 1961, remembers the games through an ideological filter: "These games manifested a form of the peoples' distaste of the occupation. They were a repudiation of it. And when a Dominican player would do something great, the people would shout their hurrahs. The game was seen as to go beat the North Americans."[27]

The latter didn't always see it that way. Before the U.S. occupation, James Sullivan, the United States diplomat in Santo Domingo, in a November 1913 letter to Secretary of State William Jennings Bryan, stated, "The American national game of baseball is being played and supported here with great enthusiasm." For Sullivan, "The remarkable effect of this outlet for the animal spirits of the young men is that they are leaving the plazas where they were in the habit of congregating and talking revolution and are resorting to the ball fields where they become widely partisan each for his favorite team." He thought baseball offered Dominicans a way to gain national salvation on U.S. terms. At the very least, Sullivan believed it soothed their anti-American passions. But it did not stop Dominican guerrillas opposed to the occupation from clashing with U.S. forces outside the capital a few years later.[28]

When a ball club emerged in Santiago de los Caballeros, the Cibao's central city, in 1929, its founders called it Sandino. Naming the team for Nicaragua's Augusto César Sandino, who was then in his mountain stronghold of El Chipote, fighting the U.S. Marines, was a statement of Dominican solidarity with the Nicaraguan rebels. Sandino was known as *el aguila del Chipote* (the eagle of Chipote) and the name of the Santiago ball club evolved from Sandino into Las Aguilas (the Eagles). "We had an empathy, a sympathy for Sandino and the Nicaraguans," baseball chronicler Pedro Julio Santana recalled. "Here was this hero who was resisting the invasion of the United Sates, fighting patriotically for his country. He was a hero of enormous popularity." Baseball, Santana stressed, was not just a game that had originated in the United States. "You must understand that baseball is not thought of as the sport of the Yankee imperialists. That is a stupid way of thinking. Baseball is the national sport of the United States and it is the greatest thing that the United States has given us and the other countries of the Caribbean." But in the Dominican Republic, baseball was no longer just the United States' game.[29]

• • •

If baseball offered Cubans in the early twentieth century their best chance to realize founding father José Martí's vision of a nation for all, what did it mean for African Americans in the United States whose efforts to take part in America's national pastime were largely rebuffed or ignored? Rather than affirm citizenship, as it did for all Cubans regardless of color, baseball in the United States denied blacks their equality and reinforced a sense that they were marginal members of society.

From the earliest days of slavery, African Americans had played sports whenever they had the leisure to do so. Abolitionist Frederick Douglass recalled "playing ball" during the brief holiday he and his fellow slaves received on their plantation after Christmas each year.[30] Such opportunities to play, however, were severely limited.

When baseball took hold among African Americans following the Civil War, it was largely concentrated among the black middle classes—its mulatto elite—in northern cities with substantial African American communities. These ball clubs formed alongside an array of self-help institutions that African Americans created to better cope with daily life and elevate their standing in society. Most teams, like black benevolent, literary, and fraternal organizations, were led by better-off, better-educated, and usually lighter-skinned African Americans.

Ball clubs, often affiliated with fraternal societies or social clubs, took shape in Philadelphia, New York City, Washington, D.C., Albany, and New Orleans. They connected black metropolitan elites at a time when there were few national black institutions. They also reflected class tensions within black America. Some of these ball clubs, like the elite Cuban social clubs, were keen to display their status and respectability. The Excelsior and Pythian clubs, Philadelphia's two most prominent teams after the Civil War, held ball games as the centerpiece of social gatherings, with picnics, dances, and banquets feting visiting clubs. These efforts to build ball clubs, mutual aid societies, and debating associations, historian Michael Lomax argues, were designed to "demonstrate their capacity for self-determination, self-improvement, and freedom."[31]

But endeavors to display respectability did not win them entry into baseball's mainstream. The Pythians, for instance, unsuccessfully applied for membership in the Pennsylvania section of the National Association of Base Ball Players in 1867. The NABBP, founded in 1857, was the first organization to legitimize baseball on a national scale, sanctioning competition and setting rules. Given that professional teams had yet to emerge, the organization was as powerful an entity as could be found in baseball.

The Pythians had proved themselves worthy on the field, and the novelty of a white team playing a black team often attracted good crowds, but acceptance by the association was another matter. White delegates—even those who stated they were in sympathy with the Pythians—asserted that their club members would not approve admission of a black club. No delegate would speak openly about the substance of these objections but the prospect of integration off the field—at banquets and in the stands—likely provoked their opposition. Rather than be voted down, the Pythians' delegate withdrew the club's application for membership. A few months later, the NABBP adopted explicit rules barring black teams and players from its ranks. Amateur baseball, even in the North, was not ready for integration.[32]

But the association's grip on baseball was weakening. After the formation of the Cincinnati Red Stockings and their profitable national tour in 1869, professional baseball became ever stronger. Amateur organizations conceded control over the sport to the play-for-pay men and pro leagues proliferated. The National League, American Association, Union Association, and the short-lived Players League (organized by the Brotherhood of Professional Base Ball Players) contested for markets and players. No single league monopolized the baseball industry until the twentieth century, when the National and American Leagues united in an attempt to control the industry.

The commercialization of baseball was largely a boon for African American teams and players during the 1870s and 1880s. The Pythians folded in 1872, not long after the murder of their leader, the militant black rights activist Octavius Catto, during Election Day riots that sought to stop African Americans from voting. But other black semiprofessional and professional teams began play. Some were run on a cooperative basis in which players split the gate; others were organized by entrepreneurs and mostly played against white teams.[33]

A couple of black teams gained membership in pro leagues, and over fifty African Americans played professionally for otherwise white clubs. A few of them, like brothers Moses and Weldy Walker, joined what were considered major league clubs in the 1880s. But African American participation was never more than tenuous. Before long, blacks faced capricious and arbitrary decisions that shoved them off the field, off the squad, and finally out of the league. Future Hall of Famer Cap Anson became the poster boy for intolerance when he declared that he would not play "with no damned Nigger" in 1883.[34] Soon the only black faces left in major league baseball were African American mascots, objects of derision lampooned as childish creatures. The best known mascot, the Chicago White Stockings' Clarence Duval, was described in the press as a grinning, shuffling, woolly-headed boy as black as the ace of spades.[35]

At least white professionals recognized the commercial benefits of competing against black teams. A game with an attractive black opponent was often more lucrative than league contests or exhibitions with other white teams. In stark contrast to Cuban organizers, black clubs, for their part, depended on white promoters, teams, and fans to survive. There were not enough African Americans in northern communities to otherwise sustain black professional baseball. With the overwhelming majority of the nation's black population still in the South, spread out over rural areas, black professional baseball's options would remain limited until the great migrations of the twentieth century.

Because black teams depended on playing against white teams in front of white fans to make a go of it, they sought creative ways of entertaining audiences who might otherwise lose interest when their team was being beaten by a black opponent. At times, their performance—cakewalking along the base paths, pantomiming play during infield practice—reinforced minstrel show stereotypes. In later years, the Ethiopian Clowns and the Indianapolis Clowns dressed up in grass skirts or featured a midget in the lineup. Black clubs were further handicapped by their lack of control over playing fields, their inability to join leagues and benefit from established schedules, and by chronic undercapitalization. Some of the top clubs—the Cuban Giants, the Page Fence Giants, and the Cuban X-Giants—relied on white entrepreneurs for capital and connections.

Black teams and players—like African Americans overall—lost ground in the 1880s. Two major efforts by black clubs to form their own leagues, one in the North, the other in the South, quickly fell apart. Black baseball languished, relegated to the interstices of the white professional baseball industry. Meanwhile, the few African Americans performing for white teams in organized leagues, like the eight playing in the International League (one of several major leagues) in 1887, were soon banished from their circuits. As most leagues began barring African American players outright, the white press wished them good riddance. The *Harrisburg Patriot* described black ballplayers as "dirty foul mouthed" men lacking the respectability of their white counterparts.[36]

But across the racial divide, baseball affirmed white Americans' capacity to shed the disadvantages of class or nationality and qualify for citizen-

ship. By the early twentieth century, the sandlots had become the bap-
tismal font of Americanization. Sons of immigrants who had grown up
speaking Gaelic, Italian, Polish, or Yiddish at home, but English on the
streets and in the classroom, played baseball to fit in. Baseball modeled
what many Americans liked best about their country: a sense of fair play
and opportunity. It was a meritocracy, where class, religion, and nationality
were not supposed to matter. If a boy was good enough, he belonged on
the team. And if he was on the team, he was an American or capable of
becoming one.

Baseball celebrated American individualism within the workings of a
team; the ball field, like the classroom, was perceived as a vehicle for Amer-
icanizing immigrant children. It would instill white Anglo-Saxon Prot-
estant values of efficiency, hard work, and teamwork. Writer Zane Grey,
who had played baseball professionally, called the sandlots a place "where
caste is lost. . . . Ragamuffins and velvet-breeched, white-collared boys
stand in that equality which augurs well for the Stars and Stripes."[37] After
World War I, as the nation confronted the task of digesting its sizable immigrant population, sportswriters often spoke of baseball's civic virtues. As
Atlanta Constitution sportswriter Hugh Fullerton wrote, "Baseball, to my
way of thinking, is the greatest single force working for Americanization.
No other game appeals so much to the foreign-born youngsters and nothing, not even the schools, teaches the American spirit so quickly, or incul-
cates the idea of sportsmanship or fair play as thoroughly." The *Pittsburgh
Post* agreed, arguing that baseball in the twilight and on weekends "brings
the foreigner of the steel mill in direct touch with native born Americans,
teaches him the language and the customs." Without it, the newspaper
warned, "Pittsburgh will suffer."[38]

The common wisdom was that any group of immigrants capable of
citizenship would display its worthiness in sport. The Irish were seen as
the best-case example of Americanization through sport. By the 1880s, no
fighter was better known than heavyweight John L. Sullivan, and Irish immigrants and their sons comprised more than a third of all major leaguers. Baseball's Michael "King" Kelly, John McGraw, Wee Willie Keeler, and
Cornelius Alexander McGillicuddy, who fans knew as Connie Mack, had
become American heroes.

Former Civil War officer George Wingate, discussing New York City's public school athletic leagues, which he had helped to found, wrote in 1913 that nothing developed "the robust, manly qualities of courage, nerve and hardihood" more than competitive athletics, especially for "school boys of foreign birth whose ancestors for hundreds of years before them have been so oppressed as to have been almost slaves in the countries from which they came." But little was said of the schoolboys of native birth whose ancestors for hundreds of years *had* been so oppressed—not almost as slave but *as slaves*. What then did Americans make of African Americans' fresh absence from these arenas?[39]

Most white Americans believed that slavery had degraded African Americans in long-lasting ways. Their absence from baseball conveyed the message that African Americans were not good enough to be there in the first place, that they did not belong. And if they weren't good enough to be on the team, they weren't good enough for citizenship either. That led to the conclusion that when it came to sport, as in the rest of life, African Americans were naturally inferior. Therefore, color lines were as natural in sport as they were elsewhere in society.

These views reflected prevailing social attitudes. African Americans were perceived as genetically inferior athletes, plagued by weak abdominal muscles, a lack of endurance, and an emotional makeup that would fail them in the heat of competition. Such an essentialist characterization of African Americans dovetailed neatly with the ascendancy of scientific racism and social Darwinism, which saw racial groups around the world as biologically inferior to Caucasians, especially those from western and Nordic Europe.

If African Americans excelled in sport, popular wisdom concluded that they had been better able to harness their animalistic nature. U.S. Olympic track coach Dean Cromwell believed that African American success at sprinting and jumping was a function of how much closer they were to the primitive: "It was not so long ago that his ability to sprint and jump was a life-and-death matter to him in the jungle."[40]

As a result, white Americans did not need to be convinced that African Americans were incapable of playing baseball. Their exclusion from such a visible and mesmerizing institution simply reinforced white assumptions about black inferiority. Segregation, of course, made it difficult for African Americans to directly challenge these beliefs. And if baseball had the capacity of teaching immigrants American values and habits, African Americans' exclusion from the game suggested that they were not up to attaining these ideals. They were not worthy of real American citizenship. And that view, with some notable exceptions, shaped popular opinion and practice until after World War II.

But on the other side of America's color line, black America would soon create a sporting world of its own.

CHAPTER TWO

Blackball's Heyday

On many a Sunday afternoon in the 1930s, Greenlee Field atop the Hill District in Pittsburgh was the crossroads of a black baseball world that stretched over a thousand miles southward into the Caribbean. The Hill, perched above downtown, had long been the traditional destination for Europeans and African Americans coming to Pittsburgh. Now, with Cool Papa Bell blazing around the base paths, Josh Gibson swatting balls farther than anybody had ever seen before, and Satchel Paige telling his fielders to sit down and watch while he struck out the side, it witnessed black baseball's renaissance. Baseball fans were seeing a similar rebirth in Kansas City, where jazz bandleader Count Basie sat elbow-to-elbow with ministers and slaughterhouse workers at Muehlebach Stadium, home to the Kansas City Monarchs. Back East, forty-five hundred paying customers routinely packed the Dyckman Oval in upper Manhattan; on game days there, the staccato cadence of Caribbean migrants mixed with southern dialects, Italian, and Yiddish. But nowhere was the rise of black baseball more obvious than during the East-West Classic, when tens of thousands of African Americans gathered at Chicago's Comiskey Park to celebrate what had become black sport's biggest event, an annual all-star game featuring baseball's best black players.

As far as Major League Baseball was concerned, these hotspots for black baseball bubbling up across the country hardly existed. The National and American Leagues had established themselves as *the* major leagues after the Pittsburgh Pirates and Boston Americans inaugurated World Series play in 1903. Their power depended on eliminating competitors in the most lucrative markets and controlling an all-white labor force. By the 1920s, the major leagues had fended off would-be rivals, instituted a reserve clause that bound players to clubs, and smashed efforts to unionize. Major league executives like White Sox owner Charles Comiskey, who bullied his own players so much that several agreed to fix the 1919 World Series, and Branch Rickey, who was building a minor league farm system for the Cardinals so that he could monopolize as much talent as possible, dominated baseball. Other leagues collapsed or accepted minor league status, while the players, chastened by repeated defeat, acknowledged that owners held the whip hand.

Although major league executives aggressively sought dominion over all of white professional baseball, they felt no compulsion to control black ballplayers or fight for their fans. Nor did they or their players protest African Americans' exclusion from the major leagues. White players benefited from segregation, which relieved them of competition for the mere four hundred jobs available in the majors. It also eliminated owners' worries of alienating white fans, especially in southern cities like Washington, D.C., and St. Louis.

Moreover, white players and owners profited directly from black baseball. White major leaguers took advantage of black ballplayers' drawing power by competing against them in lucrative postseason barnstorming games. Major league owners gained by renting their ballparks to black teams on days their facilities would have otherwise stayed shut. The Caribbean leagues, meanwhile, were far enough away to pose little competition for players or fans. But like black baseball, they offered Major League Baseball a source of income. Major league clubs profited by playing in the islands, especially Cuba, during the winter. These trips were often the difference between making or losing money for the year. Some major league ballplayers also headed to the Caribbean on their own to play for island teams and make a living doing what they did best.

But while Major League Baseball clung to its color line, African Americans were rebuilding a vibrant baseball domain in their rapidly growing northern and midwestern beachheads. Resonating as far away as the Mississippi Delta and San Pedro de Macorís in the Dominican Republic, where fans knew of Oscar Charleston, Satchel Paige, and Josh Gibson and longed for the chance to see them play, organized black baseball was rapidly establishing the race's sporting bona fides.

These ball clubs did more than display African American sporting excellence against segregation's backdrop. They helped knit black America together, giving African Americans teams and heroes of their own. Sport offered a cultural counterpoint to the discrimination African Americans encountered at work and in politics. It became an arena affirming their business competence and athletic artistry. Yet baseball was also a bridge to white communities, as black teams played thousands of games against major league barnstormers and white semipros. Though whites participated in black baseball as opponents, spectators, promoters, and owners, this was a realm that black America created and sustained largely on its own. It rebuilt a baseball world that African Americans had first established in the aftermath of World War I, only to see it collapse during the Great Depression.

•   •   •

As long as 90 percent of all African Americans lived in the South, as they did at the end of the nineteenth century, the chances of a viable black baseball league emerging were slim. The wrenching poverty of rural southern blacks, for whom segregation and sharecropping had come to replace slavery, left them little with which to build much of anything.

When conditions in the South deteriorated even further during the 1890s, thousands headed northward during the onset of what would become known as the Great Migration. They left behind Jim Crow laws, lynchings, and plunging cotton prices for the better jobs, educational opportunities, and relative freedom of the North. Most of these early migrants came from the upper South, especially Virginia, Maryland, and the District of Columbia. Often from bigger towns and cities, these upper South transplants were somewhat better off and better educated than African Americans from the rural black belt that swept across the Deep South from Georgia to Texas. Decades later, World War I triggered a far more sizable exodus. As wartime demand for labor increased, the supply of available white workers fell due to the influx of men into the military

Andrew "Rube" Foster
*(Carnegie Library of Pittsburgh).
Date: approx. 1920.* After a
spectacular pitching career,
Andrew "Rube" Foster managed
and owned the Chicago
American Giants. In 1920, the
Texas native pulled together
black teams in the Midwest
to create the Negro National
League, black America's first
viable sporting league.

and the dwindling number of European immigrants arriving from their war-torn continent. That allowed African Americans to enter factories and workplaces previously off-limits. Most of these newcomers were from the rural Deep South.

By the 1920s, the Great Migration had carried well over a million African Americans north aboard the "exodus trains," on the Illinois Central, the Erie, and New York Central lines. Although New York, Chicago, and Philadelphia were the top destinations, black communities also grew substantially in Cleveland, Detroit, and Pittsburgh. Chicago became the "bronze metropolis" as its black population more than quadrupled between 1910 and 1930 to over 225,000. With black professionals, merchants, and politicians establishing a power base on the city's South Side, Chicago became black baseball's capital and Andrew "Rube" Foster its mayor.

A Calvert, Texas, native, Foster left school after the eighth grade and pitched his way northward, starring for teams in Chicago, New York, and

Philadelphia. Fans began calling him Rube after he outpitched future Hall of Famer George Edward "Rube" Waddell in a barnstorming duel. Foster established his reputation as black baseball's top pitcher in 1903 by winning four of five games for the Cuban X-Giants in a series with the Philadelphia Giants billed as the "world's colored championship." But his enduring legacy would be founding the Negro National League, one of the first national black institutions to emerge after slavery.

After forming the Chicago American Giants in 1910, Foster set the bar for black teams by insisting that his squad receive at least 50 percent of the gate when playing white opponents. He partnered with White Sox owner Charles Comiskey's son-in-law, John Schorling, who had refurbished the White Sox's old ballpark on the South Side, near Chicago's booming black community. Foster used South Side Park as his home field. Relinquishing playing for managing, Foster became a midwestern power broker, booking games for white semipro clubs as well as his own team, which toured Canada, California, and Cuba.

In 1917 the *Freeman*, a black paper in Indianapolis, made a public appeal for a "Moses to lead the baseball children out of the wilderness."[1] Three years later, Foster answered its call. The increasing vibrancy of black communities in the North created new possibilities, and Foster understood the benefits of a league with fixed schedules, high-profile rivalries, and championships. Unhappy with allowing white promoters to dictate the terms by which he played in the East, Foster gathered black club owners and sportswriters at the Kansas City YMCA in February 1920. They formed the eight-team Negro National League and elected Foster as the NNL's first president.

The clubs were located in the Midwest, with two franchises in Chicago and one each in Dayton, Detroit, Indianapolis, Kansas City, St. Louis, and Cincinnati, where Cuban promoter Abel Linares based his Cuban Stars. There was one white owner among them, J. L. Wilkinson, who had earned his credentials with the All Nations ball club he founded in 1912. The All Nations had shattered accepted racial mores by fielding black, white, Native American, Latin, and Asian ballplayers, including future Hall of Famers John Donaldson, José Méndez, and Cristóbal Torrienti. The All Nations disbanded during World War I when several key players were drafted into military service. Afterward, Wilkinson added Kansas City sandlotters and players from the U.S. Army's Twenty-fifth Infantry Wreckers, an all-black service team, to the core of his old All Nations squad and formed the Kansas City Monarchs.[2]

Foster was not the first African American to organize a black league. But while earlier efforts had stumbled, Foster capitalized on his connections as an owner and promoter as well as good timing—the North's black population was swelling larger every day. The Negro National League achieved greater stability and success than any previous effort at black professional sport. Players enjoyed salaries that surpassed most black workers' wages and traveled on Pullman cars, which allowed them to finesse some of segregation's indignities. Their exploits were acclaimed in the black press and even drew attention in white newspapers.

Foster was an outspoken "race man," a representative of the "New Negro" emerging during the 1920s. This incipient black nationalism preached a familiar ethic of self-help emphasizing economic and social power. Foster said he wanted "to do something concrete for the loyalty of the Race" and "keep Colored baseball out of the control of whites."[3] He envisioned a black alternative to the major leagues, one that would control black teams and leagues the way that the National and American Leagues commanded its minor leagues. But he could not persuade black teams in the South or the East to accept his leadership. The southern squads, including the Birmingham Black Barons, the Memphis Red Sox, and the Atlanta Black Crackers, were never as strong as Negro National League teams either on the field or at the box office. Few had much success outside the region.

Nor were the better eastern clubs willing to subordinate themselves to Foster's Negro National League. Instead, in December 1923, they formed the Eastern Colored League, with franchises in Philadelphia, Brooklyn, New York City, and Baltimore, in addition to the Cuban Stars, owned by Alejandro Pompez and based in New York City's Washington Heights neighborhood. Several ECL owners were white, as was promoter Nat Strong, who managed most of their bookings. A familiar problem plagued both leagues. Few NNL or ECL clubs controlled ballparks, leaving them at the mercy of minor league and major league clubs willing to rent their facilities on dates they did not need them. Strong, New York City's most powerful booking agent, determined who had access to the city's choicest venues, including Yankee Stadium, Ebbets Field, and the Polo Grounds. One silver lining of the fractious rivalry was that the creation of the Eastern Colored League allowed the two leagues to begin playing a Negro World Series in 1924. The Kansas City Monarchs beat Philadelphia's Hilldale Club in the inaugural championship, when José Méndez, the by-then legendary thirty-seven-year-old player/manager, pitched a two-hit shutout in the finale of the ten-game series.

In *Invisible Men*, his pioneering 1983 study of the Negro Leagues, Donn Rogosin called the 1920s black baseball's zenith. It was an era of unprecedented stability featuring a cluster of baseball's all-time stars, including pitcher Smokey Joe Williams, who might have been black baseball's greatest pitcher ever; Bullet Rogan, who was among black baseball's best pitchers *and* best hitters; centerfielder Oscar Charleston, often called the black Ty Cobb; and shortstop John Henry Lloyd. When Pittsburgh Pirates shortstop Honus Wagner heard that Lloyd had been called the black Wagner, he said he was honored by the comparison.[4]

Frequent victories against white teams showcased NNL and ECL squads and proved they could compete with white major and minor leaguers. To the delight of black Kansas City, the Monarchs swept a doubleheader from Babe Ruth's All-Stars in 1922 and, later that season, defeated their white Kansas City rivals, the Blues, in a championship to determine local bragging rights. But when black teams began winning too many of these interracial contests, Major League Baseball commissioner Kenesaw Mountain Landis intervened. Rather than chance major league teams losing face by losing games to black teams, the commissioner barred teams under his jurisdiction from playing black squads. Only "all-star" aggregations of major leaguers could face black teams in the off-season, and they could not wear their major league uniforms in these contests. After Landis forbade a barnstorming tour between Rube Foster's Chicago American Giants and a team put together by Detroit Tiger and future Hall of Famer Harry Heilmann, Foster confronted him. When asked why he had canceled the games, the commissioner reportedly answered: "Mr. Foster, when you beat our teams it gives us a black eye." While Landis publicly dismissed African American and Latino players as unworthy, he and the white major leaguers who barnstormed against them in the United States or played with them in the Caribbean knew these men were their athletic equals.[5]

As the Roaring Twenties tore along, the Negro National League became more successful than anybody imagined possible. Its ballplayers, who earned about a fourth of what white major leaguers earned, made more than most black workers.[6] Tragically, just as the league he had founded was realizing his vision of establishing black baseball as a viable business, Foster suffered neurological damage after being asphyxiated during a gas leak at his home in Indianapolis. Although he returned to work, his health did not improve, and he collapsed in 1926. Foster was committed to a state asylum for the insane, where for the next four years he labored under the delusion that he was scheduled to pitch in the World Series. After he died at the age of fifty-one, his body lay in state for three days; the *Chicago Defender* eulogized him as "a martyr to the game, the most commanding figure baseball had ever known." The Negro National League, hobbled by the loss of its indispensable leader and a deepening economic depression, succumbed in 1931. It was not long at all, however, before it experienced a second life in Pittsburgh.[7]

•   •   •

Pittsburgh was a microcosm of the prospects and perils that African Americans across the North experienced during the Great Migration. Its black population exploded from twenty thousand in 1900 to fifty-five thousand in 1930, with another twenty-three thousand African Americans living in nearby mill towns along the Monongahela, Allegheny, and Ohio rivers. Despite the advantages that African Americans enjoyed in the North, it was no promised land. Discrimination pervaded the workplace, and the gains that African Americans enjoyed in the mills during World War I did not endure after its end. Last hired, first fired, they never achieved the seniority that allowed some white workers to withstand the chaotic ups and downs of local industry. Frequent layoffs undermined their chances at home ownership; the greater likelihood that they worked at a small shop made it difficult to bring sons and friends on to the job. As a result, African Americans found it harder to bequeath to their children what many European immigrants were able to deliver to theirs: jobs and housing.

Nor could Pittsburgh absorb the waves of new black residents arriving in droves as a result of the Great Migration. The sudden population increase taxed already inadequate housing and public health systems. And unlike most northern cities where blacks coalesced into one contiguous ghetto, African Americans in Pittsburgh lived in scattered neighborhoods, reaching a plurality only in the multiracial Hill District. The lack of a central African American neighborhood hurt their ability to wield political or economic power.

The Great Migration also exacerbated tension between African Americans born in the North and those coming up from the Deep South. In Pittsburgh, that tension divided the Old Pittsburghers, or "OPs," who had grown up in the city, from southern migrants. Place of birth usually correlated with income, education level, and skin color. The OPs, more accustomed to city life, fretted that the newcomers and their country ways would jeopardize the already tenuous status of black residents.

Black Pittsburgh's two most illustrious teams, the Homestead Grays and the Pittsburgh Crawfords, reflected these contrasts. The Grays were the by-product of the late-nineteenth-century migration of African Americans from the upper South, while the Crawfords were created by the sons of migrants from the black belt who came during World War I. By the 1930s, all African Americans shared a growing pride in the two teams and their stellar lineups. In time, these clubs transcended the divisions based on place of birth and class, and offered African Americans in Pittsburgh much-needed common ground.[8]

The Grays and the Crawfords evolved on western Pennsylvania's sandlots, where hundreds of black and white neighborhood and workplace teams played independent baseball. Though professional baseball remained segregated, these sandlots, especially in northern working-class and immigrant neighborhoods, were frequently integrated. Often in and out of each other's homes, black and white residents of the Hill recalled getting a "whupping" from their "black mamas" and their "white mamas" when they got into trouble as children. Boys often grew up playing ball together before being forced to sort themselves by race in order to join organized leagues. Even then, black teams played white teams. The better clubs charged admission or passed the hat at games, and split whatever was

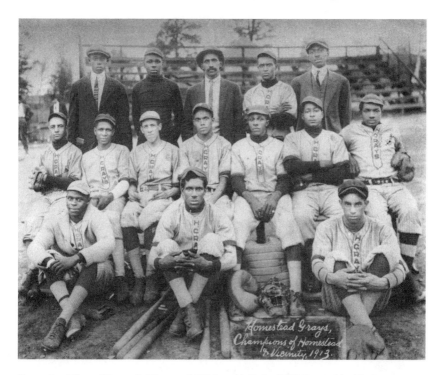

Homestead Grays *(Carnegie Library of Pittsburgh). Date: 1913.* Formed by black steelworkers in Homestead, a mill town abutting Pittsburgh, the Homestead Grays were black baseball's longest-running and possibly greatest all-time franchise. Homestead native Cumberland Posey Jr. joined the team as an outfielder, and later became its manager and owner. Left to right, front row: Ben Pace, Jerry Veney, Emmett Campbell; middle row: Pete Peatross, Eric Russell, Cumberland Posey Jr., Sellers Hall, John Veney, Bob Hopson, Hubert Sanders; top row: Henry Saunders, Sam Smith, B. F. Alexander, Roy Horne, Ralph Blackburn.

left after paying for balls and the umpire. But these athletes played to play, not for pay.

In 1900, black men in Homestead, a municipality bordering Pittsburgh, formed a team called the Blue Ribbons. They fielded a moderately successful squad each season for the next decade. Though they changed their name from the Blue Ribbons to the Murdock Grays, the players continued to come from Homestead's black community.

Homestead was an anomaly in that it boasted a sizable cohort of skilled black workers in the steel mill that stretched along the Monongahela River. In 1910, the Grays changed their name again, this time to the Homestead

Grays, and elected Jerry Veney as manager. Veney, his brother John, and several of the team's founders had come to Homestead during the 1890s to work at the Steel Works. They held skilled jobs and lived in the tree-lined Hilltop neighborhood a few blocks above the river. Captain Cumberland Willis Posey Sr., the region's most prominent African American, lived nearby. Later-arriving black migrants lived in denser, more polluted neighborhoods in the shadow of the mill along the river.

The Grays excelled, winning forty-two consecutive games against an array of sandlot teams in 1913. They recruited other teams' top players, including Captain Posey's son, Cumberland Jr., and sometimes even fielded a white player. Because Manager Veney strictly observed the Sabbath, the Grays never played on Sunday, the best day of the week to draw a crowd. Several players, however, hired themselves out to rival squads for Sunday games. Fights over Sabbath play finally convinced Veney and other men who had been with the team since its inception to step aside. Cumberland Posey Jr., who had joined the team as an outfielder in 1911, was elected the squad's new captain. Posey was soon managing and promoting the Grays; in the early 1920s, he became the team's owner.

Cum Posey Jr. had been born in 1890, two years before an epic labor conflict at the Homestead Steel Works riveted the nation's attention. As he transformed the Grays into arguably the greatest black franchise ever, Homestead came to be thought of for something other than steel and discontented workers resisting efforts by industrialists Andrew Carnegie and Henry Clay Frick to destroy their union. Cum Posey's father, Captain Posey, had earned a ship engineer's license before leaving the river and becoming an entrepreneur. His Diamond Coke and Coal Company was the largest black-owned business in Pittsburgh. President of the elite Loendi Club, the Warren Methodist Episcopal Church, and the *Pittsburgh Courier* newspaper, Captain Posey embodied the Old Pittsburghers who had established themselves economically and socially in the city and surrounding towns.

His son, Cum, became the city's best all-around black athlete. Starring for several sandlot baseball and football teams, Cum Posey played baseball and basketball at Holy Ghost College (later Duquesne University) under the name Charles Cumbert to conceal the fact that he was no longer an amateur, having received money to play baseball and basketball.

Given Posey's prominence as an athlete, it was a ruse that fooled few but was accepted by all. At Holy Ghost, Posey schooled a younger student, Art Rooney, in how to succeed in sport. They became lifelong friends, and Rooney, later the patriarch of the Pittsburgh Steelers football club, came to consider Posey his mentor on and off the field.

Sportswriter Wendell Smith called Posey "the outstanding athlete of the Negro race" of the 1920s, perhaps its most colorful personality. His Monticello and Loendi basketball squads were recognized as national black champions before and after World War I. Like Posey, most of these basketball players came from the black middle class; several were welfare workers employed by companies to help black migrants adjust to factory work. They supervised teams and athletic programs for workers, activities designed to reduce absenteeism and turnover and make employees more loyal to the company. The welfare workers, like the original Homestead Grays, were from better-off backgrounds, but after World War I, Posey began recruiting the best players regardless of class, first from the region, then from around the nation, to come to Pittsburgh.

As these Negro Leaguers bolstered the lineup, the Grays became the region's top independent team and a popular draw throughout the East. After pitcher Smokey Joe Williams joined them in 1925, the Grays won 260 games, lost 29, and tied 11 over the next two seasons. Williams, a six-feet-five-inch veteran almost forty years old when he came to Pittsburgh, had beaten Hall of Famers Walter Johnson, Grover Alexander, Chief Bender, Rube Marquard, and Waite Hoyt in barnstorming games during his career. After the Grays won 43 games in a row in 1926, Posey celebrated with a banquet at their Wylie Avenue clubhouse on the Hill. Black Pittsburgh's most prominent citizens danced to a jazz band and applauded the team. In subsequent years, Posey added Oscar Charleston, Cool Papa Bell, Willie Foster, Judy Johnson, and Cuba's Martín Dihigo to his squad, building a financially successful, athletic powerhouse that capitalized on the 1920s golden age of sport.

• • •

In 1926, the season that Posey presented his players with "gold" baseballs emblematic of their athletic achievements, a team made up of the sons of migrants from the Deep South represented the Crawford Bath House in a local league. The Bath House was a city recreational center in the Hill District whose mission was to help migrants from both the South and Europe adjust to life in Pittsburgh. Gus Greenlee, the owner of the nearby Crawford Grill, bought the boys pinstriped uniforms with CRAWFORD emblazoned across the front. After winning the league championship, they posed for a photo on the steps of the Hill's Carnegie Library.

In 1928, after the Crawfords had severed ties with the Bath House, six members of the Edgar Thomson Steel Works ball club joined the team. The newcomers included a player by the name of Harold Tinker. As a young boy recently arrived from Birmingham, Alabama, Tinker had watched the Homestead Grays play at Forbes Field. "I had an ambition," Tinker recalled. "I told myself, 'One day I'm gonna be on a team that will beat these Homestead Grays.' That was my life's desire. And every team that I became a part of, I took that nucleus of players that I knew in my heart would be coming toward that aim."

Building a team that could compete with Posey's Grays, a club made up of men who made a living from baseball, seemed a far-fetched goal for a sandlotter like Tinker. But Tinker, who managed the Crawfords and played centerfield, recruited another son of the Great Migration to the team, one whose potential dwarfed that of every other player on the field. Josh Gibson's father, Mark, had left sharecropping in Buena Vista, Georgia, for a job in a Pittsburgh steel mill. Josh quit school after the ninth grade and worked at Westinghouse Airbrake and the Gimbel Brothers department store before finding his calling on the diamond. Tinker discovered him playing third base on a dirt field on the city's Northside. Impressed by Gibson's agility and arm, he thought: "This boy is a marvel." Then Josh came to bat. "He hit the ball out of existence," Tinker would often say. "They didn't even go after it. It went over a mountain. And I said to myself, 'This is part of my plan. He needs to be with us.'" Gibson, only sixteen years old but already a well-muscled 180 pounds, took over as the Crawfords' catcher at their next game at Ammon Field on the Hill. "Those people up there went wild over him," Tinker recalled, "and so did we, from the very first day."[9]

After beating the best white independent clubs in Pittsburgh, the Crawfords were dubbed the Little Homestead Grays. But before Grays owner Cum Posey agreed to play his young rivals, he recruited Gibson away from them in 1930. Though sad to see Josh go, the Crawfords did not begrudge him the chance to play professionally. Besides, the Crawfords soon gained an owner of their own, Gus Greenlee, who put them on salary.

Everyone in black Pittsburgh knew Gus Greenlee. They might have listened to jazz at his Crawford Grill, played his numbers game, or come to him when they needed help paying the rent or buying a load of coal. Big Red, as he was known, had hopped a freight train from North Carolina to Pittsburgh before the war. He shined shoes, tended blast furnaces at Jones & Laughlin on the Southside, and drove a taxi before shipping overseas with the 367th Regiment. Wounded at Saint-Mihiel, France, he returned to Pittsburgh, where he bootlegged liquor during Prohibition and ran nightclubs. His Crawford Grill attracted a mix of African American and white patrons, as did his new baseball team.

Greenlee, like Tinker, envisioned topping the Grays. He added several reinforcements to his team, including Satchel Paige, a lanky pitcher from Mobile, Alabama. "By the grace of God," Tinker remembered, "that's when we beat the Grays." Greenlee then raided the Grays, bringing Josh Gibson back to the Crawfords, and adding future Hall of Famers Oscar Charleston, Judy Johnson, and Cool Papa Bell for good measure. As Greenlee revamped the team, Tinker and most of the original Crawfords found themselves on the bench or off the squad. In addition to transforming the Crawfords into a topflight ball club, Greenlee resurrected the Negro National League in 1933, and placed its office above the Crawford Grill. A few blocks away, he built the seven-thousand-seat Greenlee Field, the finest black-owned ballpark in the country.

Greenlee Field hosted black college football games, boxing cards, and soccer matches, and generally became a meeting place for black and white Pittsburghers. Whites frequently attended Negro League games, just as they watched sandlot contests between black and white teams in their own neighborhoods. Art Rooney, Gus Greenlee's political ally, had his fledgling football team practice and play exhibitions there in 1933, its first season in the National Football League.

Like the sandlots and other venues where black and white teams played, Greenlee Field offered the chance for athletes to compete in an arena where white and black players and fans shared the same sporting values. They could judge for themselves if African Americans were good enough to compete.

Black baseball in Pittsburgh benefited from the city's central location as well as from the charismatic men driving it, especially Posey, Greenlee, and Gibson. Pittsburgh was a stop on the chitlin' circuit, the black entertainment network, and any musician or ball club traveling between major black population centers in the East and the Midwest played there. Harlem Renaissance poet Claude McKay called the intersection of Wylie and Fullerton avenues on the Hill the "Crossroads of the World."[10] Pittsburgh-bred musicians like Earl "Fatha" Hines, Mary Lou Williams, Roy Eldridge, and Billy Eckstine played at Greenlee's Crawford Grill. So did Cab Calloway, Count Basie, and Lena Horne. There, they mingled with ballplayers and folks from all strata of the black community. "All the people flocked to the games and after the games, they would flock to the Crawford Grill," Newark Eagle outfielder Monte Irvin remembered. "Had good entertainment, great food, and there were plenty of girls."

Pittsburgh quickly recaptured the élan that black baseball had achieved during the 1920s. Its teams were at the top of Negro National League play through the 1930s and 1940s and fielded several of its most iconic figures, including Paige, Bell, Gibson, and slick-fielding, hard-hitting first baseman Buck Leonard. Many of the Negro Leaguers later elected to the Hall of Fame played for one or both of these teams, which together won over a dozen Negro League championships. The 1935 Crawfords might have been baseball's best team ever, while the Grays won nine NNL pennants in a row from 1937 to 1945. "Coming to Pittsburgh was a big thrill," Monte Irvin recalled. "If you had a four-game series, the fact that you could win one game was really something! You were lucky. You see, the Pittsburgh Crawfords and the Homestead Grays, they dominated baseball at that time."[11]

• • •

Greenlee's ability to turn the Crawfords into a stellar club, build a ballpark, and reform the Negro National League rested on the revenue he generated from a system of organized gambling popularly called the numbers game. For that matter, so did the viability of most NNL teams. The "numbers"

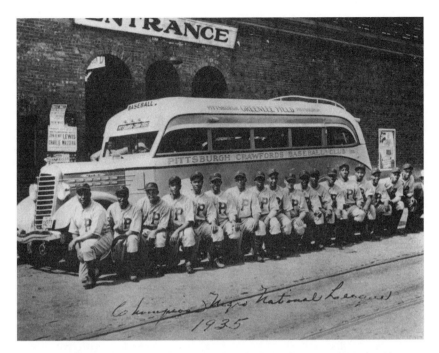

Pittsburgh Crawfords outside Greenlee Field *(public domain). Date: 1936.* Formed by youth in Pittsburgh's Hill District in 1926, the Pittsburgh Crawfords became a professional squad owned by numbers baron Gus Greenlee. Posed in front of Greenlee Field on the Hill, the 1936 Crawfords' lineup featured five future Hall of Famers. Left to right: Oscar Charleston, Jimmie Crutchfield, Dick Seay, Sam Bankhead, Bill Harvey, Sam Streeter, Bill Perkins, Chester Williams, Theolic "Fireball" Smith, Harry Kincannon, Judy Johnson, Cool Papa Bell, Leroy Matlock, Ernest "Spoon" Carter, Josh Gibson, Jasper Washington, Satchel Paige, Duncan Escota.

derived from similar gambling games known by different names across diverse locales, including European peasant lotteries, *la bolita* in the Caribbean, and "policy" in New Orleans. In this poor person's lottery, people could bet as little as a penny on a three-digit number based on daily stock transactions or the outcomes of horse races. Although the numbers bank paid off at 600 to 1, the odds against picking the number were 1,000 to 1. But for people who were unlikely to save much of their meager wages, the numbers game provided action and the chance for an occasional windfall.

In Pittsburgh, the numbers began on the Hill but swept through the rest of the city and nearby mill towns by the 1930s. The profits allowed Greenlee to not only support his ball club but make hundreds of never-to-be-repaid loans to people in need. Numbers men like Greenlee backed black teams in several cities. When Cum Posey found himself in financial trouble during the depression, he turned to Homestead's Rufus "Sonny-man" Jackson. The owner of the Sky Rocket Café in Homestead, Jackson ran the numbers game in the Monongahela River Valley. Abe and Effa Manley's Newark Eagles, Alejandro Pompez's New York Cubans, James "Soldier Boy" Semler's New York Black Yankees, and Tom Wilson's Nashville (later Baltimore) Elite Giants also depended on the numbers to stay afloat. Most of the men running these grassroots gambling operations were highly regarded in their communities. "You realized," Homestead native Mal Goode recalled, "that here are some men involved in the numbers who are not just throwing their money up and down the street." Goode saw Greenlee and the other numbers men's investment in baseball as their way of giving back to the community.[12]

The numbers became the black community's bank at a time when most African Americans lacked financial institutions of their own and white-controlled banks were leery of lending to them. No other source of capital in the black community was big enough to invest in black baseball or willing to see if it could become a going concern. Black boxing also benefited from the numbers men's largesse. Greenlee managed John Henry Lewis, the first African American light heavyweight champion of the world, while numbers men Julian Black and John Roxborough guided Joe Louis to the heavyweight throne.

"They would have been steel tycoons, Wall Street brokers, auto moguls had they been white," author Richard Wright wrote of the numbers men.[13] In Pittsburgh, Greenlee was dubbed the Caliph of Little Harlem. One former player called him the Jesus of Negro sport, while another contended that Greenlee and his partner Woogie Harris were responsible for keeping "Pittsburgh on the block as far as black people were concerned" during the Depression.[14] "He was never slow when a fella needed a favor," Negro Leaguer Ted Page recalled. "His hands were just as fast as you could hope they would be when he'd come across people who needed help."[15] Greenlee distributed turkeys at Thanksgiving, ran a soup kitchen across from the Crawford Grill, and paid tuition for youth to attend college. His numbers revenue funded an array of black businesses, including legal and medical practices, restaurants, bars, and even the old Hot Sauce Williams barbecue stand.

Greenlee also supported Bethune-Cookman College, sandlot sport, and Homer Brown's successful campaign to become Pittsburgh's first African American representative in the state legislature. Nor was he the only numbers-man-cum-philanthropist. Most of the numbers men who backed black ball clubs in other cities enjoyed similar reputations. While some players disliked James Semler and American Giants owner Robert Cole, considering them cheap or dishonest, few had anything bad to say about the Manleys, Sonnyman Jackson, or Alejandro Pompez.

Pompez connected Caribbean baseball to the Negro Leagues and later the major leagues like no other individual. His father, José, part of the Cuban diaspora of the 1870s, settled in Key West, where Alejandro was born in 1890. A fierce proponent of Cuban independence, José Pompez left his estate to the movement, prompting his suddenly impoverished family to return to Cuba after his death. As Alejandro came of age, he moved to Tampa, where he began running numbers and promoting baseball. The dark-skinned, multilingual Pompez was conversant with baseball in Cuba and the United States, and unusually adept at operating in black, Latin, and white settings. His Cuban Stars began touring the Caribbean in 1916, following the sun and playing baseball year-round.

Pompez relocated his numbers game and ball club to New York in the 1920s. Because of his base in the Caribbean and his entrée to New York City's growing Latino market, Pompez was able to negotiate more favorable rental terms than most black club owners when dealing with power broker Nat Strong, who controlled access to local ballparks. Through their teams, Pompez and fellow Cuban Abel Linares introduced soon-to-be legends like José Méndez, Adolfo Luque, Cristóbal Torrienti, Armando Marsans, Rafael Almeida, and perhaps the greatest of all Latin players, Martín Dihigo.

In the early 1930s, when Jewish gangster Dutch Schultz began taking over Harlem's numbers business, Pompez had to choose between leaving the racket or accepting Schultz as his boss. Always adept at self-preservation, he made his accommodation with the mob but was reduced to working for Schultz on salary until the mobster's murder in 1935 freed him to recapture much of his former empire. In 1937, however, New York district attorney Thomas Dewey indicted Pompez and was preparing to arrest him as he arrived at his Harlem office building one morning. When the elevator operator alerted Pompez to what awaited him upstairs, he fled the building and then the country. Arrested months later in Mexico, Pompez turned state's evidence against New York City's Tammany Hall regime and avoided prison. He was soon back in baseball, his reputation barely diminished.[16]

"Any person who has the honor of knowing Pompez personally is well aware that he is in no way a hardened criminal and does not look at life through the eyes of a criminal," Cum Posey wrote in his defense. "Pompez has been many more times a benefactor in the life of Harlem than he has been a nuisance."[17]

The same could have been said for Abe Manley, who ran the numbers in Camden and backed the Newark Eagles. Abe turned the Eagles over to his considerably younger wife, Effa. Effa's parents were a biracial couple. But her biological father was her white mother's white lover. Effa grew up with her mother, her mother's African American husband, and black half-siblings, unaware of her unusual racial background until she was older. Even when she found out about her biological father, Effa identified herself as African American. A onetime treasurer of the New Jersey chapter of the National Association for the Advancement of Colored People, she was involved with "Don't buy where you can't work" and anti-lynching campaigns. She often used ballgames to raise awareness of civil rights causes.[18]

Greenlee, Pompez, the Manleys, and others like them kept black baseball nourished and deeply rooted in the community. As bleak as conditions were in the black community during the Great Depression, they would have been far tougher without the numbers men, who contributed to its welfare by funding soup kitchens and political campaigns, and employed thousands, including baseball players, in its underground economy.

• • •

Perennially undercapitalized, lacking control over ballparks, and dependent on fans battered by the Great Depression, black leagues were never very profitable or stable. Running a club during the 1930s was not for the faint of heart. Major League Baseball had also suffered since the onset of the Depression, with attendance contracting by 40 percent from 1930 to 1933, salaries shrinking, and profits turning into losses.[19] Black owners were neither as deep-pocketed as their white counterparts nor able to tap similar lines of credit. They often lost money and some survived only because they had the numbers to back them up. Instability encouraged players to jump contracts, sparking infighting among owners who were often already at odds. But despite its economic shortcomings, black baseball offered the community the chance to build greater unity and a stronger identity.

Baseball encouraged that sense of cohesion both locally in cities such as Pittsburgh and Chicago, and nationally, across an increasingly dispersed black America. In Pittsburgh, the Grays and Crawfords offered heroes for an otherwise fractured black community. Nationally, black teams created a highly visible institution with an aura of accomplishment that fostered a positive sense of an emerging black America.

The Negro American League, which began play in 1937, extended black baseball's professional presence into the Midwest. Its footprint fit into the area that Rube Foster's league had once covered. Southern teams—the Atlanta Black Crackers, Birmingham Black Barons, and Memphis Red Sox—capitalized on growing black urban populations and the relatively more liberal atmosphere that prevailed in cities to further expand this baseball world. The best of these teams met in four-team doubleheaders at Yankee Stadium that drew strong reviews in the white press and further enhanced black baseball's image. *Life* ran a story and photo spread after one Sunday doubleheader in the spring of 1941, touting Satchel Paige as one of the best pitchers in baseball.[20]

Spring training for black teams meant barnstorming through the South in order to drum up enough cash to start the season. That kind of movement connected the nation's still largely southern black citizenry to their mostly northern baseball leagues.

African Americans followed their teams and the exploits of their heroes by word of mouth and in the black press. The *Chicago Defender, Pittsburgh Courier, Afro-American,* and other papers circulated nationally, often carried by Pullman porters along the all-important railroad lines. Fans who rarely attended ball games devoured stories by Rollo Wilson, Ches Washington, Sam Lacy, and Wendell Smith, sportswriters who traveled with black musicians and ballplayers on the trains and buses that tied this network together.

No event bathed black baseball in more favorable light than its annual East-West Classic. In 1933, the same year that Major League Baseball began playing an annual all-star game, black baseball created one of its own. Gus Greenlee, Pittsburgh Crawfords secretary Roy Sparrow, and *Pittsburgh Courier* editor William Nunn Sr. worked in tandem to create the event. Most often held at Comiskey Park in Chicago, the East-West Classic drew as many as fifty thousand fans. Millions more took part by casting ballots published in black papers to select the teams.

Like a Joe Louis or Henry Armstrong fight, the East-West Classic attracted African Americans from around the country. They traveled to Chicago by special railroad coaches and stayed on the South Side, which had become the nation's most important black community. Politicians, sportsmen, fans, celebrities like Louis Armstrong and Bill "Bojangles" Robinson, and the leaders of fraternal organizations like the Elks and Alpha Phi Alpha congregated in Chicago for what were likely the largest gatherings of African Americans seen during these years. The all-star contest underscored the drawing power of the black game and further elevated its pantheon of baseball demigods. It didn't just display black athletic talent; it sustained the growing consciousness of the entire national black community.

● ● ●

Black baseball fit snugly into the world that African Americans were creating for themselves during the Great Migration. By denying African Americans access to white-controlled schools, stores, and leisure activities, segregation had encouraged the creation of black businesses and institutions: an infrastructure of colleges and newspapers, mutual aid and literary societies, funeral parlors and nightclubs, rackets and ball clubs. In Pittsburgh, scores of black-owned businesses lined Wylie Avenue on the Hill. African Americans had their hair cut at Woogie Harris's Crystal Barbershop and their prescriptions filled at Goode's Pharmacy. They dined at the Crawford Grill and watched ball games at Greenlee Field. African

Americans in Chicago, Kansas City, and Harlem had similar black-owned options for how to spend their time and money.

Playwright August Wilson grew up on the Hill in Pittsburgh, where he set his play, *Fences*, about an ex–Negro Leaguer who became a garbageman. "If you are all together standing outside the doors of white American society and you cannot participate in this society," Wilson emphasized, "then there is a certain strengthening in who you are as a people." Wilson saw the Negro Leagues as representing tangible social and economic ownership by African Americans. For Wilson, black baseball mattered. "It gave you a sense of belonging."[21]

This social and cultural significance outweighed black baseball's shaky economic underpinnings. Mal Goode grew up near Cumberland Posey Jr. in Homestead. "Sport," he reflected, "was segregated in those days, but when you found blacks playing white teams, our pride was showing. It had to be. There was so much negative living that we had to do over which we had no control. Remember that you didn't go into a bank and see a black teller in those days. You didn't see a black man driving a streetcar or a bus for a long, long time—until the civil rights movement became strong in the late '40s and early '50s. So anything that you could hang onto from the standpoint of pride, it was there and it showed."[22]

"We didn't just play and think we were inferior," Homestead Grays infielder Clarence Bruce argued. "We thought we were great ballplayers and I think we walked with that air. When we walked into a town, we held our heads high. We knew we were great players, and the fans knew it. I think the white fans knew it."[23]

In 1963, a year after Mal Goode became the first African American to become an on-the-air correspondent on ABC's national news, another Pittsburgh native, John Edgar Wideman, became the nation's second-ever African American Rhodes scholar. "When I grew up," Wideman explained, "all the talk was about sport. Nobody ever said, 'Here now, we're going to discuss the possibilities of manhood and realizing ourselves in this culture,' but that was the sub-theme, that was the hidden agenda." In the barbershops and on the corners, Wideman observed men who had never been very good athletes. "What they talked about," he said, "was not deals on the market or jobs or selling cars—they talked about hitting a home run or stealing a base.

That was entrée. You had to have that sports knowledge or sport ability to prove yourself. So behind every black man was that archetypal athlete."[24]

Black baseball was central to black social life and a place where fans could also show themselves off. "They wore their finery," Kansas City Monarch Buck O'Neil observed. "They'd have their fur stoles on and their hats on—just like they left church."[25] The Monarchs' Booster Club organized opening-day parades, held dances and "Frolics," and counted on the backing of the black Ministerial Alliance and businessmen. In return, the Monarchs played benefits for community groups, churches, and the NAACP.[26] Ministers often scheduled services earlier than usual to accommodate their parishioners who would go from church to the ballpark for a Sunday-afternoon game.

"It didn't hit me until later," Hall of Famer Monte Irvin said, "that we were living in a special era. In other words, we had provided a form of entertainment for people, for a group of people who were downtrodden, who had no hope, who didn't get much encouragement. But then on a Saturday or a Sunday or a Tuesday night, they could come out to the ballpark and see some guy that could play baseball very well and that would give them hope. And say, well at least somebody is making it."[27]

With so many other arenas closed to African Americans, baseball was more than entertainment. "The very best black athletes," Wideman observed, "who not only competed among themselves and put on a good show, but who would go out and compete against their white contemporaries and beat the stuffing out of them—even if they didn't win—produced in the folk stories that are better than winning in which the exploits get exaggerated and fabled. All that was very important, particularly at a time in America when race relations were at their nadir." During the 1930s and '40s, African Americans from all over the country savored and clung to their teams and players. They would need to hold on tight—an unexpected threat was brewing much farther south than anyone could have anticipated.

CHAPTER THREE

A Latin Challenge

If you had asked most fans during the 1937 season where the best baseball was being played, most would have pointed to Yankee Stadium or the Polo Grounds, where the Yankees and Giants were winning pennants that summer. They would have been wrong. Hispaniola, the island that the Spanish-speaking, baseball-playing Dominican Republic uneasily shared with the French- and Kreyòl-speaking, soccer-playing Haiti could claim that distinction. There, beneath a fierce Caribbean sun, the best Cuban, African American, and Dominican players met in El Campeonato Nacional de Base Ball 1937: Pro Reelección Presidente Trujillo (President Trujillo's Reelection 1937 National Baseball Championship). Their presence, as much about politics as sport, reflected the coming of age of an alternative baseball world that had grown up alongside the major leagues and the Negro Leagues and now threatened to siphon away their lifeblood.

The Dominican championship posed the first significant foreign challenge to professional baseball in the United States. Until then, Caribbean baseball had coexisted peacefully with both the major leagues and the Negro Leagues. Each had its respective season, and players circulated between the United States and the Caribbean, abiding by the former's color line in the summer while enjoying the latter's racial inclusiveness during the winter. In the summer of 1937, however, Dominican baseball challenged the Negro Leagues head-on and left one of black baseball's most storied teams, the Pittsburgh Crawfords, in tatters by summer's end.

That the Dominican Republic defied U.S. baseball was the result of island politics, not sport. Cuba remained the headwaters of Caribbean baseball, the fount of the game throughout the region. But after Cuban expats introduced baseball to the Dominican Republic in the late 1800s, young, better-off Dominicans quickly claimed it as their own. "These boys were exposed to baseball while they were in school in the United States or Puerto Rico," Manuel Báez Vargas recalled. "But we who were not from such affluent backgrounds were not far behind." Báez Vargas, a carpenter's son, grew up in Ciudad Nueva, Santo Domingo's old colonial zone, playing ball with his cousin, whose father was a shoemaker. Báez Vargas became an educator; his cousin Tetelo Vargas became the greatest Dominican player of his era.

As baseball permeated the urban working classes along with the well to do, clubs proliferated. Báez Vargas and his friends organized Los Muchachos de las Ruinas de San Nicolás, drawing on boys who lived near the ruins of an old church.[1] Baseball offered cheap diversion that cut across class lines, and teams met in tournaments with trophies, not cash, for the winners.

Ruminating as to why Dominicans rejected Spanish sports—*fútbol*, jai alai (a fast-paced ball game from the Basque region of Spain played on a court) and bullfighting—Báez Vargas dismissed the mother country's legacy to its Dominican colony: "The Spanish never really had much love for this country. They came here, made their money, and abandoned us. They did not leave much. Perhaps that is the reason that Dominicans did not take much to their sport."

Báez Vargas also stressed the growing influence that the United States exerted during its World War I intervention. "Even though Cubans introduced the sport," he explained, "it was during the epoch of the North American occupation that baseball was really ignited."[2] Dominicans had traded Spanish colonialism for a brief but bloody nineteenth-century Haitian occupation and then a series of their own homegrown dictators until the United States invaded in 1916. Before they left in 1924, U.S. forces fought intermittently against Dominican guerrillas, built roads, and played baseball. "In the east," Báez Vargas recalled, "the guerrillas were fighting the Marines, but in the capital, we played ball with them." Though Dominicans bristled over the occupation, they welcomed games against U.S. sailors, soldiers, and Marines.

"The North Americans were not trying to win our hearts and minds," Báez Vargas protested. "They just wanted to play baseball."

For Báez Vargas, sport was a way to bring people together. "There is something about sport that unites people," he reasoned. "Sometimes we felt humiliated by the occupation, but in sport, we fraternized. The crowds were full of this fervor and wanted us to win because we were their team and because we represented the Dominican flag."[3]

His compatriot, Juan Bosch, was less sanguine about sport's fraternal nature. In 1963, two years after dictator Rafael Trujillo's assassination, Bosch became the first democratically elected Dominican president. Ousted by a coup several months later, he was on the verge of returning to power when the United States occupied the country a second time, in 1965. "These games were not a form of collaboration with the North Americans," Bosch insisted. They were a way to assert Dominican independence against the North Americans.[4]

Sportswriter Pedro Julio Santana shared his countrymen's sense of patriotic resistance to the occupation, but downplayed sport's overt political overtones. "We had gone through a sad experience—eight years under the invaders' boots! This is a shameful thing for a country and there are scars that have been left on the body of our *patria*. That is something for which the United States cannot be forgiven." Baseball, though, was different. It had intrinsic worth and could be incorporated into Dominican culture on Dominican terms. "They [the United States] have not given us anything else that, in my opinion, is of any value but baseball! And here, baseball is the king." On that, Báez Vargas, Bosch, and Santana agreed. "Perhaps most of all," Báez Vargas reflected, "baseball was more appropriate for us. It's more exciting; it has more *acción*. Dominicans became more inclined to baseball the moment it appeared on the scene."[5]

Baseball was one of the few aspects of life—like merengue—that could be savored and shared by all in a society wracked by dictatorship and underdevelopment. And the ballpark was one of the few arenas where Dominicans could shout and argue without fear of political retribution. The more they played baseball and the better they got at it, the more Dominicans branded the game as their own.

Baseball caught on in cities like San Pedro de Macorís on the south-east coast and in Santiago, the major city in the Cibao, the valley to the north of the capital. It knit these urban centers together, connecting them through sport. By 1921, the four cornerstone teams of Dominican baseball were in place: Licey (named for a river in the Cibao) and Escogido (the "chosen ones," selected from the top players of three other teams) in Santo Domingo, Aguilas (the Eagles) in Santiago, and the Estrellas Orientales (the Eastern Stars) in San Pedro. A few Puerto Rican, Cuban, and U.S. expats or hired guns played now and then, but most of the players were Dominican. The teams' rivalries became epic, their clashes with clubs from elsewhere in the Caribbean part of national lore.

In 1922, El Campeonato de la Reina (the Championship of the Queen) between Escogido and Licey attracted a total of twenty thousand paying fans to twenty-one games at a time when Santo Domingo's population was barely thirty thousand. The teams were hardly distant institutions; most residents of the city knew players or team directors through family, friendship, work, or school. Baseball became a fraternity that all Dominicans could aspire to join. Athletic rivalries reinforced local identities, but rather than splitting the republic along the lines of class or color, they encouraged Dominicans to transcend their differences and collaborate in sport.[6]

"We played for the love of the game," Pedro Julio Santana attested. "The yearning for lucrative gain had not awakened yet in the athlete." Then hardware stores and liquor companies began sponsoring teams so that their names would adorn jerseys and appear in the press. Players started to be put on salary and foreign players began appearing more frequently. When a player made a sensational catch, Santana recalled, "they would pass the baseball cap around and from the higher seats, the bills would fly." In the 1920s, the best Dominican players entered the larger baseball world, performing in Cuba, Puerto Rico, and North America. "After 1929," Santana confessed, "we were lying to ourselves, fooling ourselves to call ourselves amateurs and these teams amateurs."[7]

Although Dominicans had embraced baseball with passion, their nation remained a baseball backwater until the 1930s. By then, Dominican baseball was reaching the end of its romantic epoch as semiprofessionalism crept into the game. In 1936, the Estrellas Orientales, fielding a mostly Cuban lineup, won the Dominican championship, beating Santiago, as well as the capital's two teams, Licey and Escogido. The San Pedro team's victory triggered changes that rippled northward through the baseball world.

The outcome embarrassed dictator Rafael Trujillo, who found it unacceptable that the two teams from his capital city, which had been renamed from Santo Domingo to Cuidad Trujillo, could lose. That prompted the men behind the capital's clubs to combine Licey and Escogido into one powerhouse, El Dragones de Ciudad Trujillo, for the 1937 summer tournament. But even that combination was not enough to satisfy the team's anxious directorate, who dispatched its chairman, Dr. José Aybar—a dentist, loyal Trujillista deputy in congress, and the dean of the University of Santo Domingo—to the United States. His mission was to bring Satchel Paige back to the island to pitch for the Dragones.

Aybar found Paige in New Orleans, where the Pittsburgh Crawfords were preparing for the regular season, which would begin in April. According to Paige, Aybar said: "President Trujillo has instructed me to obtain the best possible pitcher for his team and our scouts recommend you."[8] He also asked Paige to recruit eight additional players. Paige, renowned for jumping contracts, accepted Aybar's offer, which vastly exceeded what Gus Greenlee would pay him to pitch in Pittsburgh that summer. He said that Aybar gave him $30,000 to split as he saw fit among himself and eight other players. After appraising the Dominican competition, Satchel contacted Crawford teammate Cool Papa Bell and persuaded him to join him in the Dominican Republic. Centerfielder Bell, catcher Josh Gibson, shortstop Sammy Bankhead, pitcher Leroy Matlock, and several other Crawfords were soon flying south aboard a Pan American Clipper, leaving a devastated Crawford team in the plane's wake.

Gus Greenlee may have been the most powerful man in black Pittsburgh, but Rafael Trujillo ruled his nation with near-absolute authority. He had seized power in 1930 after a stint in the National Guard that the United States organized during its 1916–24 occupation. Trujillo's megalomania knew no bounds. Not only had he renamed the country's capital in his honor, the nation's highest peak, towns, streets, and much else also bore his name. In every Dominican home, a plaque on the wall stated *En esta casa, Trujillo es el jefe* (In this house, Trujillo is the chief).

Trujillo was unassailable for most of his thirty-one-year reign. Whether it was your land or your vote, your business or your prettiest daughter, they were there for Trujillo's taking. And take he did. A sexual predator who few dared oppose, Trujillo acquired wealth by confiscating whatever attracted his attention. He preferred horses and women to baseball, but the game, like everything else in his Dominican fiefdom, was subject to his whims. If Trujillo paid baseball little mind, those who backed him manipulated the game to their desired outcomes—his greater glory and political quiescence among the populace. "Trujillo's minions," Báez Vargas remarked, "understood that professional baseball should be given all the help possible. . . . It kept people happy, in such a condition that they didn't bother with politics."[9] And though the revenues generated by Dominican baseball hardly justified the salaries necessary to lure Paige, Gibson, and Bell to the island, the symbolism of the championship outweighed such considerations. "Government here never neglects sport," Pedro Julio Santana emphasized.[10]

Nor did governments elsewhere in the Caribbean. In Cuba, first General Gerardo Machado, then Fulgencio Batista, who took over after the army ousted the dictatorial Machado in 1933, diverted state funds to baseball, especially at the amateur and grassroots level. As president, Batista often watched games at La Gran Stadium Cerveceria Tropical, his presence duly noted on the radio and in the press. His government created the Direccíon General Nacional de Deportes (National General Sports Administration), a government agency that reformed professional baseball and organized amateur sport.

As governments around the globe became more powerful and inclined to intervene in domestic matters during the 1930s, they began to cast sport in nationalistic terms. Caribbean basin governments focused on the Central American Games and the Mundiales, the world amateur baseball championship. The Central American Games, a regional Olympic-type competition that began in 1926, were played every few years. The Mundiales, held every year but two between 1938 and 1953 and later on a biannual basis, sought to capture some of the élan of soccer's World Cup, but never gained comparable attention. After their inaugural games in London, the next six Mundiales were staged in Havana, with most participants coming from the region. Caribbean basin nations won every competition played from 1940 through 1972. Cuba accounted for most of these victories, to the delight of fans, Batista, and his Direccíon General Nacional de Deportes, which hosted the Havana tournaments. Cuban leaders saw the games as a way to display Cuban accomplishments on a grand stage.[11]

Although largely ignored in the United States, these international rivalries captivated the Caribbean, where Cuba was the team to beat. The deciding game of the hard-fought 1941 Mundiales between Cuba and Venezuela was broadcast on radio throughout the region. Although Cuba lost, its fans were so enamored of Venezuela's play that they carried pitcher Chino Canónico, who had won five of Venezuela's eight victories, including the deciding game, around the field in homage afterward. When the gunboat bearing the champions neared the Venezuelan coast, planes flew out to meet them and dropped roses on their vessel. The city of Caracas emptied as people lined the twenty miles of road from the port to the capital, waiting to applaud their heroes. Poet Andrés Eloy Blanco thanked them "in the name of the Venezuelan people, for this enormous joy." Venezuelans still consider the nation's 1941 Mundiales victory its most important sporting triumph ever.[12]

The Dominican Republic and Nicaragua had similarly transcendent moments at the Mundiales. In 1948 Dominicans were stunned when the plane carrying their top club, the Caballeros from Santiago, crashed by the Río Verde, with no survivors. But then, a few months later, a hastily assembled Dominican team shocked the Caribbean baseball world by winning the Mundiales in Managua, Nicaragua. Mourning gave way to celebration and Dominicans took to the streets. It was the first time that the Dominican Republic had beaten Cuba, Venezuela, and the United States in just about anything.

For Nicaraguans, sporting catharsis came decades later. Like Trujillo, whom the U.S. military anointed to lead the Dominican National Guard during its occupation, Nicaragua's omnipotent dictator, Anastasio Somoza García, had come to power due to a 1920s U.S. occupation. Fernando "Bolo" Vicioso, who later organized the Dominican Republic's amateur sporting system, became close to Somoza while working in Nicaragua. "Somoza loved baseball *muchísimo*," Vicioso remembered, "much more than Trujillo." During the 1948 Mundiales, Somoza even jailed Nicaragua's manager after the team lost several games and took to the dugout to direct the team himself.[13]

In 1972, with the Somoza family still in power, Nicaragua beat Cuba in the final game of that year's Mundiales to claim the bronze medal. The victory, which took place in Nicaragua's capital city of Managua was consecrated as "the miracle of 1972." The games acquired an even more special meaning because of the presence of Roberto Clemente, the beloved Pittsburgh Pirates right fielder, who had become the greatest major leaguer to emerge from the Caribbean. A devastating earthquake struck weeks after the Mundiales concluded. Clemente, who had managed the Puerto Rican team playing in Managua, immediately began to organize earthquake relief efforts from Puerto Rico's San Juan. On New Year's Eve, his chartered plane, en route to Nicaragua with relief supplies, disappeared into the sea. The earthquake marked the death of the player writer David Maraniss would honor as "baseball's last hero," as well as the beginning of the end to the Somoza dynasty.[14]

But thirty-five years earlier, in the Dominican Republic, nationalism was less of a factor in baseball than Rafael Trujillo's looming presence. The three teams entering the 1937 Dominican tournament—Estrellas Orientales from San Pedro de Macorís, Aguilas from Santiago, and Ciudad Trujillo from the capital—fielded mostly foreign ballplayers, including the freshly acquired Satchel Paige. Cubans Martín Dihigo, Silvio García, Santos Amaro, Alejandro Oms, and Lázaro Salazar, Puerto Rican Perucho Cepeda, and Dominicans Horacio Martínez and Tetelo Vargas joined a score of Negro Leaguers in a tournament that would run from late March into July.

It was not the first time that an international all-star medley had played on the island. Foreign-born players first appeared in Dominican tournaments in the 1920s. In 1934 and 1935, a star-studded Venezuelan club, Concordia, played several games against Escogido. Luis Aparicio Sr., Martín Dihigo, Josh Gibson, Perucho Cepeda, Luis Tiant Sr., Tetelo Vargas, and other Caribbean and Negro League stars dazzled Dominican fans. Like Ciudad Trujillo, Concordia was the baseball proxy of a political strongman, Venezuelan dictator Juan Vicente Gómez, whose son directed the club. Later in 1937, the Cincinnati Reds became the first major league club to visit the Dominican Republic. Yet all of these games occurred during the winter, when they posed no direct threat to baseball in the United States.[15]

The head-on Latin foray for U.S. players commenced in March 1937 when Alejandro Pompez's brush with the law over his involvement in the numbers game forced him to abruptly disband the New York Cubans. Martín Dihigo and Lázaro Salazar, two extraordinary players who both pitched and played the field, were suddenly left stranded without a U.S. team. Quickly surveying the baseball landscape, they found teams to play for in the Dominican Republic and induced several Negro Leaguers to join them there. At Dr. Aybar's urging, Satchel Paige followed a few weeks later.

Then in May, Federico Nina, one of the San Pedro club's directors, and Luis Mendez, a Dominican consular employee, traveled to Pittsburgh to recruit additional Negro Leaguers to bolster San Pedro's largely Cuban lineup. By this point, Negro League teams were *en garde* for foreign raiders. After making inquiries about ballplayers during a Negro League game, Nina and Mendez approached Crawford pitcher Ernest Carter at the Crawford Grill that evening. They were negotiating terms with Carter at his hotel when Crawford manager Oscar Charleston stormed into the room. "I came here to whup you," Charleston snarled, "but since you're so little, I won't do it." Accusing Nina and Mendez of stealing players who were under contract, Charleston vowed to have them arrested. Before leaving, he spat: "Why don't you go into the white leagues and get your players?" The irascible manager knew the answer to that question; the Negro Leagues were easier pickings. Charleston, one of baseball's more intimidating characters, did not harm Nina and Mendez, but they were jailed on charges of conspiracy. Released on bail, Nina returned to San Pedro with several ballplayers only to have them sequestered by General Federico Fiallo and ordered to play for Ciudad Trujillo, the club for which Fiallo was a director, instead of San Pedro.[16]

Reeling from multiple defections, Gus Greenlee and the Negro National League lobbied the U.S. State Department to intervene. League commissioner Ferdinand Morton wrote U.S. senator Robert Wagner seeking redress. "Our problem," he stated, "is a grave one for the very existence of our league is threatened. All the work which we have done to secure for the colored ball player a decent wage will go for naught unless we are able to prevent further inroads."[17] Morton was prescient; black baseball's Achilles' heel would be its helplessness to rebuff efforts by better-financed leagues seeking its most precious asset—players. But the most that the State Department was willing to do was to speak with the Dominican government about rearranging schedules to minimize future conflict.

Negro League protests weren't able to force the return of its ballplayers, meaning that more than a roster's worth of Negro Leaguers defected in 1937. To these men, the advantages of Dominican baseball were obvious. They made more money for fewer games. Instead of barnstorming and playing two, even three, games a day, Dominican clubs played only two or three games a week. Nor did black players face segregation on the island, where they were put up in the finest hotels and toasted as celebrities. But they did encounter a more politicized atmosphere than in the United States.

Pointedly, Paige, Gibson, and company got the not-so-subtle message that Trujillo's team must win the Dominican tournament. Kansas City Monarch Chet Brewer, who pitched for the rival Aguilas, visited Paige's hotel one day looking for his buddy. When a boy told him that Paige was *en el carcel* (in jail), Brewer figured that the players were being held in protective custody "so they wouldn't rouse around." Paige later recounted tales of soldiers escorting them during the day and guarding their rooms at night. Before the championship game, he said, "You'd have thought that war was declared. We were guarded like we had the secret combination to Fort Knox."[18]

Paige's recollections often tended to the apocryphal, but Trujillo's influence could hardly be exaggerated. Rafael Antun remained an unreconstructed Trujillista long after the dictator's downfall, but he grew up rooting for San Pedro's club, which he later owned. "We had a Cuban team here," he said about 1937. "They were the only ones that could beat Ciudad Trujillo, so the army came and arrested all our Cubans before the game one day. We could play only with *Criollos*—Dominicans. This happened two or three times and then they would free them after the games. Why did they do this? Because they said Ciudad Trujillo, a team with Trujillo's name, could not lose."[19]

Dominicans were elated that their island occupied the center of Caribbean baseball, even if only for a few months. San Pedro's *cocolos*, dark-skinned immigrants from other islands who worked on the sugar estates, identified with the Negro Leaguers and savored their elevated stature in Dominican society. "My older brother used to carry me to the ballfield," *cocolo* millworker Roberto Caines recalled. "I remember everything I see then," he said as he rattled off the lineups. Paige, Bell, and other Negro Leaguers played golf on the Consuelo sugar mill's estate. "Only black men to do that!" Caines whooped. Coleridge Mayers, from the nearby Santa Fe sugar estate, befriended the African American players. "I knew them personally," he explained. "Those who played here in San Pedro would dance on Monday nights and we would get to know them." Josh Gibson was Mayers's favorite. Half a century later, he described a home run that Gibson hit off Ramón Bragaña. "Whooooo! It was the biggest home run I ever saw in all these Lord's days." [20]

Ciudad Trujillo got its money's worth for the reported $30,000 it spent on Negro League reinforcements. In the Dominican tournament, Paige led all pitchers with an 8–2 record and Gibson hit well over .400, won the batting title, and drove in the most runs. Aguilas's Martín Dihigo, the top Cuban in the tournament, was the next-best pitcher, and coleader in home runs. His compatriot, twenty-four-year-old Lázaro Salazar, managed Ciudad Trujillo. Salazar led the league in several batting categories and skillfully managed a diverse roster of men, some of whom spoke only Spanish while others understood only English. Most all of them were older than he was. [21]

In the deciding game of the tournament, the Aguilas faced the menacing Ciudad Trujillo. Chet Brewer, who had thrown a one-hitter to beat Ciudad Trujillo the previous week, started the game. When the Dragones exploded in the fifth inning, Aguilas player-manager Dihigo came in from center field to relieve Brewer.

Dihigo, the only ballplayer enshrined in the Hall of Fame in the United States, Cuba, Mexico, Venezuela, and the Dominican Republic, played every position with virtuosity. This was the third time that he had faced Josh Gibson in postseason play. In 1930 Gibson and the Homestead Grays had beaten Dihigo and the Philadelphia Hilldales for the Negro League championship. In one game, Gibson walloped a ball over Forbes Field's 457-foot center-field wall, a prodigious blow for an eighteen-year-old. In the 1935 NNL championship, Gibson and the Pittsburgh Crawfords played Dihigo and the New York Cubans. Gibson homered in game seven as the

Crawfords rallied in the ninth inning and won the series. This time, in the Dominican Republic, Dihigo was determined that he would finally beat a Gibson-led team. But he could not quiet Ciudad Trujillo's bats, and when he gave up a grand slam to shortstop Sammy Bankhead, Ciudad Trujillo won the game and the championship.[22]

After raucous parades in the colonial zone celebrating Ciudad Trujillo's victory, the players were feted at a lavish banquet and flown back to the United States. When the Negro National League issued two-year suspensions to those who had jumped contracts to play in the Dominican Republic, the players formed their own barnstorming club, the Trujillo Stars. Realizing that it could ill afford to do without these marquee players, the league scaled back its punishment to a modest fine for all but Satchel Paige, who had routinely flouted contractual obligations. Though his suspension stuck, Satchel's drawing power was such that his income hardly suffered. He sold his services to an array of independent clubs and was soon back in organized black baseball. In the meantime, he received offers to play elsewhere in the Caribbean.

The Crawfords, however, never recovered from the defection of their best players. Making matters worse, Gus Greenlee had hit a rough patch with his numbers business and began losing money at Greenlee Field as the Depression plunged to its second severe trough in 1937. After mediocre records on the field and at the box office in 1937 and 1938, the Crawfords folded and Greenlee sold Greenlee Field for less than what it had cost him to build. The ball field was torn down, replaced by Bedford Dwellings, a public housing project. Greenlee focused instead on his stable of boxers. His protégé, John Henry Lewis, had won the light-heavyweight championship in 1935 and Greenlee was angling to get him into the ring with heavyweight champ Joe Louis. They met in January 1939, the first time two African Americans fought for the heavyweight title. Although it was the biggest payday of John Henry Lewis's career, Joe Louis knocked him out in the first round. Greenlee resigned as NNL president a month later and then left baseball for several seasons.

Cum Posey and the Homestead Grays benefited from the Crawfords' demise. Josh Gibson returned to the Grays and, along with Buck Leonard, powered the team to the top of the Negro National League, a perch they would hold for most of the next decade. Meanwhile, with his legal troubles behind him, Alejandro Pompez reformed the New York Cubans and rejoined baseball in 1938.[23]

Dominicans often say that there is never political turmoil during a baseball season, only afterwards. With sugar exports bottoming out at only a penny a pound during the Depression, poverty endemic, and baseball no longer distracting Dominicans from their woes, Trujillo sought another outlet for the people's frustrations. In October 1937, after the ballplayers had left, Trujillo ordered the roundup and massacre of Haitians living in the Dominican Republic. Attacking Haitians appealed to Trujillo's profoundly racist attitudes; he had received a copy of Adolph Hitler's *Mein Kampf* the previous month and had an almost primal fear of Haitians, although he was partially Haitian himself. Trujillo sought to "whiten" the Dominican Republic; he even applied makeup to lighten his own mulatto appearance. His command to rid the nation of Haitians, given while inebriated at a party celebrating his rule, had horrific results. The death count topped thirty thousand; some Haitians were decapitated in the courtyards of government buildings, others bound and thrown alive into the sea, and still more hacked to death with machetes, their bodies pushed into the Río Massacre, which marked the border between Haiti and the Dominican Republic. Though the river had been named in the eighteenth century, it would henceforth be associated with the genocidal attack. Baseball was quickly forgotten as Trujillo exploited deep-seated racial fears to consolidate his by-now nearly unlimited powers.[24]

•   •   •

Despite the genocide, the Dominican Republic remained a stopover on a broader Caribbean baseball circuit that included Mexico, Nicaragua, Panama, Venezuela, Puerto Rico, and above all, Cuba. This network had its own rivalries and infrastructure. Caudillos (political strongmen) like Somoza and Trujillo, factory owners, priests, politicians, and activists sponsored teams and leagues. Some sought to win goodwill and political support, others to sell products, and a few to promote community development. These clubs were similar to sandlot and factory teams in the United States; like them, they constituted the indispensable grassroots foundation of the game.

As Caribbean baseball's guiding light, Cuba set the bar for regional play. Cubans had introduced baseball to many of these nations and became their template for the game. Dominicans listened to Cuban games on the radio and delighted when their countrymen proved themselves good enough to play there. "Much of the structure we set up in Dominican baseball," Pedro Julio Santana explained, "was an attempt to follow the efforts of the Cubans. We even copied their metaphors and expressions for the game." The Dominican Republic modeled its amateur sport system after Cuba's Direccíon General Nacional de Deportes while Cuba's professional leagues became the gold standard by which others in the Caribbean basin measured themselves.[25]

Major league baseball in the United States would have supplanted Cuba in this regard but for its color line. That barrier meant that Caribbean baseball developed a schizophrenic relationship to U.S. sport—men who played together in the Caribbean were divided by race in the United States. As long as that color line prevailed, Cuba remained the Caribbean game's center of gravity. Adolfo Luque, José Méndez, and Martín Dihigo might have starred in the major leagues or the Negro Leagues, but Cubans cared more about their exploits on the island. Similarly, Dominicans were less interested in Tetelo Vargas and Horacio Martínez's appearances in black baseball's East-West Classic than their success in Caribbean play.

More importantly, the boys who grew up playing baseball in the street, on banana plantations and cigar factory teams, and in the shadow of sugar mills aspired to play in Caribbean leagues—not in the United States. American baseball mattered mostly when its stars visited. Babe Ruth's appearance in Cuba, Hall of Fame first baseman Johnny Mize's play in the Dominican Republic, and Gibson and Paige's participation across the basin were cherished moments. But they were only moments, not the stuff of enduring legend.

At times, however, the play of Cubans in the major leagues—if not the Negro Leagues—did bring acclaim back home on the island. Adolfo Luque was a gun-toting carouser called the Pride of Havana (the name of a well-known Cuban cigar) in the United States and Papá Montero (after an infamous rumba dancer and pimp) in Cuba. Yale professor Roberto González Echevarría described Luque as "a snarling, vulgar, cursing aggressive pug, who, though small at five-seven, was always ready to fight."[26]

Luque played for parts of twenty major league seasons, winning more major league games than any Latino pitcher until another Cuban, Luis Tiant Jr., surpassed him half a century later. In 1923 he had a phenomenal year, leading all National League pitchers with a 27–8 won-loss record, six shutouts, and a 1.93 earned run average. His stellar campaign came at a time when Prohibition in the United States was boosting tourism in Havana and contributing to Cuban prosperity.

Luque's return to Havana after his triumphant 1923 season was the occasion, sportswriter Guillermo Pi enthused, "to show our gratitude for the noble, imponderable achievement that he has made in the powerful and fraternal Yankeeland." Thirty thousand Cubans, including bands, floats, groups of amateur and professional ballplayers, and army units marched to the waterfront to greet their conquering hero when his ship docked in Havana. The multitude, Pi wrote, encompassed "the most distinguished to the most humble, from the richest to the poorest, all equals, all embraced by the same feelings of action." [27]

The next day, Luque performed in a skit at the Marti Theatre in which he played himself beating up an actor dressed as New York Giant Casey Stengel. That season, Luque had pummeled Stengel after several New York Giants yelled racial slurs, including "Cuban Nigger," at him from their dugout during a ballgame. It's unclear whether Stengel was among those Giants insulting Luque (although he had a reputation as a bench jockey), but he was the one who took it on the chin. Patrons at the Marti Theatre howled and stomped their feet as Luque reenacted his vengeance upon the hapless Stengel.

When they played together on the island, José Méndez was Luque's teammate. In the U.S., Luque's light skin color gave him entrée to the major leagues. Méndez's African heritage, by contrast, meant that his only choices were performing in the Negro Leagues or on barnstorming teams. Méndez was revered in Cuba for his pitching brilliance in winter baseball as well as his gentlemanly ways. In the United States, he starred for the multiracial All Nations team and then the Kansas City Monarchs, for whom he played and managed. He led the Monarchs to the Negro League World Series title in 1924 and then again in 1925, the first two times that a postseason tournament was played between the winners of black leagues.

But no crowds or bands met him upon his return to Cuba. Unlike Luque, who was wildly applauded for his exploits in the United States, Méndez's triumphs there were all but ignored.

• • •

From the early twentieth century through World War II, top ballplayers of all nations and races gravitated each winter to wherever Caribbean salaries were the highest. Many of the very best congregated on particular squads or in particular locales—Havana, Caracas, or Mexico City—for a season or more. The 1923–24 Santa Clara Leopardos are still regarded as Cuba's greatest team ever. Concordia of the mid-1930s occupies a similar place in Venezuelan baseball lore, while the 1937 Ciudad Trujillo squad was a virtual facsimile of the 1936 Negro National League champion Pittsburgh Crawfords. After playing for Ciudad Trujillo, Lázaro Salazar and several of the Crawfords reunited in Cuba the next two winters to lead Santa Clara to league titles. Each of these clubs featured ballplayers from multiple countries, races, and leagues. In the summer, most of them played in the Negro Leagues, while those who were white or able to pass appeared in the majors. But during the winter, these men of all skin colors became teammates again.

Latin baseball gave as good as it got. Cubans Adolfo Luque, José Méndez, Cristóbal Torriente, and Martín Dihigo (all but Luque future Hall of Famers), Puerto Ricans Perucho Cepeda and Luis Tiant Sr., and Dominicans Tetelo Vargas and Horacio Martínez enriched baseball in the United States, while Negro Leaguers and future Hall of Famers Rube Foster, Cool Papa Bell, Willie Wells, Mule Suttles, and Satchel Paige brought their pizzazz to the Caribbean. Baseball knew no borders. Just as Negro Leaguer Josh Gibson astonished fans from Pittsburgh to San Pedro with his staggering blasts, Cuban Lázaro Salazar won batting championships in Cuba, Mexico, and the United States, and managed fourteen teams to titles in four different nations.[28]

While few questioned the caliber of Caribbean play, baseball in the islands often sputtered financially. Weather, economic downturns, political upheaval, and undercapitalized owners savaged schedules, rosters, and franchises. A few seasons ended abruptly when owners could not meet payroll; no professional season was held at all in Cuba after the ouster of

Horacio Martínez *(Carnegie Museum of Art, Pittsburgh; Heinz Family Fund copyright 2004, Carnegie Museum of Art, Charles "Teenie" Harris Archive). Date: Late 1930s.* A "have glove, will travel" shortstop, Horacio Martínez was one of five baseball-playing brothers. He and outfielder Tetelo Vargas were the top Dominican players before integration. Martínez later scouted for the Giants, signing Juan Marichal, the Alou brothers, and Manuel Mota.

dictator Gerardo Machado in 1933 or in the Dominican Republic after the 1937 Trujillo championship and ensuing Haitian massacre. The tournament's unusually high costs, including the salaries of its glittering Negro League stars, bankrupted Dominican professional baseball at season's end and the league did not resume play until 1951.

Major League Baseball commissioner Kenesaw Mountain Landis added to Cuban baseball's difficulties when, in a calculated move, he banned major leaguers from barnstorming after the first week of November in 1927. Cuban major leaguers Adolfo Luque and catcher Miguel Angel González saw their way around Landis's dictate by playing in the Cuban League under the names of friends, a ruse that delighted Cubans and escaped the imperious commissioner's attention.[29]

But the economic woes of Caribbean leagues did not deter baseball's vigor at the grass roots of the game. By the 1930s, baseball was at the center of social life, the sport of peasants, workers, and the middle classes. According to González Echevarría, baseball was closely associated with physical pleasure, especially liquor, coffee, and sugar, connections that "gave the game the allure of the forbidden."[30]

• • •

If Rafael Trujillo shattered Gus Greenlee's Pittsburgh powerhouse before it solidified into a Negro League dynasty, Jorge Pasquel posed a far more daunting challenge to baseball throughout the hemisphere. The wealthy Mexican mogul not only convulsed the Negro Leagues, he defied Major League Baseball in the United States and compromised the game in Cuba. Charismatic, driven, and highly competent, Pasquel had the resources that made his vision of a Mexican alternative to the major leagues instantly credible. Moreover, his timing was impeccable. He entered the baseball scene on a wave of Mexican nationalism and power flexing.

Mexico would pose a greater threat to baseball in the United States than the Dominican Republic did in 1937. It sparked a stampede of players from the Negro Leagues and, for the first time, attacked the major leagues directly. The confrontation weakened Major League Baseball's control over its players, cast doubt on its color line, and triggered realignment of its relationship with Caribbean baseball.

Baseball's beginnings in Mexico were more complex than elsewhere in the Caribbean, with Cubans spreading the game in the Yucatán and Veracruz, and foreign oil company and railroad workers introducing it elsewhere. Perhaps because of its hybrid origins, Mexican baseball was not nearly as developed as it was in Cuba. A few Mexicans had played in the major leagues before World War II, but not many held their own at the higher levels of the game. Most Mexican players were less concerned with playing abroad than with establishing themselves in the Mexican League, which became Pasquel's realm during the 1940s.

Pasquel was more ambitious than Trujillo and his Dominican underlings, with their inward-looking focus. Pasquel's goal was to elevate Mexican baseball to a status comparable with the best leagues in the world.

Taking advantage of Mexico's growing economic heft and his own fortune, he planned on importing a majority of its league's players from Cuba and the United States.

Pasquel and his four brothers had parleyed their father's Veracruz-based export-import business into a diversified economic juggernaut, Pasquel Hermanos, making them one of the most powerful families in Mexico. The business gave Pasquel considerable leverage; his personal experiences, meanwhile, had instilled a strong sense of Mexican identity bound up with his country's tortured relationship with its northern neighbor. U.S. forces had seized Veracruz on Pasquel's seventh birthday in April 1914, after President Woodrow Wilson had ordered its bombardment to force General Victoriano Huerta from power. Pasquel's attitudes toward the United States were further colored by the racial contempt U.S. citizens commonly displayed toward Mexicans and Mexican Americans. Signs reading NO DOGS, NEGROES, MEXICANS were commonplace throughout the American Southwest before World War II. Pasquel never forgot the time that he and his chauffeur, who had been his valet since childhood, stopped at a restaurant in Texas in the 1930s and the manager told the driver to leave. While Pasquel could pass for "white," his chauffeur's darker Indian features labeled him as Mexican.

Nor was Pasquel the sort of man to be intimidated. Physically fit and tremendously disciplined, Pasquel rode, shot, and fought with aplomb. He ran for an hour each morning in Mexico City's Chapultepec Park and had acquitted himself in fights and even a duel. He was well connected politically; boyhood friend Miguel Alemán, who had huddled with Pasquel in a basement during the shelling of Veracruz, assumed the Mexican presidency in 1946.

Mexican baseball had begun bringing in outside players, mostly Cubans, in the 1930s. Pitcher Ramón Bragaña, who arrived in 1931, would play twenty seasons in Mexico, marry a Mexican woman, and die in his adopted land. He and other Cuban players were later elected to the Mexican Hall of Fame. In 1938, the year after Trujillo destroyed the Pittsburgh Crawfords, Satchel Paige became the first African American to play in Mexico. Although the Negro Leagues had won a restraining order to prevent him from leaving the United States, Paige waited until it lapsed before crossing the border. Four other Negro Leaguers and an even greater number of Cubans, including Martín Dihigo and Lázaro Salazar, joined him; most had played in the Dominican Republic the previous summer.[31]

Because Mexico was the only significant league outside the United States to play during the summer, it directly competed for Negro Leaguers. The 1939 season, when a dozen Negro Leaguers played in Mexico, served as a prelude to a significantly larger infusion of African American and Cuban talent in 1940.

Pasquel was the catalyst. He entered Mexican baseball in the wake of President Lázaro Cárdenas's nationalization of U.S. and British oil company holdings. Accustomed to having their way, the oil companies had refused to abide by a Mexican Supreme Court ruling that ordered them to pay contested wages despite the fact that they had originally agreed to accept the court's decision. Pasquel's chum, Miguel Alemán, then governor of oil-rich Veracruz, mobilized support for President Cárdenas and the expropriation. Although the oil companies retaliated, organizing a boycott of Mexican oil, Mexicans cheered Cárdenas's bold move. They reveled in confronting foreign interests that had traditionally trampled on Mexican honor. Pasquel sought to do the same over U.S. baseball interests.[32]

Prior to the 1940 season, he bought the Veracruz Azules (Blues) and moved the team to bustling Mexico City, already home to 2 million residents, where they shared Delta Park, which he also purchased, with the Mexico City Diablos Rojos (Red Devils). By owning Delta Park, Pasquel controlled the city's best facility and kept rival league teams from playing there. After buying the Veracruz club, Pasquel flew to Havana and convinced Martín Dihigo to manage and play for him. Dihigo quickly filled the Veracruz lineup with top African American and Cuban players.

Pasquel directed the more powerful of the two Mexican leagues, the Mexican Major League, and dictated policies emphasizing collective survival. He intuitively understood what National Football League owners in the United States realized during the 1930s and 1940s when their enterprise was struggling: survival required the smaller-market, weaker franchises to succeed. Accordingly, Mexican League teams shared a greater portion of revenues than teams in other leagues, with three-quarters of the gate distributed evenly. Players were likewise allocated to teams to promote competitive balance. Pasquel was optimistic that the league could exploit his country's size. Mexico's population of 20 million dwarfed the rest of Latin America's baseball world.

Over sixty Negro Leaguers ventured to Mexico in 1940, including seven future Hall of Famers. In all, the Negro Leagues lost a fifth of their players to Mexico that season. The Newark Eagles were hit especially hard, unable to retain three future Hall of Famers, third baseman Ray Dandridge, pitcher Leon Day, and shortstop Willie Wells. Dandridge would reward Pasquel's generous treatment by playing eight of the next nine summers for Veracruz, which fielded thirteen Negro and Cuban Leaguers in 1940.[33]

Stunned by the flight of so many talented players, the Negro National and Negro American Leagues adopted common cause in 1941. Players who jumped to Mexico or other foreign leagues would be suspended for three years. Seeking to further isolate and punish the jumpers, they also barred Negro Leaguers from barnstorming against the outlawed players. Clemency, however, would be granted to any ballplayer who returned to his Negro League team by May 1, 1941, and paid a $100 fine.

When Josh Gibson, who had signed with the Homestead Grays for $6,000, took Pasquel's offer of $10,000 plus living expenses and went to Mexico in March 1941, Grays owner Cum Posey sued for breach of contract. Allegheny County courts awarded Posey $10,000 and ordered Gibson to return or forfeit his house on the Hill in Pittsburgh. Gibson, as well as thirty-eight other Negro Leaguers, including future Hall of Famers Cool Papa Bell and Willard Brown, went anyway. Gibson had close to a Triple Crown season (leading the league in home runs, batting average, and RBIs) in Mexico but returned to Pittsburgh in 1942 and the suit was dropped.[34]

African American and Cuban ballplayers prized the economic and social splendor that Pasquel lavished upon them. Newark Eagle Monte Irvin described the time he spent playing in Mexico as "one of the best years of my life . . . the first time in my life that I felt free. We could go anywhere we wanted, eat anywhere we wanted, do anything we wanted and not have to worry about anything." Making only $150 per month for the Newark Eagles when he joined Veracruz, Irvin surpassed that sum in a week in Mexico, where the cost of living was also much lower than back home in the States. He had a terrific season, leading the league in batting average

(.397) and home runs (20). If he had driven in a few more runs, he would have won the 1942 Triple Crown.[35]

Far from simply being tolerated, black players were revered in Mexico. "We saw the black players as gods," Mexican baseball historian Jaime Cervantes recalled. "We sought their friendship. We wanted them to recognize us and to talk to us." Pasquel made sure that Negro Leaguers and their wives were well cared for, treated in ways that they had never experienced in the United States. He had suits custom-tailored for pitchers who threw shutouts and gave cash bonuses for timely home runs.[36]

Despite Pasquel's solicitude, playing in Mexico had its downside. Teams took excruciatingly long bus and train rides, sometimes traveling with livestock. Ballparks often lacked locker rooms or showers, and playing conditions and fields were subpar. In Tampico, a city on the Gulf of Mexico, a railroad spur crossed through the outfield and games were sometimes stopped to allow a train to pass by. For some, the language and the food presented difficult hurdles. But for most, the benefits outweighed these drawbacks.

When Willie Wells spoke with the *Pittsburgh Courier*'s Wendell Smith about why he had decided to return to Mexico in 1944, the Newark Eagle shortstop's words resonated with many of the men who had joined him. "I came back to play ball for Veracruz because I have a better future in Mexico than in the States. Not only do I get more money playing here, but I live like a king. I am not faced with the racial problem in Mexico. . . . I didn't quit Newark and join some other team in the States. I quit and left the country. I've found freedom and democracy here, something I never found in the United States. I was branded a Negro in the States and had to act accordingly. Everything I did, including playing ball, was regulated by my color. Well, here in Mexico, I am a man."[37]

Cuban, Puerto Rican, and Venezuelan players also favored Mexico to the United States. If light-skinned enough to be able to play in the major leagues, they were routinely paid less than American major leaguers of comparable merit. But being paid less because they were darker-skinned was not an issue in Mexico. Some, like Cuban outfielder Santos Amaro, declined opportunities to play in the United States because of an unwillingness to contend with discrimination on a daily basis. Amaro liked Mexico enough to settle there. His Mexican-born son Rubén would play for the Yankees, and his Philadelphia-born grandson, Rubén Jr., would play with the Phillies and eventually become their general manager.[38]

Perucho Cepeda won batting championships in Puerto Rico, where he twice hit over .400. But while the light-skinned Hiram Bithorn and Luis Olmo became Puerto Rico's first major leaguers during World War II, Cepeda's color prevented him from joining them. Although courted by Alejandro Pompez, Cepeda refused entreaties to join the Negro Leagues. "My father was a proud man," his Hall of Famer son Orlando explained. "As a black man, he had neither the inclination to endure segregation nor the temperament to buck racism in the United States."[39]

Luis Tiant Sr., for his part, was deeply embittered by his own experience in the United States. When his son signed with the Cleveland Indians in 1961, he tried to dissuade him from leaving Cuba. The elder Tiant, like his son Luis Jr., had been a marvelously canny pitcher with an assortment of off-kilter windups and off-speed pitches. During his career with the New York Cubans, he endured months, even years, away from Cuba and his family and never reconciled himself to the racial insult he faced. "He went through so many bad things," his son explained. "I think he was afraid I would have bad luck, too." In 1975, after watching his son pitch for the Red Sox in the World Series, the senior Tiant told the press: "I didn't want him to come to America. I didn't want him to be persecuted and spit on and treated like garbage, like I was." Like many Negro Leaguers, Amaro, Cepeda, and Tiant Sr. preferred playing in Mexico and Cuba.[40]

By 1942, most of the Negro Leaguers who had relished playing abroad were back in the United States. The conflicts raging in Manchuria, Spain, and Poland during the 1930s had escalated to world war. While opposition by the Negro Leagues had done little to restrain black players bent on leaving for Mexico, military conscription was an effective deterrent. Moreover, the Negro Leagues prospered during wartime and could finally pay competitive salaries. World War II stemmed the hemorrhaging of Negro Leaguers to Mexico and cast a shadow over baseball, as it did over everything else in the world for the next four years. Following the war, Mexico's Jorge Pasquel would attempt to renew his bold challenge to U.S. baseball. By then, World War II had eroded segregation's foundation stateside, and integration—Major League Baseball's great experiment—was on the horizon.[41]

CHAPTER FOUR

The Winds of War

World War II was America's long-delayed catalyst to racial change, drastically reconfiguring almost every aspect of the home front, including baseball. For the Negro Leagues, the war posed a bittersweet paradox, pumping them up economically before unleashing the social and political forces that would soon undercut them. During the war, black baseball would soar to new heights of popularity, allowing a few years of unparalleled viability as Negro League owners began pulling in cash from gate receipts hand over fist. Yet World War II also forced integration onto the nation's agenda; how such monumental societal change might play out at the ballpark was still anybody's guess.

The war itself was a paradox; the United States was fighting a viciously eugenicist Nazi regime while sanctioning racism and segregation at home. Nowhere were the country's racial contradictions and those of its national pastime more glaring than in Washington, D.C. The capital's racial patterns were a patchwork of segregated zones, including the public schools, most workplaces, and housing, with spliced-in integrated wedges, primarily federal institutions and public spaces. Sport belonged primarily to the former. During the 1930s, black prizefighters could not enter the ring against white opponents in the District of Columbia, and Washington Senators owner Clark Griffith forbade interracial ballgames at the stadium that bore his name. Griffith Stadium was one of only two major league ballparks that segregated fans; the other was Sportsman's Park in St. Louis. Segregation at Senators games was de facto; African Americans could attend, but only if they kept to their allotted place, mostly the right-field pavilion. Yet the ballpark was located in a black neighborhood, between Howard University and the Freedmen's Hospital.[1]

Despite its federal status, Washington remained a southern city at heart, and Clark Griffith refused to place black players on the Senators. But Griffith had always been willing to juggle when racial boundaries came up against bottom lines. During his time managing the Cincinnati Reds in 1911, the club signed Cubans Rafael Almeida and Armando Marsans and then labored to convince skeptics that both were of pure Castilian heritage. In Washington, Griffith continued to negotiate racially ambiguous terrain when it made financial sense. Throughout the 1930s and '40s he exploited the Cuban market more than any other major league executive. Papa Joe Cambria, an Italian-born, American-bred ex-ballplayer, had begun scouting Cuba for Griffith before the war. He signed scores of Cubans for the Senators and their minor league teams at bargain prices. Several of them were almost certainly of mixed Afro-Cuban racial origins, prompting sportswriter Red Smith's classic line that "there was a Senegambian somewhere in the Cuban batpile where Senator timber is seasoned."[2]

In 1940 Griffith, who rented his ballpark to black clubs when the Senators were out of town, gained a new tenant, the Homestead Grays. Despite a sizable black population, the nation's capital had been a graveyard for black ball clubs. But Cum Posey, who had by then emerged as one of baseball's most astute entrepreneurs, envisioned the city as a second venue for his Grays, who played home games at Forbes Field in Pittsburgh. He figured that Washington, coming alive due to the wartime frenzy, could become a profitable second city for his team. Still, the Grays drew poorly at Griffith Stadium in 1940 and not much better when they returned for a second season in 1941. By the summer of 1942, however, with the world at war, Posey gave Washingtonians something they hadn't seen in years— terrific baseball—and they responded in record numbers. Success was largely due to World War II. The runup to war that began after Germany invaded Poland in September 1939 jump-started a moribund American economy. After Pearl Harbor, unemployment vanished, overtime became readily available, and wages and salaries more than doubled. Because new homes, cars, and consumer durables were not being produced, spending on entertainment and recreation skyrocketed, boosting black baseball's attendance. For the next few seasons, the Homestead Grays and the Kansas City Monarchs rode the rising tide of profits spilling over from a national economic boom to become the two most profitable clubs in black baseball history.

World War II also spurred women's professional baseball. Seeking to capitalize on the times, what became the All-American Girls Professional Baseball League (AAGPBL) started play in 1943. Based in the Midwest, with teams the first season in Racine and Kenosha, Wisconsin; Rockford, Illinois; and South Bend, Indiana, the league would play through 1954. At its peak in 1948 the ten-team circuit attracted nearly a million fans.

The league benefited from liberalized gender roles as the image of a more physical and capable woman temporarily supplanted the traditional idealized notion of woman atop the pedestal—passive, demure, and averse to sweating. Like African Americans, women would gain greatly from the war's impact on social norms. Most of these gains, however, would be eclipsed during the 1950s before gaining greater purchase in the late 1960s and 1970s with the emergence of a women's liberation movement. The AAGPBL, like MLB, rejected integration, and maintained its exclusivity even after MLB's racial walls were breached.

Perhaps no segment of the population benefited more in relative terms from this war-induced economic turnaround than African Americans. The conflict shattered the status quo, recharging the Great Migration, expanding employment possibilities, and energizing black activists.

In 1940, before the United States entered the war, three-fourths of all African Americans still resided south of the Mason-Dixon Line, many in bleak rural hinterlands. More blacks labored as sharecroppers, tenant farmers, and domestics than in any other occupations, and less than 2 percent of the U.S. Army was black.[3] The war persuaded many to search for better lives elsewhere. Millions headed for the North and the West; millions more relocated within the South, forsaking the countryside for towns and cities. Black workers flooded shipyards, aircraft factories, and steel mills; some four hundred thousand black women traded mops for factory or government jobs. Soon, a quarter of the iron and steel workforce was black, while the ranks of African American government employees tripled to two hundred thousand. Even the number of black skilled workers and foremen—fiercely held, traditionally whites-only positions—doubled.[4]

These gains did not go uncontested. Discrimination still prevailed in many industries and more than a dozen international trade unions denied African Americans membership. Some white workers rioted or sabotaged efforts by blacks to gain a foothold in previously all-white workplaces or win promotion to skilled positions. Elsewhere, African Americans were recognized as vital to organizing efforts and welcomed into the labor movement, especially by unions that belonged to the Congress of Industrial Organizations (CIO).

Comparable steps forward were made in the military. In August 1939, only thirty-six hundred African Americans were in the Army. The Army Air Force and Marines were lily-white, and the Navy and Coast Guard assigned African Americans to duty only as stewards and kitchen workers. The war's demands would force the government to make better use of African Americans. By December 1942, almost half a million were in the military, albeit in segregated units. Enlisting at a rate 60 percent higher than the national average, more than 1 million African Americans served by war's end.[5]

Most population and job gains came in northern cities or on the West Coast, where African Americans were beginning to concentrate. During the 1940s, metropolitan Chicago's black population increased to half a million, while New York City's shot past 1 million, and Detroit and Philadelphia's black communities more than doubled to 300,000 and 465,000 respectively. African American enclaves on the West Coast also exploded in size. By 1960, three-fourths of all African Americans lived in urban areas, a remarkable transformation over a stunningly short amount of time. Such dramatic demographic shifts augured well for black baseball.[6]

• • •

Nowhere did the wartime bustle generate a more sweeping makeover than in Washington, D.C. As African Americans gained jobs in the federal government during the war, the city's black population soared by almost 100,000, to over 280,000. During the 1950s, Washington would become the nation's first majority-black city.[7]

The Homestead Grays, who wore a *W* for Washington on their sleeves when they played at Griffith Stadium, capitalized on the city's growing African American community and its substantial black middle class. They also benefited from Satchel Paige, who had achieved a folkloric celebrity that crossed racial lines. No black athlete, with the exception of Joe Louis, was better known. And even Louis did not give rise to as many fables as Paige.[8]

Given that major league baseball was not yet broadcast on television and remained confined to dense urban centers in a region of the country north and east of St. Louis, it's likely that more people saw Paige play in person than any other player in baseball history. He performed everywhere. Pitching a few innings almost every day, he combined dexterity on the mound with a mythic persona, enigmatically admonishing: "Don't look back, something might be gaining on you," and "Keep your juices flowing by jangling around gently as you move."

Although Paige had a well-deserved reputation as a contract jumper, the Negro Leagues needed him more than he needed them. Because he was black baseball's biggest attraction, his past indiscretions—leaving teams for the Dominican Republic, Mexico, or parts unknown—had been forgiven if not forgotten. "When Satchel got to the ballpark," teammate Jimmy Crutchfield said, "it was like the sun just came out."[9] While not every Negro Leaguer liked Paige, they all appreciated the paydays he generated.

Paige, who now played for the Kansas City Monarchs, pitched three times at Griffith Stadium in 1942. He pitched for the Grays versus St. Louis Cardinal pitcher Dizzy Dean and a barnstorming team of white ballplayers in May in a game the Grays won 8–1, then twice for the Monarchs *against* the Grays later that season. The three contests collectively drew over seventy thousand fans with one of the Monarchs-Grays games attracting the largest crowd any teams—white or black—had drawn at Griffith Stadium since 1933. In a marquee showdown, the Monarchs-Grays games pitted Paige against rival legend Josh Gibson. Although they had been teammates in Pittsburgh, on Ciudad Trujillo, and through the barnstorming circuit, the duo had rarely played against each other. Satchel got the better of Josh in these two contests, but the Grays won both games.[10]

The Grays enjoyed several advantages that season. Most of all, they had not been hard hit by the draft and enlistments. While about 125 Negro

Satchel Paige (on left) **and Josh Gibson** *(Courtesy Dennis Goldstein). Date: 1940s.* Satchel Paige and Josh Gibson were more than the best black players of their time. They became mythic figures throughout black America and the Caribbean. Teammates in Pittsburgh and the Dominican Republic, they were opponents after Paige joined the Kansas City Monarchs.

League players and 500 major leaguers entered the service, and many others took defense jobs, the Grays managed to hold onto both Josh Gibson and Buck Leonard. Advancing age and accumulated injuries had rendered both stars 4-F.[11] The capital also had terrific rail connections, which became more important with gasoline and tire rationing. Moreover, in 1942, Clark Griffith's pecuniary instincts got the better of him and he permitted interracial games at the ballpark. As a result, the Grays staged lucrative contests with white clubs like Dizzy Dean's All-Stars and Griffith profited commensurately. The Grays won the 1942 Negro National League pennant, part of a nine-year span in which they ruled the league, and drew a record 127,690 fans to Griffith Stadium. They averaged 11,608 paid attendance per game, far more than the hapless Senators attracted.[12]

Cum Posey called the 1942 season black baseball's best ever, pointing out that the Negro Leagues had done over a million dollars in business. He contended that a key reason for their success was that most clubs were finally playing in major league parks, enhancing their appeal to fans. From 1922 until 1935, only the Homestead Grays had played home games regularly at a major league venue. Posey was just as upbeat regarding the 1943 season and argued that a consolidated eight-to-ten-team league that merged the best of the two Negro Leagues would elevate black baseball even higher, making it in effect baseball's third major league. But Posey's optimism was tempered by the realization that integration could jeopardize this steadily growing enterprise. Black owners had more at stake than ever before.[13]

The Grays played twice as many dates in Washington in 1943 than they had during the previous season, averaging about nine thousand fans per game and winning another NNL pennant. Overall, the Negro Leagues drew a record 3 million fans that year. They continued to thrive through 1945, their best run ever, but profits did not mask black baseball's limitations. Its owners were still perpetually undercapitalized, black fans had considerably less discretionary income than whites, and no black club owned its own venue and controlled what dates it played.[14]

Black clubs also faced serious problems of their own making. Black baseball had long been roiled by disputes between the NNL and NAL, by personality squabbles that undermined sound collective decision making, and by arguments over the role of white booking agents. Teams failed to sign players to formal contracts, leaving them vulnerable when players jumped to other teams, leagues, or countries. Scheduling was inconsistent and unbalanced, causing disputes over league standings. The officiating was substandard and statistics were haphazardly recorded. And unlike Major League Baseball and its autocratic commissioner Kenesaw Mountain Landis, Negro League commissioners were comparatively weak figures, unable to resolve differences among feuding owners. Black baseball had overcome these self-inflicted wounds in the past, but time was about to run out.[15]

•   •   •

The war did more than allow the Negro Leagues to turn a profit; it changed what Swedish sociologist Gunnar Myrdal called the "Negro problem" from a southern issue into a national dilemma. As African American populations grew in the North and the West, their concerns could no longer be dismissed as pertaining only to the South. Changed circumstances, meanwhile, energized black consciousness. "World War II has immeasurably magnified the Negro's awareness of the disparity between the American profession and practice of democracy," NAACP executive secretary Walter White observed. "The majority [of black soldiers] will return home convinced that whatever betterment of their lot is achieved must come largely through their own efforts."[16]

The right to play became part of the larger struggle. While paling in significance when compared with efforts to end lynching, desegregate workplaces, and enfranchise voters, sporting equality resonated with African Americans. Access to recreation and the chance to compete appealed to a sense of fairness and the desire for respect. It is "when they set out in pursuit of pleasure and recreation," journalist George Schuyler wrote, that "the Ethiops are made to feel most keenly their lowly status." He rued that the simple act of seeking access to a beach or park outside their own neighborhood sorely tested their patriotism.[17] The war brought these racial contradictions into bold relief.

Even before the United States entered the fray, Washington, D.C., had become a national focal point for protest. In the spring of 1939 virtuoso black contralto Marian Anderson's concert before an integrated audience at Constitution Hall was blocked by the Daughters of the American Revolution, which controlled the venue. After Eleanor Roosevelt intervened, Anderson sang instead at the Lincoln Memorial before seventy-five thousand people. The incident—and Anderson's stunning performance—drew widespread attention to the race question.[18]

So did A. Philip Randolph in early 1941. The charismatic editor of the socialist newspaper the *Messenger*, Randolph had spearheaded the organization of the Brotherhood of Sleeping Car Porters, the first national union of African American workers and a lynchpin of the fight for civil rights, in the 1920s. Now, turning to industry, Randolph sought pledges from tens of thousands of African Americans to march on Washington that summer and demand that defense work be desegregated.[19] The specter of a mass march on the capital alarmed President Franklin Delano Roosevelt, who issued Executive Order 8802, barring racial discrimination in defense work and creating the Fair Employment Practices Commission to address complaints. After forcing FDR's hand, Randolph channeled the energy he had unleashed into the March on Washington Movement and set up chapters across the country. It became the crucible in which activists who organized the Montgomery Bus Boycott, the 1963 March on Washington, and other campaigns were forged.[20]

As the capital of a nation preparing for war, Washington had a heightened symbolic profile, and Anderson's concert and the March on Washington campaign became galvanizing victories. Nor could African Americans, who were becoming a substantial northern voting bloc, be so easily ignored anymore. The Democrats had been the beneficiaries of black voters—despite the retrograde policies of their southern wing—ever since *Pittsburgh Courier* publisher Robert L. Vann had urged blacks to turn Lincoln's picture to the wall and vote for FDR in 1932. Now, their numbers were growing in states where they were able to register and vote. So were the ranks of black workers in industrial unions, which were steadily gaining influence. The migration also strengthened the political infrastructure in many black communities and reinvigorated the black press, which pushed the envelope regarding segregation.

While integrating baseball was not African Americans' highest priority, the cause benefited enormously from a rapidly morphing political environment. The black press led the way, as it had for years. A few weeks after Kristallnacht, the infamous "night of broken glass" when Nazi gangs attacked Jews throughout Germany in November 1938, *Pittsburgh Courier* sportswriter Wendell Smith took Major League Baseball to task. "They play the same game as Hitler," he wrote. "They discriminate, segregate and hold down a minor race, just as he does." But Landis and other major league executives, he scoffed, lacked Adolf Hitler's courage and truthfulness. At least Hitler was forthright in his hatred. "When asked about the inclusion of black 'jews' in baseball, they [Landis and the owners] beat around the bush."[21]

Not all of the black press's dispatches were so searing. Smith's editor Ches Washington telegraphed Pirate manager Pie Traynor at the winter baseball meetings to tell him that he possessed the elixir for Pittsburgh's mediocre lineup. "HAVE ANSWER TO YOUR PRAYERS RIGHT HERE IN PITTSBURGH." He listed several names—Josh Gibson, Buck Leonard, Satchel Paige, Cool Papa Bell, Ray Brown—each a future Hall of Famer. "ALL AVAILABLE AT REASONABLE FIGURES." Traynor, however, could not accept the offer, even though he worked for one of baseball's few progressive owners, William Benswanger. Integration was still virtually unimaginable.[22]

But Ches Washington, Wendell Smith, Sam Lacy, Rollo Wilson, and other black sportswriters did not let the issue of racial barriers in sport fade from the headlines. They celebrated victories, decried discrimination, and featured efforts to desegregate swimming pools, parks, ball fields, and most of all, teams. These writers addressed doubts over the abilities of black players, defused concerns that white players, especially those from the South, would not tolerate black teammates, and confronted the notion that fights between black and white players on the field would provoke race riots in the stands. In 1939 Wendell Smith interviewed players and managers on the eight National League teams for a lengthy *Courier* series. These men, who had played against blacks in the off-season, had no doubts that they could succeed in the major leagues; most of the managers acknowledged they would sign black players if they could. "I would certainly use a Negro player who had the ability," Pirate manager Pie Traynor said. But he did not seek to do so.[23]

The campaign to desegregate the nation picked up momentum after Pearl Harbor. Because the United States saw itself as fighting a racialist enemy in Nazi Germany, people began to look at discrimination and the war effort differently. As Gunnar Myrdal contended in his classic 1944 study, *An American Dilemma*, by fighting fascism, America stood before the world in favor of racial tolerance, cooperation, and equality.[24] The war encouraged many to embrace previously unthinkable reforms and brought new allies to the struggle. The *Pittsburgh Courier*, the black press's most widely circulated newspaper, launched its Double V campaign, calling for victory over fascism abroad and racism at home. Other black papers echoed the cry for full citizenship for African Americans in all avenues of life.

Activists in black organizations, the labor movement, and the Communist Party took aim at baseball's color line, although there was no fixed target to attack. The owners had never voted to ban African Africans; on the other hand, not one of them was willing to sign black players. As activists searched for a way to force integration, some picketed, others wrote and spoke out, and many more gathered signatures for petitions. A few even tried to force Major League Baseball's hand through direct action.

In the spring of 1942, *Courier* correspondent Herman Hill arrived at the Chicago White Sox training camp in Pasadena with two black players, Jackie Robinson and Nate Moreland, and asked for a tryout.[25] The White Sox flatly refused his request. But later that summer, the *Courier* reported that William Benswanger, who had taken over the Pirates after the death of his father-in-law, Barney Dreyfuss, had agreed to a tryout for players the paper would select. An elated Wendell Smith saluted the Pittsburgh owner as "the greatest liberal in baseball history," and reminded readers that Benswanger had reignited efforts to desegregate the majors in 1937 when he became the first owner to state publicly that blacks should be in the major leagues. Anticipating a historic breakthrough, the *Courier* selected Josh Gibson, Willie Wells, Leon Day, and shortstop Sam Bankhead for the tryout. All but Bankhead would eventually win election to the Hall of Fame. But the tryout never took place, and Smith castigated Benswanger for reneging.[26] Such setbacks, however, did not deter black writers or their white allies like Communist Party member Lester Rodney, who used his *Daily Worker* pulpit to lambaste baseball commissioner Kenesaw Mountain Landis and the owners.

When the *Courier* reported that Brooklyn Dodgers manager Leo Durocher considered Landis the primary obstacle to integrating baseball, the imperious commissioner denied that there was a ban on black players "either by rule, agreement or subterfuge."[27] Landis, who as a federal judge had ruled against black heavyweight champion Jack Johnson and members of the Industrial Workers of the World, often relied on precise legal wording to defend his positions. Not only black writers, but white journalists like *New York Daily Mirror* sports editor Dan Parker and *Pittsburgh Sun-Telegraph* sports editor Harry Keck lashed into Landis for blatant hypocrisy. Keck scoffed about what Landis would do if Cum Posey requested a major league franchise and stocked it with black players. Calling the commissioner out, Keck concluded: "Why lie about it and say white is black, or vice versa, and expect the fans to believe it just because the great Judge Landis says so?"[28]

Ironically, some black owners joined Landis in opposing integration outright. Many more black players and owners were simply ambivalent; the players knew that if the best Negro Leaguers entered the majors, their leagues would suffer and they could lose jobs or face pay cuts. "Might be a good thing," Homestead Grays player-manager Vic Harris said about the possible integration of the major leagues, "and then again, it might not be." Acknowledging that the best black players would benefit, he asked: "How could the other 75–80 percent survive?" Some owners protested that major league clubs might take their players without offering compensation, devastating their teams. Other owners and sportswriters, however, embraced the prospect of integration and thought it would help black baseball. The more far-sighted and optimistic of them argued that the Negro Leagues could affiliate with the majors and become a high minor league that developed players. And if they could place a black team in the majors, sportswriter Joe Bostic wrote, "all of the money and jobs . . . would come to us."[29]

When asked in August 1942 how he would feel about playing in the majors, Satchel Paige responded: "It wouldn't appeal to me." He neither relished facing hostile white players nor wanted to risk his income, which came to $37,000 in 1941 and surpassed that of most ballplayers, white or black. Criticized for his remarks in the black press, Paige felt compelled to address the forty-eight thousand fans gathered at the 1942 East-West Classic in Comiskey Park. Before Paige took the mound to pitch in the seventh inning, the umpire halted play so that Paige could speak over the public-address system. Claiming that he had been misquoted, Paige said he did not oppose black players in the majors. But he posed an alternative to the majors accepting a handful of Negro Leaguers. Instead, he suggested, "It might be a good idea to put a complete Negro team in the majors."[30]

For all the high-minded debate, major league clubs had little concrete incentive to integrate. Before accepting a military commission in September 1942, Brooklyn Dodger president Larry MacPhail echoed black owners' concerns that integration could wreck the black leagues and cost "hundreds of negro players" their livelihood.[31] MacPhail, however, was hardly a disinterested party. In Brooklyn and again after the war in New York as the Yankees general manager, his teams profited from the Negro Leagues. In fact, the Yankees gained more than any other major league club, renting Yankee Stadium and several minor league parks to black teams. The Giants, Dodgers, Pirates, and Senators also benefited from symbiotic relationships with black teams.

The Senators organization, which made $35,000 to $40,000 a year from the Grays, helped with their ticket sales and publicity, but never seriously considered signing their players. During a game in 1938, Clark Griffith called down to the dugout and asked Buck Leonard and Josh Gibson to come to his office afterwards. He asked them whether they thought they were good enough to play in the majors. Leonard responded that they would welcome the chance to find out. When Griffith asked if they could hit major league pitchers, Leonard chuckled: "Well, we could hit some of them and some of them we couldn't." Griffith, who knew that they could hit big-league pitching as well as anyone in baseball, ended the conversation by saying: "The reason we haven't got you colored baseball players on the team is that the time hasn't come." Years later, Leonard said that he still could not figure out why Griffith had bothered asking in the first place.[32]

Realizing that black and white owners were conflicted about integration and unlikely to lead the fight for desegregation, Wendell Smith called for citizens, especially black ones, to mobilize and apply pressure directly on the major leagues. "The final blow to be struck in this long-waged war for Negroes in the majors remains to be struck by the fans," he concluded. "Nothing else can do the trick." The journalist issued a dramatic call to arms. "An army of baseball fans from coast to coast must rise and fire the final shot demanding that the owners hire Negro players." Change, he argued, would come only if fans pushed hard for it. "Now is the time for the NAACP, Urban League, Elks and all other organizations to join the fight for Negroes in the majors. The issue must not die. Shoulder arms, you sons of Ham, and carry on!"[33]

Many did just that. Unions, especially those with black members like the eighty-thousand-member Ford United Auto Workers local in Detroit, passed resolutions against segregation in baseball. Black and white voices within the church also joined the pro-integration chorus. The Catholic Interracial Council demanded that black ballplayers be given a chance. "Nothing less will meet the standards of democracy and fair play." Ad hoc groups organized petition drives and protested at ballparks.[34]

Just what baseball's integration would look like, however, was subject to debate. Some writers and owners had suggested in the mid-1930s that the Negro Leagues could affiliate with Major League Baseball and accept minor league status. Such a relationship would prevent major league teams from raiding their rosters without compensation if integration were to occur. But *People's Voice* writer Joe Bostic, Satchel Paige, and others countered that instead of accepting designation as minor leagues, entire clubs should enter Major League Baseball with black ownership remaining intact.[35]

On December 3, 1943, over forty white owners, general managers, and front-office executives met with a delegation of black publishers, sportswriters, and actor-turned-activist Paul Robeson to address Major League Baseball's fears of integration. Sam Lacy, then working for the *Chicago Defender*, had arranged the meeting at the Hotel Roosevelt in New York City. But Negro League owners were noticeably absent from the conference. And other than Landis (who had already been forced to state for the record that there was no rule barring blacks from the majors) acknowledging that any club could sign anyone it sought, nothing came of the meeting. Landis might have been willing to make a gesture by holding the meeting, but he would not disrupt baseball's racial status quo. No owner said or did anything publicly that suggested integration was on its way.[36]

Outspoken opponents of integration often focused on black baseball's weak organizational standards. The major leagues, by contrast, stressed the importance of structure, and referred to their own system of major and minor leagues as organized baseball. Even black owners and writers tempered their boosterism of the Negro Leagues with the admission that the leagues were compromised by their own faulty internal dynamics. Still, Joe Bostic declared, black baseball was a business worth protecting. "To kill it would be criminal and that's just what entry of their players into the American and National would do."[37] If the majors accepted even a token number of African Americans, the Negro Leagues could lose players, fans, and the interest of the black press. Black owners, despite needing the help of the black press, had taken sportswriters for granted, failing to provide them with adequate and accurate stats, box scores, and access.

With Major League Baseball unwilling to integrate on its own, activists sought government intervention. While veteran sportswriter Rollo Wilson fumed that "a one-armed man, a one-legged man, Cubans, Chinese, Mexicans—anyone except a known colored man is welcomed into the big leagues at this time," politicians in New York and Massachusetts began legislating for change.[38] A bipartisan effort in New York led to passage of the Ives-Quinn law in March 1945, creating the state equivalent of the federal Fair Employment Practices Commission. Employers who discriminated in hiring on the basis of race would be subject to fines and jail sentences. That included the state's three major league clubs. In Boston, city councilman Isadore Muchnick threatened to block renewal of the Red Sox' and the Braves' Sunday baseball licenses unless they allowed tryouts regardless of race. And in early April, Harlem newspaper man Joe Bostic showed up without warning at the Dodgers spring training camp at Bear Mountain, New York, accompanied by two black players, for whom he demanded tryouts. Although Dodger president Branch Rickey rebuked Bostic for his tactics, the players—neither a strong prospect—did receive perfunctory tryouts.

Protests against Major League Baseball's segregation gathered steam as the war reached its victorious conclusion. In 1945, Colonel Hubert Julian, the famous "Black Eagle" who commanded the Ethiopian Air Force during the Italian invasion, and radical black politician James Pemberton organized opening-day boycotts. An End Jim Crow in Baseball committee picketed Yankee Stadium with photos of black soldiers who had died in the war, captioned "Good Enough to Die for Their Country, But Not Good Enough to Play." In Los Angeles, both the CIO and AFL backed integration of the city's Pacific Coast League team, the Los Angeles Angels. After the Angels backed out on a promise to give Negro League pitcher Chet Brewer a tryout, over one thousand white workers at the aircraft factory where he was employed signed a petition protesting the club's action. In New York City, Brooklyn Communist councilman Peter Cacchione sought scrutiny of the city's three teams, while in Washington, radical U.S. congressman Vito Marcantonio called for an investigation of Major League Baseball's hiring practices.[39]

A major barrier to integration fell when Commissioner Landis died in November 1944. The following April, MLB owners selected U.S. senator Albert "Happy" Chandler from Kentucky as his replacement. The *Courier's* Ric Roberts rushed over to Capitol Hill to interview Chandler, who told him that he opposed barring African Americans from the majors. "I am for the Four Freedoms," Chandler stated, referring to President Roosevelt's Address to Congress in January 1941. Roosevelt had spoken of the "perpetual peaceful revolution" by which the United States had—and would again—adjust itself to changing conditions. Chandler, too, looked to a fairer, freer future. "If a black man can make it at Okinawa and go to Guadalcanal," he declared, "he can make it in baseball." Meanwhile, unbeknownst to Chandler and all but a few confidants, Brooklyn Dodgers president Branch Rickey was already scouting black players and plotting to make that happen.[40]

•   •   •

Rickey's motives and machinations were complex, befitting a man once described as having taught Machiavelli the strike zone. During the 1920s, he had revolutionized player development as the St. Louis Cardinals' general manager by creating a farm system of minor league teams. Monopolizing a huge stable of players, Rickey was able to keep salaries down and gather together the talent that allowed St. Louis to win several World Series in the 1930s and 1940s. He was about to change the game again.

In May 1945, Rickey called a press conference to announce his involvement with Gus Greenlee's United States League. The Caliph of Little Harlem, as Greenlee was known in Pittsburgh, had reorganized the Pittsburgh Crawfords in 1944. Denied readmission to the NNL, in part because Cum Posey did not want competition from a rival black club in Pittsburgh, he operated the Crawfords independently and raided Negro League teams for players. Unable to find common ground with the Negro National League, Greenlee launched the USL in 1945 and put franchises in many of the same cities as the NNL.

Although Greenlee was the league's founder, Branch Rickey was its surprising godfather. Now the president of the Brooklyn Dodgers, Rickey pledged his support to the venture and announced that its teams would play at Ebbets Field and Brooklyn's minor league parks. Using the press conference to denigrate the Negro National and Negro American Leagues as poor excuses for a sports league, he declared: "There does not exist in a true sense such a thing as organized Negro baseball."[41] Rickey's involvement in the USL—especially the extent of his backing for the USL's Brooklyn Brown Dodgers and what he hoped to gain by it—has puzzled historians. It is also unclear if Rickey, who railed against the Negro Leagues as little more than rackets, knew of Greenlee's history as a numbers baron.[42]

Rickey's participation and public endorsement of the USL, however, startled Negro League owners. Newark Eagles owner Effa Manley, who attended the press conference, challenged Rickey's newfound interest in the welfare of black baseball. Washington Senators owner Clark Griffith, meanwhile, disputed Rickey's right to "set himself up as the czar of Negro baseball." Griffith, who had milked the Negro Leagues for considerable sums by renting his ballpark to the Grays, saw Rickey and the USL as threatening those easy revenues. The black press was just as skeptical, but no one fully realized what Rickey was attempting behind the scenes.[43]

While the United States League never rivaled the two established Negro Leagues, it did challenge their legitimacy. And though Greenlee touted the USL as a way to achieve integration by making it a minor league affiliated with Major League Baseball, the circuit never fulfilled his vision. It struggled through two shaky seasons before folding, and became little more than an afterthought as Branch Rickey revealed his plan to transform baseball on a much larger stage.

• • •

On October 29, 1945, Rickey stunned the entire baseball world when the Brooklyn Dodgers organization announced that it had signed African American Jack Roosevelt Robinson to a contract with its top farm club, the Montreal Royals of the International League. After evaluating the aging Dodgers and the wartime shortage of players, Rickey had devised an ambitious strategy to revamp the organization. Though most clubs were cutting back, Rickey asked his board of directors in January 1943 for the go-ahead to expand scouting and sign younger players, including African Americans and darker-skinned Latinos. Even before Commissioner Landis's death late in 1944, Dodger scouts had been discreetly appraising players who might integrate the organization.[44]

Rickey initially considered signing Latin players first, but once he fully appreciated the linguistic and cultural obstacles they would face, he shifted his focus to African American prospects. He had settled on Jackie Robinson in August 1945 and signed him to a contract a full two months before the October announcement, which came hot on the heels of the end of World War II. Many connected the signing to the war's end. As Montreal

Royals president Hector Racine (unaware that the U.S. military had kept its units segregated during the war) declared, "Negroes fought alongside whites and shared the foxhole dangers, and they should get a fair trial in baseball." Elmer Ferguson of the *Montreal Herald* echoed Racine's sentiments, arguing, "Those who were good enough to fight by the side of the whites are plenty good enough to play by the side of whites!" The *Pittsburgh Courier* proclaimed that Robinson carried "the hopes, aspirations and ambitions of thirteen million black Americans heaped on his broad, sturdy shoulders," while the *Crisis* and other black journals wrote that he personified optimism for the future. Fans, meanwhile, were still wondering who Robinson was. He had played but one season in the Negro Leagues, at shortstop for the Kansas City Monarchs. Though Robinson had appeared in the East-West Classic that summer, he had little experience in professional baseball and, for many, represented not a savior, but a question mark.[45]

• • •

Born in Cairo, Georgia, to a family of sharecroppers in 1919, Jackie Robinson moved with his mother and siblings to Pasadena, California, as an infant. His brother Mack was the silver medalist in the 200 meters at the 1936 Berlin Olympics, coming in behind Jesse Owens. But the best job Mack could find upon his return home was as a street sweeper. Jackie attended Pasadena Junior College in 1937, transferred to the University of California at Los Angeles in 1939, and became the school's first four-sport athlete.

At UCLA, Robinson was part of an exceptional cohort of black student athletes. Bill Terry, his roommate and teammate on the basketball squad, would be convicted—and later pardoned—for his role in the Freeman Field Mutiny, an effort by black officers to force the integration of an officers' club in Indiana during the war. Two of his teammates in UCLA's backfield, Kenny Washington and Woody Strode, would integrate pro football in 1946. Robinson twice led the Pacific Coast Conference in scoring in basketball, averaged eleven yards per carry in football, and won the NCAA championship in the broad jump. He also won the conference golf championship, swam competitively, and played baseball. After leaving UCLA for financial reasons his senior year, Robinson worked for the

National Youth Administration (a New Deal program) and barnstormed
with the Los Angeles Bulldogs football team before he was drafted into the
Army in the spring of 1942.[46]

When Robinson was denied entry to the Officer Candidate School
at Fort Riley, Kansas, Sergeant Joe Louis successfully interceded on the
young soldier's behalf. The reigning heavyweight champ, who was also stationed there, spoke out frequently on racial matters during the war. After
becoming a second lieutenant, Robinson was waiting to hear whether he
would be deployed overseas when he boarded an Army bus on the Fort
Hood, Texas, base in July 1944. He sat with a light-skinned African American woman who was married to a black officer he knew. The bus driver,
believing that Robinson was sitting next to a white woman, accosted him
and demanded that he move to the back of the bus. Robinson, knowing
that the military had directed that its buses be desegregated, refused to do
so. Nor did he back down when the military police arrived. The incident
led to a court-martial on charges ranging from insubordination to drunk-
enness and insulting a civilian woman.

With black soldiers rallying around Robinson, his court-martial became a well-publicized test of the military's racial practices. Robinson
stood his ground during the August trial and was acquitted of all charges.
He left the military with an honorable discharge a few months later
and began playing with the Kansas City Monarchs in 1945. Robinson
soon began attracting attention in the black press as a possible candidate
to crack Major League Baseball's color line. He got Branch Rickey's attention too. After months of scouting black players and closely investigating
their backgrounds, Rickey settled on Robinson, who he saw as combining exceptional athleticism, unusual poise, and a background in integrated
collegiate sport and the military.[47]

When the Dodgers signed Robinson, they ignored the Kansas City
Monarchs, his Negro League team. Rickey, pointing out that Robinson
did not have a signed contract with the Monarchs, dismissed black baseball as unfit to be called a league. "As at present administered," he scoffed,
"they are in the nature of a racket."[48] The Monarchs, meanwhile, were in
a bind—not wanting to be perceived as hurting Robinson's chances, but
unhappy over losing a player without compensation.

Several MLB owners protested that Robinson's signing shamelessly exploited black teams. Those who complained the loudest, Senators owner Clark Griffith and Larry MacPhail, who had become the Yankee's chief executive after World War II, had the most to lose from integration. Griffith was making more money from the Grays' rentals at Griffith Stadium than Cum Posey was making as their owner. MacPhail's Yankees were doing even better, banking about $100,000 in 1945 from ballpark rentals to Negro League teams and concession sales during their games.[49] Rickey ignored his critics and soon signed three other Negro Leaguers, pitchers John Wright and Don Newcombe, and catcher Roy Campanella. The die was cast. Integration would proceed, and it would occur on Major League Baseball's terms.

• • •

Still reeling from the Robinson signing, the Negro Leagues took another body blow when they lost fifty-five-year-old Cum Posey to cancer in March 1946. "In his death," the *Courier*'s John L. Clark wrote, "the race lost one of its most dynamic citizens, baseball lost its best mind, [and] Homestead lost its most loyal booster." Ches Washington hailed Posey as "the sagacious sportsman who made the Homestead Grays as magic a name in the baseball world as Joe Louis in the fistic firmament." Pittsburgh's political and sporting elites poured out to attend his funeral; Josh Gibson and Cum's close friend, Pittsburgh Steelers owner Art Rooney, were among his honorary pallbearers.[50]

As the 1946 season began, the degree to which integration would savage the Negro Leagues was not yet apparent. Robinson's appeal, however, was. More than fifty-one thousand tickets were sold for his minor league debut in Jersey City, twice the number that could squeeze into the ballpark. After Robinson homered in his second at-bat, Wendell Smith wrote: "Our hearts beat just a little faster and the thrill ran through us like champagne bubbles." For his colleague Joe Bostic, the game meant that baseball had taken up "the cudgel for Democracy."[51]

Negro League attendance held its own in 1946, but that would be black baseball's last decent season. After an abrupt but short postwar downturn, the consumer demand that had been pent up because of enforced wartime saving launched the U.S. economy on a skyward trajectory. The major leagues took terrific advantage of the economic bounce and sold a record 18.5 million tickets that season. A few black clubs, particularly the Newark Eagles and the Kansas City Monarchs, also drew well thanks to the strong economy. In May, Branch Rickey signed another black player, Roy Partlow. Because the pitcher had actually signed a contract with his Negro League team, the Philadelphia Stars, Rickey paid the team $1,000. Partlow's signing represented the first time that a major league club compensated a Negro League team for a player. Still, there were cautionary signs; black teams that played within the International League's footprint found that swarms of their fans were traveling to Newark, Jersey City, and Baltimore to watch Jackie Robinson play whenever the Montreal Royals came to one of these towns.[52]

Owners on both sides of the color line fretted as Major League Baseball's large-scale integration became more and more likely. While black owners saw impending financial doom, white ones had a more amorphous set of fears. Never known for their foresight, major league executives formed a committee that reported back to the owners in the summer of 1946 on a series of problems, including what they called the "race question." The internal document, whose existence several owners later denied, drew a dire portrait. Its authors complained that their game was besieged by "political and social-minded drum beaters" with an agenda that would damage both MLB and the Negro Leagues. While allowing that every boy "should have a fair chance in baseball" regardless of his race, the report concluded that no African Americans were ready for the majors. Furthermore, it argued that integration would jeopardize a $2-million-a-year black business that employed thousands and would cost major league teams rental and concession fees. Most noxiously, the report expressed the concern that large crowds of black fans at major league games in New York and Chicago, where four of the sixteen major league teams played, could "threaten the value" of these clubs by scaring off white fans.[53]

The next year began badly for black baseball. Josh Gibson, perhaps its best player ever, died in January 1947 at the age of thirty-five; the cause of his death would never be definitively determined. Misfortune continued

Josh Gibson and kids at Forbes Field *(Courtesy Dennis Goldstein). Date: likely early 1940s.*
The son of a Georgia sharecropper who moved to Pittsburgh to work in the mills, Josh
Gibson became black baseball's greatest all-around player. He led the Crawfords and
Grays to a slew of Negro National League championships and starred throughout the
Caribbean.

that spring when bad weather forced many games to be canceled, sinking
struggling teams deeper into the red. But it was Jackie Robinson's debut
with the Brooklyn Dodgers on April 15 that sounded black baseball's death
knell. Black fans went gaga over Robinson, taking Jackie Robinson Special
trains to see him play. The Dodgers' attendance rose by over three hundred thousand on the road, black attendance at Ebbets Field quadrupled,
and all but one National League club set a single-game attendance record
that summer when playing Brooklyn. "Jackie's nimble, Jackie's quick, Jackie
makes the turnstiles click," the *Courier*'s Wendell Smith wrote. But Negro League baseball hemorrhaged as a result. "After Jackie," Buck Leonard
sighed, "we couldn't draw flies."[54]

In July, Cleveland Indians owner Bill Veeck signed Newark Eagles outfielder Larry Doby to a contract with his team, and Robinson was no longer the sole African American in the majors. Three other Negro Leaguers—outfielders Hank Thompson and Willard Brown, and pitcher Dan Bankhead—arrived later that season. In each case, the player's Negro League team was compensated. The sale of players to major league organizations recouped some of the losses that the Negro League clubs were facing, but without formal affiliation with Major League Baseball, their long-term prospects were bleak.

Those prospects became even bleaker after the season ended. In December 1947, with their options narrowing, the Negro Leagues applied for membership in the National Association of Professional Baseball Leagues. Their request to become a minor league was denied on the pretext that Negro League territories overlapped with preexisting territorial rights of current members. The handwriting was on the wall; black clubs would not be accepted into white baseball's fraternity.

Negro League attendance continued to plummet in 1948, as radio and limited television broadcasts of Dodgers games further siphoned away crowds. It didn't help that coverage of Robinson and a handful of other black major leaguers in the black press overshadowed that of the Negro Leagues as a whole. The Newark Eagles, who had drawn 120,000 fans in 1946, attracted only 35,000 in 1948. Negro League games at Yankee Stadium pulled in a third as many fans as they had in 1946, and the Eagles and the Grays lost money for a second consecutive season. The Eagles, Grays, and the New York Black Yankees left the NNL following the 1948 season; the three remaining NNL clubs joined the NAL, but that league wasn't viable either. The storied Homestead Grays barnstormed for a few more years, then shut down for good.[55]

Interestingly, segregation offered some protection for black teams in the South, where minor league baseball remained all white. The Kansas City Monarchs, located outside major league territory, also remained profitable, in part due to player sales. But the number of players who could be sold to major league teams was dwindling and by selling their best or most promising players, black baseball was mortgaging its future. At the same time, more black prospects were entering organized baseball directly from high school, sandlot, or college ball, bypassing the Negro Leagues altogether. Nor could black teams continue to make up for diminished crowds at league contests by playing what had often been lucrative games with white independent clubs. Even white independent baseball was withering under the onslaught of television and suburbanization.

For many African Americans, the erosion of segregation in baseball, if not its total disappearance, had weakened the Negro Leagues' reason for being. Separate black institutions were now perceived as less worthy, even backward, at a time when African Americans were moving forward into white institutions. Moreover, integration had freed the relatively captive audience that the Negro Leagues and other black businesses had relied upon for lifeblood.

Most major league teams, despite Brooklyn's success, were in no rush to follow suit. Although Jackie Robinson first took the field as a Dodger on April 15, 1947, only six of sixteen clubs had fielded black players by 1952. All of them, however, would integrate their minor league systems by August 1953. Former Negro Leaguers Roy Campanella, Willie Mays, Ernie Banks, Henry Aaron, Monte Irvin, Ray Dandridge, and Satchel Paige were now the property of major league organizations. In July 1959, the Boston Red Sox reluctantly became the final team to integrate when, amid a wave of political pressure, they called up infielder Pumpsie Green from the minor leagues.

By then, the Negro National League had been history for a decade, disbanding after the 1948 season. The league's inability to defend itself against Jorge Pasquel and the Mexican League in 1940 had foreshadowed its helplessness to withstand a much more powerful predator less than a decade later. Little was said about its disbandment. The black press, with its attention newly riveted on MLB, had all but dropped the Negro Leagues. After the Homestead Grays beat the Birmingham Black Barons to win the 1948 Negro League World Series—the last ever played—the *Pittsburgh Courier* devoted just two paragraphs to the victory, which was buried by coverage of black major leaguers.[56]

Amid mounting financial losses, black teams were unable to reconstruct themselves in ways that would return them to profitability or persuade the major leagues to accept them as affiliates—not that the latter ever seriously considered that outcome. The Negro American League limped along during the 1950s with an ever-changing roster of teams. Clubs barnstormed, clowned, cut rosters, instituted salary caps, and promised to elevate their standards of organization. But none of these efforts stopped the bleeding of talent, fans, and dollars to the major leagues. Black baseball became a pallid shadow of its former self, soon to become a thing of the past. Few seemed to mind: everybody was watching Jackie Robinson anyway.

CHAPTER FIVE

Integration's Curse

With a runner on first base, one out, and the score tied in the top of the fifth inning, Jackie Robinson, wearing the away uniform of the Brooklyn Dodgers, stepped into the batter's box at Pittsburgh's sold-out Forbes Field. A man in the right-field stands screamed: "Stick that nigger in his ear!" Two rows away, Mal Goode put a hand on the arm of a friend who was about to jump out of his seat. "Charley," the veteran journalist implored, "don't say anything." Local ministers, African American newspapers like the *Pittsburgh Courier*, and Dodgers president Branch Rickey had urged black fans to show restraint whenever Robinson played that summer in 1947. Fights at the ballpark over race might jeopardize integration.

On the mound, Pirates pitcher Fritz Ostermueller leaned forward, rocked back, and delivered the ball with the exaggerated windup that had become his trademark after fourteen major league seasons. Robinson scorched the pitch, but right at third baseman Frank Gustine. Gustine threw to second base, forcing the runner out; Robinson, however, beat the relay to first to prevent an inning-ending double play.

Earlier that season, an Ostermueller pitch had come close to striking Robinson's skull. The Dodgers rookie threw up his arm to protect his head, but the pitch smashed into his left elbow. "When the ball hit him," the *Courier's* Wendell Smith reported, "a deathly silence hovered over the entire park. Jackie was on the ground grimacing in pain." The pitch was one of six that clipped Robinson in the first half of 1947, more than any batter had been hit in the entire previous season. It brought his teammates to the top of the dugout steps, where they angrily cursed the Pirates and threatened retaliation. "Don't forget you guys have to come to bat, too," second baseman Eddie Stanky roared. Robinson didn't say anything, but in the fifth inning he lined a ball by Ostermueller's head that "made Fritz flinch," according to *New York Times* reporter Roscoe McGowen. The next time Ostermueller faced the Dodgers, Robinson homered and hit two singles.

A month after the near-beaning, Ostermueller stared at Robinson dancing off first base. Before the game, the Pirates pitcher had sworn that Robinson was not going to exploit his idiosyncratic delivery to steal bases. Now, Ostermueller seemed to be paying more attention to Robinson on first than he was to Carl Furillo, who was at bat. When Furillo singled, Robinson advanced to third. On the third pitch to the next batter, Robinson broke for home before pulling up after several steps. Pittsburgh catcher Homer "Dixie" Howell caught the pitch, whirled toward third base, and glared at Robinson, who retreated to third. But Howell's focus on Robinson allowed Furillo to take second base.

On the next pitch, Ostermueller went into a full windup—*Pittsburgh Post-Gazette* sportswriter Vince Johnson described him stretching forward "like a Mohammedan on his prayer rug"—and Robinson dashed for home. The crowd of 35,331 at Forbes Field shrieked, alerting Ostermueller to what was happening, but the veteran left-hander had no choice but to follow through on his delivery. Otherwise, a balk would have been called and the runners awarded a base. The pitch arrived on the first-base side of home plate ahead of Robinson, but Jackie slid under Dixie Howell's tag to score what proved to be the winning run. It was the first of twenty times that Robinson stole home during his ten seasons in the majors.[1]

Ostermueller's inattention to Robinson on third base was understandable; nobody was stealing home in the major leagues in the 1940s. Stolen bases, for that matter, had been a lost art since the early 1930s, and by 1947 the number of steals per game was at a record low. Sluggers, not speedsters, were baseball's reigning aristocrats. But Jackie Robinson, who had already stolen as many bases that season as the entire Pittsburgh roster, played the game differently, relying on the speed, bunting, and baserunning that typified Negro League baseball. As he went around the majors that summer, Robinson realized that many pitchers had become careless, even complacent, about base runners. He was accustomed to pitchers knocking down batters who dug in at the plate; that was common practice in black baseball. But in the Negro Leagues, pitchers respected base runners' speed and daring too. Robinson was insulted that Ostermueller would wind up when he was on third, "ignoring my movements as antics." For Robinson, that was both a license and an inducement to steal.[2]

Stealing home might have stunned most fans, but not those, like Mal Goode, accustomed to Negro League play. "In Negro baseball," he said, "you couldn't be a one-dimensional player. You had to be able to run as well as hit, and play several positions, too."[3] Jackie had demonstrated his ability to run from the first week of the season; the hitting took longer.

Although Robinson had been an instant box-office sensation—inspiring record fan turnouts in Philadelphia, Chicago, and St. Louis—he had struggled at the plate. Seething at the racial abuse he was subjected to by opposing players, but unable to respond to such provocation, Robinson pressed at the plate. After twenty consecutive at-bats without a hit, his batting average had sunk so low that some writers argued that he should be benched. The *New York Sun* ran a story headlined: "Robinson's Job in Jeopardy," while Jimmy Cannon called Robinson the "loneliest man" in sports.[4]

He was also learning a new position in the field—first base—since Dodgers management didn't want to expose him to the spikings and collisions he would have faced at second, his regular position. Besides, Brooklyn had the famously crafty Eddie Stanky at second base. "He can't hit, can't run, can't field. He's no nice guy," Dodger manager Leo Durocher famously said about Stanky. "All the little SOB can do is win."

By midseason Robinson's difficulties were behind him, and the twenty-eight-year-old rookie was off to a Hall of Fame career, demonstrating uncanny baseball intelligence and unrivaled intensity. "He was the greatest opportunist on any kind of playing field," sportswriter John Crosby observed, "seeing openings before they opened, pulling off plays lesser players can't even imagine." Robinson's desire to win, meanwhile, won over baseball purists. "This guy didn't just come to play," Leo Durocher said. "He came to beat ya. He came to stuff the goddamn bat right up your ass."[5] At no time was that more apparent than when he stole home.

"When Jackie stole home on Ostermueller," Mal Goode recalled, "I was in the stands on the third-base side and this same one fellow [who had yelled: "Stick that nigger in his ear!" when Robinson came to bat] said, 'Niggers should have been in big leagues long time ago.' In broken English, that's what he said!" For Goode, the significance of Robinson's derring-do had less to do with winning baseball games than on influencing those watching. "To remember that incident," the journalist reflected, "I'm saying that there must have been thousands of incidents around the country where white businessmen sat and never hired a black to do anything except to mop or to sweep . . . who said 'What's wrong with it? Let's try it, an experiment.'" Those who witnessed Brooklyn's experiment, Goode argued, replicated it in myriad ways, translating it "from the baseball field to the corridors of businesses, banks, and corporations."[6]

By season's end, "baseball's great experiment," as historian Jules Tygiel called it in the title of his well-known book, was a surprising success.[7] Robinson was the Rookie of the Year, the Dodgers were in the World Series, and major league baseball attendance hit an all-time high.

Robinson was the avatar of a new style of play for major league baseball, one combining speed with power. A strong man with the physique and bearing of the sensational college football running back he had been at UCLA, Robinson did not forsake power for speed. No Dodger hit more home runs that season. Home-run hitters, though, were not uncommon in the majors in 1947. Speed was the dimension that had been missing for decades. Robinson bunted and ran the bases with purposeful aggression, emboldening his teammates and distracting opponents, who began paying him undue attention.

His triumph heralded the arrival of the greatest infusion of talent baseball had ever seen, as African Americans and Latin players of color began arriving in force. These men would help their teams win championships, reap disproportionate numbers of individual honors, and allow major league baseball to become what Walt Whitman, Mark Twain, and National League president John Tener felt it could be a century before—the watchword of democracy. Baseball's integration, in turn, opened doors of opportunity off the field and changed the nation's psyche in profound if subtle ways.

But baseball's integration was also a curse. The major leagues might

Jackie Robinson at Forbes Field during his rookie season *(Carnegie Museum of Art, Pittsburgh; Heinz Family Fund copyright 2004, Carnegie Museum of Art, Charles "Teenie" Harris Archive). Date: 1947.* The most transformative figure in the nation's sporting history, Jackie Robinson debuted with the Brooklyn Dodgers in April 1947. Later that summer, he stole home at Forbes Field. By season's end, he had smashed Major League Baseball's color line.

have symbolized social democratization, but desegregation came with heavy costs for the black community. Major league owners had insisted that integration occur on their terms. As a result, this grand social triumph destroyed the Negro Leagues, and black America lost control over its own sporting life. Individual African Americans became eligible to enjoy professional sport's lucrative financial rewards, but sport would now be seen primarily in terms of commercial payoff. Baseball, in particular, would come to play less of a role as a means by which African Americans forged community and identity. While baseball's integration meant that African American and Latino athletes could finally join the team, and helped the United States embrace the movement to desegregate its core institutions, it came with little consideration for its impact on those whose needs should have been foremost. As a result, baseball's integration was predatory as well as salutary. It cost black America a piece of its soul plus a crucial part of its social cohesion and economic sustenance.

• • •

Jackie Robinson's first month in the majors was marred by savage verbal abuse. When the Philadelphia Phillies visited Ebbets Field in April, manager Ben Chapman and his players unleashed a barrage of racial invective. Chapman mocked Robinson's physiognomy, ranting about thick-lipped, thick-skulled Negroes. He shouted to Robinson's teammates, Brooklyn's traveling secretary Harold Parrott later wrote, advising them that they would contract "repulsive sores and diseases . . . if they touched the towels or the combs he used."[8] So many fans voiced objections to the egregious attacks, which Walter Winchell condemned on his nationally broadcast radio show, that Commissioner Happy Chandler warned the Phillies to tone down their vitriol. Chapman defended himself by saying that bench jockeying was part of the game—that they were just trying to shake the rookie up and see if he could take it. But few players had ever been subjected to such vicious language. Robinson—as he had promised Rickey—refrained from fighting back. But he later wrote that he had been sorely tempted to say: "To hell with Mr. Rickey's 'noble experiment' [and] grab one of those white sons of bitches and smash his teeth with my despised black fist."[9]

Each city the Dodgers visited posed a different set of trials for Robinson, who received enormous amounts of hate mail and numerous death threats. On Brooklyn's first road-trip to Philadelphia, the team was denied rooms in the Benjamin Franklin Hotel.[10] In other cities, Robinson was able to stay in the same hotel as his teammates, although the Dodgers would not room him with a white player. Instead, he shared accommodations with the *Pittsburgh Courier*'s Wendell Smith, who was also in the Dodgers' employ that season. Smith had touted Robinson to Rickey in April 1945, and when Rickey decided to bring Robinson to the Dodgers, he sought Smith's assistance in making Jackie's experiences on the road more palatable. The older Smith roomed with Robinson and accompanied him off the field on many road trips that season. He would later write Robinson's as-told-to biography.

In St. Louis, several Cardinals threatened to strike rather than play against a black man. Their bluster, exposed by *New York Herald Tribune* sportswriter Stanley Woodward, was quashed by National League president Ford

Frick, who told the players that they would be suspended if they did not play. Though the seriousness of the Cardinals' intentions was likely overblown, the incident pushed more Americans into Robinson's corner. The *New York Post's* Jimmy Cannon, who had called Robinson a 1,000-to-1 long-shot to make the grade in the majors when he was signed, now thundered: "There is a great lynch mob among us and they go unhooded and work without the rope." He called the threat to strike a "venomous conspiracy."

Robinson not only endured the racial jibes, death threats, and segregated accommodations; he also turned his season around on the field, racking up points with his teammates in the process. The same day in May that Fritz Ostermueller almost beaned him, he was on a fourteen-game hitting streak. Robinson's willingness to cover first base even when runners were out to spike him and hold his ground in the batter's box when pitchers threw at him further eased his acceptance on the Dodgers. Some of his teammates must have wondered if they would have held up as well as Robinson. Most of all, they realized that if they wanted to win, they needed to stand behind him. "He's gonna help us win the pennant," pitcher Ralph Branca said at a players-only meeting.[11]

Robinson was winning over players on opposing teams, too. When Pirate infielder Frank Gustine reached first base the inning after Ostermueller decked Robinson, he told Jackie that he was sure that Ostermueller hadn't hit him intentionally. "Osty's fast ball takes off," he said. "It jumps in on you and that's what happened in your case. I'm sure he didn't mean it." It was the second time that a Pirate had made amends with Robinson during the series. The day before, Robinson was bunting for a base hit when he collided with Pittsburgh first baseman Hank Greenberg, who was trying to make the play at first. When Robinson arrived on first after a single later in the game, Greenberg said: "Hope I didn't hurt you, Jackie. I was trying to get that wild throw." Greenberg had some inkling of what Robinson was going through. As the most prominent Jew yet to play baseball, he had encountered anti-Semitic taunts throughout his career. He asked Robinson how his transition to the majors was going and urged him to "just stay in there and fight back. A lot of people are pulling for you to make good. Don't ever forget it."

Robinson wrote about these exchanges in his "Jackie Robinson Says" column that week, praising Gustine and Greenberg and absolving Oster-mueller of ill will. Of Greenberg, he wrote: "Class tells. It sticks out all over Mr. Greenberg." The Greenberg-Robinson collision, Wendell Smith wrote, was the sort of play that integration's opponents had said would provoke riots in the stands. Instead, it showed how smoothly integration was proceeding.[12]

Almost overnight, Brooklyn had become black America's team. Among African Americans that summer, the most asked question was, "How did Jackie do?" The answer usually brought a sense of elation. "To black America," Jules Tygiel wrote, "Jackie Robinson appeared as a savior, a Moses leading his people out of the wilderness."[13]

Robinson's success at the ballpark magnified his impact off the field. But like Joe Louis before him, Robinson's appeal crossed racial lines. Many whites exposed to the dangers of fascism during the war found him a sympathetic, even inspiring, figure. Baseball fans who appreciated his effort and performance gave him their respect. Playing more games and hitting more home runs than any of his teammates, Robinson led the league in stolen bases, was runner-up in runs scored, and did indeed help Brooklyn win the pennant. The Dodgers reached new highs in attendance, and the National League surpassed its overall 1946 record attendance by a million and a half fans, almost 20 percent. Few ballplayers have had more consequential rookie seasons.[14]

•   •   •

Jackie Robinson's triumph made it possible for an exceptional cohort of black ballplayers to enter the majors. Sixty-three African Americans and ten Latinos who played in the Negro Leagues got the chance to play major league baseball. Including Robinson, eight of those African American players would wind up in the Hall of Fame: Satchel Paige, Larry Doby, Monte Irvin, Willie Mays, Roy Campanella, Ernie Banks, and Henry Aaron. Another nine African Americans, who were born before Jackie Robinson debuted with the Dodgers but didn't play Negro League ball, would join the influx to Cooperstown: Frank Robinson, Billy Williams, Bob Gibson, Lou Brock, Willie McCovey, Willie Stargell, Joe Morgan, Ferguson Jenkins, and Reggie Jackson.[15] In the thirteen seasons between 1947 and 1959, black players in the National League won nine Rookie of the Year and nine Most Valuable Player awards. They led the majors in almost every conceivable category of excellence.

These men changed forever how the game was played. Before their arrival, major league baseball had gone through two distinct eras. Until Babe Ruth began knocking pitches out of the park, baseball had been known for its dead ball. Few home runs were hit (or *could* be hit, given the use of a baseball that became softer and more misshapen as the game progressed), and players relied on speed and guile. They stole bases, bunted, and won games on the base paths. Ruth, Jimmie Foxx, Mel Ott, and Lou Gehrig, however, ushered in a period in which the emphasis turned to power instead of speed. In the 1930s and 1940s, the number of home runs hit historic highs, while that of stolen bases sunk to all-time lows.

The arrival of black and Latin players introduced a third era that fused speed with power. In sportswriter Dan Daniel's estimation, Jackie Robinson, Larry Doby, and Sam Jethroe—all black—were the three fastest players in baseball. "If that race has contributed nothing else to the game," he concluded, "it has brought the consummate speed of a quality rarely demonstrated since the Ty Cobb heyday." [16] Daniel could not have been more on the mark. African Americans or Latinos have led both leagues in stolen bases almost every year since 1947. In the first fifty seasons since integration, black and Latin players won ninety-one of one hundred stolen-base titles in the two leagues. In six of the nine seasons that an African American or Latino did not lead the league, there were almost too few playing to count.

"At that time," former Negro Leaguer Buck O'Neil explained, "baseball was a base-to-base thing. You hit the ball, you wait on first base until somebody hit again. See? But in our baseball you got on base if you walked, you stole second, you'd try to steal, they'd bunt you over to third and you actually scored runs without a hit. That was our baseball." [17]

Speed changed how teams sought to score and forced opponents to adjust their pitch selection and defensive positioning. The game became more cerebral as the possible permutations for each game situation multiplied. Pitchers threw fewer breaking balls with men on base; first and third basemen played in to guard against the bunt; infielders were wary of the hit-and-run or stolen-base attempt. Defenders, particularly centerfielders and middle infielders, needed to be able to cover more ground to prevent opposing players from taking liberties on the base paths. The emphasis on speed filtered down to scouting and player development.

But black power was as critical as black speed, and even the best defensive positioning could not prevent balls from leaving the park. Three of the Negro Leaguers who debuted in the 1950s are among baseball's top twenty-five career home-run leaders—Aaron (second), Mays (fourth), and Banks (twenty-first)—and would rank even higher if players whose careers have been tainted by performance-enhancing drugs were struck from the list. Aaron and Mays, in particular, epitomized the combination of speed and power; Aaron hit 755 home runs and stole 240 bases, while Mays hit 660 home runs and stole 338 bases. Fifteen of the top twenty-five home-run hitters of all time and twenty-two of the twenty-five career stolen-bases leaders since Robinson are black or Latino.

Individual rankings aside, the two National League teams with the most black players—the Dodgers and the Giants—won eight of ten pennants between 1947 and 1956. After Robinson, the Dodgers brought up Roy Campanella, who would become a three-time National League MVP, and pitcher Don Newcombe, who would win 112 games and lose only 48 over his first six seasons. They added future Rookie of the Year winners Joe Black and Jim Gilliam, as well as Cuban-born Edmundo "Sandy" Amorós and became the National League's dominant squad. The Dodgers met the Yankees in the World Series six times in Robinson's decade-long career and finally won their first title in 1955. The signature moment of the 1955 World Series came in Game 1 when Robinson stole home.

National League clubs, fielding twice as many black players as their American League counterparts in 1959, won ten of sixteen World Series between 1954 and 1969. When the two leagues met in the All-Star Game in these seasons, the National League team won fourteen, lost five, and tied once. (Between 1959 and 1962, two All-Star games were played each season.) Except for 1950, the World Series has featured black and Latin stars every year since Jackie Robinson. The Cleveland Indians, the New York Giants, the Brooklyn Dodgers, and the Milwaukee Braves won championships in the 1950s with former Negro Leaguers in their lineups. Even the

New York Yankees, the dominant franchise in baseball since the 1920s, dipped into the Negro League market. Their first black player, former Kansas City Monarch Elston Howard, became a versatile Gold Glove defender and the first African American to win MVP honors in the American League. In contrast, teams like the Boston Red Sox, who whiffed on Robinson despite grudgingly giving him a tryout in April 1945 and who were the last team to integrate when they signed Pumpsie Green in 1959, lagged clubs willing to cross the racial divide.

• • •

Both Major League Baseball and a cohort of African American athletes benefited enormously from integration. The major leagues, by denying African Americans and Latinos of color a place in the game, had become inbred and one-dimensional. African Americans and Latinos would introduce new styles and emphases of play and expand baseball's potential talent pool exponentially. Those newcomers who survived its racial gauntlet would see the rewards in terms of fatter paychecks and exposure to the limelight. But the death of independent black baseball meant that thousands of other African Americans who depended on the Negro Leagues for employment lost their jobs. Only a few players entered the major leagues. Some of the others hung on in the minor leagues or abroad, but most found their careers suddenly over. For many, integration had come too late.

"If the majors had taken or accepted the black player ten years before," Monte Irvin lamented, "they would have gotten the real stars." Before Rickey chose Robinson, many Negro Leaguers believed that Irvin was the best candidate to integrate the majors. A four-sport high school letterman who played football at Lincoln University, Irvin starred for the Newark Eagles and several Latin American teams before entering the military in 1943. After the war, he won the NNL batting championship and led the Eagles to the Negro League World Series title. The perennial Negro League all-star, who debuted in the majors in 1949 at the age of thirty-one, would become a major league all-star too. He sparked the Giants' remarkable comeback to win the 1951 pennant and entered the Hall of Fame in 1973. But Irvin regretted that men he considered better players than he was—especially Josh Gibson—never got a chance. "All of a sudden [Gibson] got sick and died without feeling the thrill of playing in the majors. He never played one game in the majors. And all the black players will tell you he was our best, our best hitter, our best all-around player."[18]

"Most of those boys with the original Crawfords would have played in the high minors," the Reverend Harold Tinker recalled of his Pittsburgh sandlot teammates as he sat inside Central Baptist Church on the Hill. "Wasn't none of them couldn't have made the minor leagues, and of course, quite naturally, three or four of them would have been stars in the majors, including Josh [Gibson], and Josh never made it. He never got that opportunity. And Campanella couldn't have held Josh's glove. We went crazy over Campanella. Campanella used to sit on his haunches and throw 'em out, but he couldn't throw 'em out like Josh could. And I know Campanella hit home runs, but he never hit home runs like Josh. And all he needed was the chance to do it in the majors. He would have been something. I believe that, and I'm sitting on holy ground right now and I sure wouldn't say it if I didn't believe it."[19]

"I wish that people could have seen Ray Dandridge play third base," Monte Irvin said about his Newark Eagle teammate. "If you saw him, you'd never forget him. He played just like Brooks Robinson and all those other great third basemen. He had that certain flair, the way he would throw that ball. He would have been a natural attraction. He was so flashy that the people would have come just to see him field the ball."[20]

The New York Giants did acquire Dandridge in 1949, sending him to their Minneapolis farm club, where he became the American Association's Rookie of the Year in 1949 and its MVP the following season. But the Giants kept the future Hall of Famer in the minors, because of either his age or his tremendous drawing power in Minneapolis, or, even more likely, because of the informal quota that major league teams observed on the number of black players on their rosters. Monte Irvin, Dandridge's teammate on the Newark Eagles, who joined the Giants in 1949, urged the club to bring him to the majors. "But they said he was too old. I asked what difference it made if he could play? I know it was the old quota system."[21] Dandridge never did step into a major league batter's box. "The only thing I ever wanted to do was hit in the majors," Dandridge said later. "I just wanted to put my left foot in there. I just would have liked to have been up there for one day."[22]

At least Satchel Paige made it to the majors, as a forty-two-year-old rookie with the Cleveland Indians, in 1948. He won six games (two of them shutouts), lost only once, and became the first African American to pitch in the World Series. Paige's first three starts drew more than two hundred thousand fans to Cleveland's Municipal Stadium, including a record seventy-two thousand for a night game.[23] But Buck Leonard, Cool Papa Bell, Willie Wells, and other stars who were already in their thirties or older as of 1947 never got a chance. Many played ball in Latin America for a few more seasons, then found jobs where they could. Leonard became a probation officer in Rocky Mount, North Carolina; Bell was a guard at City Hall in St. Louis; and Wells worked at a delicatessen in New York City.

While African Americans and baseball fans celebrated the arrival of a handful of black players, black owners, general managers, managers, coaches, and front-office personnel disappeared from the game and remained absent for decades. Not many seemed to notice; issues regarding ownership and power within Major League Baseball were largely ignored in the aftermath of integration. The informal quota system prevented a large cohort of black players from forming on one club; black players scattered about the majors were less likely to speak up. A black sportswriter or former Negro League owner occasionally lamented the loss of command by African Americans over their own sporting lives, but they were voices in the wilderness for decades until the notion of black power gained sway in the 1960s. It took a gaffe by Dodgers general manager Al Campanis on *Nightline* in 1987, forty years after Robinson's debut, to make most people realize how thoroughly African Americans had been whited out of positions of influence in baseball.[24]

• • •

The expectations heaped on Jackie Robinson in 1947 could hardly have been higher, the focus of African Americans on their ebony paladin any more intense. The *Boston Chronicle* had greeted his arrival in the majors with the headline, "Triumph of Whole Race Seen in Jackie's Debut."[25] Forty years later, columnist George Will wrote that: "Robinson's first major league game was the most important event in the emancipation of black Americans since the Civil War." Sixty-three years later, Blue Jays skipper Cito Gaston, among a handful of African American managers in the majors, said at the ballpark in Toronto: "Without Mr. Robinson I wouldn't be sitting here and President Obama would not be president of the United States."[26]

For all the hype surrounding Robinson's debut, there's no question that baseball's integration brought the question of civil rights to the fore. Given the prominence of baseball in American culture at that time and society's segregated bias, the Chronicle's point, Will's retrospective, and Gaston's reflections were not just hyperbole. The attention Robinson received brought the question of civil rights to audiences that might not have otherwise thought about, much less wrestled with, integration.[27]

As civil rights activist Roy Wilkins, the editor of the NAACP's magazine Crisis, observed, those who watched ballgames or read box scores might never attend a lecture on race relations or know anything about black historical figures like George Washington Carver. "But Jackie Robinson," he argued, "if he makes the grade will be doing the missionary work with these people that Carver could never do. He will be saying to them that his people should have their rights, should have jobs, decent homes and education, freedom from insult and equality of opportunity to achieve."[28]

Robinson's debut came at a moment when African Americans felt more empowered than at any time since the end of the Civil War. Despite fears that World War II's aftermath might spark a reprise of the kind of race riots that had plagued the "Red Summer" of 1919 following World War I, African Americans made gains in the workplace and at the polls. More blacks were registered to vote, even in the Deep South, than ever before and the income gap between white and black workers had narrowed considerably. Though Cold War witch hunts sidetracked the struggle for civil rights and the search for subversives made the language of social and racial justice suspect, critical victories were won. In 1948 the Supreme Court of the United States outlawed restrictive housing covenants, President Truman desegregated the Armed Forces, and African Americans played a decisive role in Truman's surprising reelection victory over Thomas Dewey. Finally, seven years after baseball's integration, the Supreme Court overturned *Plessy v. Ferguson's* decades-old "separate but equal" doctrine and ordered the integration of the nation's public schools "with all deliberate speed" in its landmark *Brown v. Board of Education* decision.[29]

It's difficult to gauge how much Robinson's acceptance in baseball factored in to such broad social gains. At the least, his well-publicized victory, which preceded these breakthroughs, affected how people felt and thought about race in complex and often subtle ways. "You have to put them together," Mal Goode insisted. "Jackie Robinson was a catalyst. Supreme Court justices were going to games like everyone else; they saw black players perform at the highest level. Jackie made people think."[30] But there were limits to these symbolic breakthroughs. The Dodgers' march to the 1955 World Series certainly hadn't prevented fourteen-year-old African American Emmett Till's murder in Mississippi that summer or the acquittal of his two white killers that fall, just days before the series began. The *Pittsburgh Courier* edition following the acquittal of the men who had tortured and killed the black youth for the invented offense of whistling at a white woman featured a dark border with a black ribbon and called the September 23 verdict "Black Friday." In the same edition's sports section, the headlines lauded Robinson for stealing home yet again.[31]

While Robinson's role as a catalyst to sweeping change is difficult to assess, there is little doubt that he affected a generation of black youth who tracked his every move. Robinson was bold, dashing, a step ahead of everybody else both physically and mentally. Pittsburgh city councilman Dr. Jake Milliones, activists Robert Curvin and Roger Wilkins, and writer John Edgar Wideman all studied Robinson when they were young. "I wanted to be like Jackie Robinson," Milliones asserted. "You know Jackie Robinson was pigeon-toed, and I can remember as a kid running pigeon-toed, although I wasn't. But you wanted to be Jackie Robinson, so you ran pigeon-toed." Curvin believed that Robinson's trials in sport pushed him into becoming an activist, that Robinson's example raised his expectations of himself. "He was important to black youths in a very special way," Curvin emphasized. "He gave America vision."[32]

Fifteen years old in 1947, Roger Wilkins would recall that Robinson "brought pride and the certain knowledge that on a fair playing field, when there were rules and whites could not cheat and lie and steal, not only were they not supermen but we could beat them." The future civil rights leader and historian believed that Robinson understood what hung in the balance. "He knew what the stakes were every time he danced off a base. If he failed, we failed." [33]

But Robinson's triumphs placed pressure on young African Americans who grew up with the admonition to "be like Jackie." John Edgar Wideman, only six when Robinson debuted, could not escape the commotion around him. "Jackie Robinson was a vexed figure for me," he recalled. "One thing you were taught is not to put your behind out there too visibly. That was a no-no." Drawing attention to yourself could cause trouble. Robinson was the focus whenever he was on base; his fiercely competitive persona made him a flashpoint, especially after Rickey took the wraps off him late in his second season and let him fight back and argue like other players. "Someone like Jackie Robinson was potentially a troublemaker and that was scary, so my response to him was ambivalent," Wideman remembered. "I was rooting for him, but he was worrisome as well as a hero, as well as somebody who was opening up vistas and possibilities. As a kid, I didn't understand politics. I didn't understand the larger movements. I worried about the guy. I thought, 'You know he's going to suffer—something's going to happen bad to him, and possibly happen bad to me.'"

Robinson instilled pride in Wideman, but watching him was unsettling. "It worried me," Wideman reflected, "in the same way that it worried me to read James Baldwin, in the same way that it worried me to read Ralph Ellison and Richard Wright, because they were demanding something of me. They were saying, 'Hey, the way things are going along now is not good and you know that. So take a chance, take a step, you have to make it better, you have to do something about it.'" [34]

Mal Goode had been doing something about it most of his adult life. He became the country's first African American network correspondent when he assumed the United Nations beat for ABC shortly before the Cuban missile crisis in 1962. That he got the job had much to do with Jackie Robinson, who had criticized ABC's all-white on-air cast to ABC News chief Jim Hagerty. Robinson, by then out of baseball and working as an executive with Chock Full o'Nuts, knew Hagerty, President Eisenhower's former press secretary, from Republican Party politics. Arriving one day at

Hagerty's office, he said: "Jim, whenever I come here, the only black people I see are mopping the floor. When are you going to do something about that?" Robinson recommended Goode as a candidate to alter the network's monochromatic makeup.

Goode had grown up a block from Homestead Grays owner Cum Posey. After watching his father labor decades at an open-hearth furnace for Carnegie Steel's Homestead Works without prospects for advancing on the job due to racially skewed hiring and promotion practices, Mal became an advocate journalist. He began working for the *Courier* and delivering news and commentary on the radio, where he punctuated victories over segregation with the closing: "And walls came tumbling down." If there was trouble in Pittsburgh, Goode covered it. Robinson and other black players were frequent visitors to the Goode home on road trips to Pittsburgh. Goode saw the ballplayers' struggles as part of the civil rights fight that consumed his life.

"How did I feel about Jackie Robinson?" Goode asked rhetorically. "I don't say I cried but I felt like crying. There were many people who went to Forbes Field and cried when they saw Jackie. People came from across the country, carloads and busloads and trainloads of them, and he didn't let us down."

But unlike most of Robinson's giddily joyful fans, Goode knew that Jackie's presence on the Dodgers came with a steep price. "Integration had its disadvantages from the standpoint of baseball and black owners knew that—including Cum Posey. He knew it was going to kill him, but the broad-minded said it's going to come eventually anyhow." The black owners, he said, thought that Major League Baseball would find a place for them in their new universe. "That was a wild dream," Goode reflected, "but they saw, which is the greater, shall we do it, shall we accept it, or shall we continue with segregated baseball." For Goode, the decisive factor was baseball's ability to open doors in the workplace and other institutions. As with integration of the schools, Goode realized that there were losses as well as gains. "But what we gained is the greater," he concluded. "We got our self-respect back, and you have to have been black to understand what that meant." [35]

Like Mal Goode, playwright August Wilson was born in Pittsburgh and became a passionate sports fan. For Goode, who had grown up in a world of rigid color lines, encountering insult whenever he boarded an airplane or entered a downtown restaurant, integration was worth almost any price. Wilson was not so sure. Jackie Robinson had never been his boyhood hero; Henry Aaron and Sonny Liston filled that role. "Every home run Hank Aaron hit," he recalled, "I helped him hit. Every time Sonny Liston knocked somebody out gave me a place in the world." Liston, who became the heavyweight champion of the world after serving time in a penitentiary for armed robbery, was an edgier figure than Robinson. So were the 1960s, when Wilson came of age and black power began eclipsing the emphasis on integration at any cost that had characterized the civil rights movement.

Wilson's cycle of plays set on the Hill in Pittsburgh explores the evolution of the black community. *Fences* is about fictional former Negro Leaguer Troy Maxson, who winds up working as a garbageman on the Hill, bitter over the opportunities he never got. Maxson is a composite of men like Josh Gibson and Wilson's neighbor, fighter Charley Burley, who were denied the chance to show their true worth on sports' biggest stage.

For Wilson, the Negro Leagues signified ownership and power. "In that time in America, there were very few blacks in any positions of authority. The streetcar driver was white. You go downtown to buy something, the person you buy your stuff from is white. All the teachers are white. Everybody in any position is white. So it's important, if you go to the Negro Leagues, to see the umpire ain't white. It's a black umpire. The owner ain't white. Nobody's white. This is our thing, and I think it's important to transfer that over into the community—and we have our everything—until integration. And then we don't have our nothing."

To Wilson, black baseball was a metaphor for a stronger, more vibrant black community. "In the '40s," he reasoned, "whatever little bit of money there was, it was our money. It was our teams, and it gave us a sense of self that we don't have anymore. You had your own thing and it gave you a sense of belonging." But that sense of power and belonging was ephemeral. Black owners tried to negotiate with Major League Baseball to become part of its landscape and join organized baseball as a high minor league. But Major League Baseball ignored them and the Negro Leagues disintegrated. For Wilson, the impact went beyond the ball field. Black baseball's obliteration heralded a wider war on black institutions nationwide with long-term consequences. "If that economic ownership in the black community could have been developed and maintained," he contended, "blacks in America would be in a very different place."[36]

John Edgar Wideman voiced similar doubts. "I think a lot was lost when the Negro Leagues went belly-up. I think a lot was lost when the black colleges began to lose students and funds. After all, this is supposed to be a culture, a society, of diversity, and losing institutions that have that long a life and play that crucial a role in the community [is] very worrisome. That is some measure of what was lost. What was contained in those institutions was not simply a black version of what white people were doing but the game was played differently." Integration, he argued, should not have been a matter of minorities divesting themselves of long-held mores but of licensing them to bring their ways into the mainstream. The black leagues and colleges had their own character that reflected a rich and deeply rooted culture, he said. "And so rather than having those institutions change the total picture, change what we all do, we lost them, and that is to me, continues to be, a great loss. That's not what integration is supposed to be about."

Integration on Major League Baseball's terms denied the legitimacy and relevance of African American culture. To Wideman, integration became little more than a prelude to "extinction, extermination, and loss." Sport's expressive dimension, especially the black version of the game, with its emphasis on improvisation, spontaneity, and self-expression, suffered. Sport had offered African Americans an arena "where the possibilities that were closed off in other areas of life, where that positive energy, could be realized." But after Jackie Robinson, sport took place in a different context with different power relationships, one where African Americans had far less say in why and how the games were played, who got to play them, and what they meant.

"Integration, the way it is understood in this country," Wideman said, "is really nothing new. Because integration the way it is understood does not involve any change in the power relationships between white and black. And so integration is just another phrase or description of white over black." The refusal to consider incorporating black teams, owners, front-office personnel, managers, and coaches insured that African Americans would be powerless in baseball—except on the field. "Integration has become simply a very bald choice for black people," Wideman observed. "Do it our way. Come on board. And we have forgotten that James Baldwin said, or posed the question, 'Should we integrate into a burning house?'"

Integration into Major League Baseball's burning house meant that making it often required leaving the black community behind. "Success in *this* culture," Wideman argued, "is seen as getting the hell out of what we mean as *the* culture as fast as you can."[37] For Wideman and Wilson, it was not just what was gained, but what could have been created if integration had not been such an either/or phenomenon. "There are two forms of black entertainment," Wilson pointed out, "entertainment for whites and entertainment for blacks. The song you sung and danced for the slave master was not the same song you sung and danced on Saturday night for yourself."[38]

As segregation collapsed, so did the institutions it had protected. Black hospitals, newspapers, banks, insurance companies, hotels, and restaurants were often decimated by competition from better-funded competitors. Many folded as a result. Only eight of over one hundred black hospitals operating in 1944 remained open fifty years later. The black press lost most of its circulation and some of its most talented writers; black banks have all but disappeared.[39]

"What was the real meaning of the Jackie Robinson revolution," baseball historian John Holway asked. "Was it to get Jackie Robinson and the great black players into the major leagues? No! They had been playing major league caliber baseball. The real significance of the Jackie Robinson revolution was that it got the black owners and the black fans out. Now the great black players played for white owners. Now, the great black players played for white fans. They entertained whites. They used to entertain blacks. Now if you go to the game you very rarely see a black in the grandstand."[40]

The Negro Leagues could be romanticized as belonging to a "golden ghetto." In reality, of course, the Negro Leagues reflected all the compromises, limitations, and troubles that plagued African American life under segregation. Many African Americans did not think that such an artifact of a segregated society was worth saving. Others were not so sure. Was there an alternative to their demise? Could integration in sport have worked out differently? Sadly, Major League Baseball did not consider those options. Why couldn't the major leagues have accepted the Homestead Grays, Newark Eagles, Kansas City Monarchs, and New York Cubans as franchises, or at the least, as a top minor league circuit? Did Major League Baseball owners really need to insist on such a limited and heavy-handed integration of the game they turned around and sold as a model for American democracy? They refused to confront these questions for decades to come. By the time they did, African Americans had stopped caring about baseball.

CHAPTER SIX

¡Viva México!

Jackie Robinson opened major league baseball to Latin players of color, but that breakthrough came at a steep price: Caribbean baseball's independence. The trickle of Latin players heading northward before Robinson's debut turned into a torrent after his 1947 rookie year. In time, Latin ballplayers came to constitute a staggeringly talented cohort that surpassed African Americans in both number and performance. Major League Baseball would become their destination of choice, and after just a few short years, the Caribbean leagues they left behind would submit to its authority.

Transforming the Caribbean into a baseball colony required the major leagues to eliminate all competitors, especially Jorge Pasquel's Mexican League. In 1946 Mexico posed the greatest challenge to the monopoly that the big leagues held over professional baseball since the upstart Federal League had sought major league status and a share of the market thirty years before. The gloves-off showdown between MLB and Pasquel, a fight that the majors were unwilling to lose, was about to shake up the baseball world.

That it was Mexicans who defied the major leagues first was less about the quality of their baseball than the wealth of their society and the weight of their history. Cuba had more and better ballplayers, but not a robust wartime economy like that of the vastly bigger, more populous Mexico. Nor did Cuban baseball have anyone willing to take on major league magnates at their own game, as Jorge Pasquel did. Pasquel's immense wealth allowed him to combine scores of Cuban and Negro Leaguers with expatriate major

Jorge Pasquel *(Courtesy Jorge Pasquel Acosta). Date: 1946.* Left to right: Mickey Owen, Pasquel, Danny Gardella, Burnis "Wild Bill" Wright, Ray Dandridge. The fiercely patriotic Jorge Pasquel used his wealth to remake Mexican baseball into an international and multiracial powerhouse, attracting top Negro League and Cuban players. After World War II, he recruited major leaguers too. MLB never faced a more formidable challenge.

leaguers in a Mexican league that posed the most serious threat that Major League Baseball had ever faced from beyond U.S. borders.

After buying a team in 1940, Pasquel funded the Mexican League's expansion as a summer circuit, putting it in direct competition for players with the Negro Leagues. Accustomed to traveling to wherever salaries were the highest, more than sixty Negro Leaguers and scores of top Cubans headed to Mexico. Perhaps one-fifth of all Negro League players jumped during the 1940 season alone—revealing how vulnerable the black leagues were to a better-capitalized rival, a lesson that Dodgers president Branch Rickey absorbed. But the war stanched further defections. The draft prevented many black players from returning to Mexico in 1942 while wartime profits let black clubs pay competitive salaries.

Two Negro Leaguers who did come back to Mexico to play in 1943 came as a result of a bizarre trade that Pasquel engineered. The U.S. government arranged for catcher Quincy Trouppe and pitcher Theolic Smith to receive exemptions from their defense-plant jobs stateside. In exchange, Mexico sent tens of thousands of guest workers to the United States to fill labor shortages caused by the war. These farmworkers harvested crops that would have otherwise rotted in the fields while Trouppe and Smith tended baseball diamonds. Except for Trouppe and Smith, few Negro Leaguers played in Mexico during the final years of the war.[1]

When the war ended, Pasquel not only renewed his assault on Negro League rosters but began pursuing major leaguers. In addition to deploying his considerable fortune to fulfill this vision, Pasquel exploited his extensive business and personal connections, including his lifelong friendship with Miguel Alemán, who assumed the Mexican presidency on December 1, 1946.

When it came to baseball, Pasquel was more of a patron and patriot than a calculating businessman. He traveled extensively, spending money with flair and noblesse oblige. One evening at a Manhattan restaurant, Joe DiMaggio stopped by Pasquel's table to chat with him and his companion, actress María Félix. After the Yankee outfielder complimented Pasquel for his blue alligator shoes, Pasquel instructed his assistant to measure DiMaggio's feet so that he could have a dozen pairs of shoes handcrafted for him.[2] Journalists likened Pasquel to Pancho Villa, the sharecropper's son who became a social bandit and a general in the Mexican Revolution. In 1916, irate over U.S. meddling in Mexican politics, Villa and his forces crossed the border, attacked a U.S. cavalry base, and raided Columbus, New Mexico, leaving the town in flames and bodies in the streets.[3]

In 1946, thirty years after Villa crossed the border, Pasquel launched his own raid. The timing was propitious. Not only was Jackie Robinson's signing reverberating through Major League Baseball, hundreds of ballplayers had recently returned from fighting abroad. As a result, hundreds of Negro Leaguers and an even greater number of demobilized veterans were all suddenly competing for jobs when the major league baseball season began in 1946.

The glut of competition that scared the ballplayers delighted and emboldened the owners, who insisted on downright insulting terms. Absent a union, players were helpless to negotiate and easily became locked into steeply one-sided contractual relationships. The infamous "reserve clause" in their contracts bound players to their current club for the following season, essentially preventing them from becoming free agents as long as they played in the majors. Appraising Major League Baseball from afar, Pasquel maneuvered to exploit player anxiety. He began his assault in Cuba.

• • •

Pasquel, Washington Senators owner Clark Griffith, and Major League Baseball commissioner Happy Chandler converged on Havana, where the first skirmishes in the Mexican baseball war were fought that winter. The Cuban League was easily the Caribbean's top winter circuit. During Cuba's 1945–46 campaign, the talent level—featuring native sons, major leaguers back from the war, and Negro Leaguers—surpassed what the major leagues fielded during their previous, war-depleted season. For demobilized players, Cuba was an opportunity to regain playing form and collect a paycheck. For Pasquel, it was a chance to sign ballplayers for the upcoming Mexican summer season.

Pasquel courted recruits at his posh Sevilla-Biltmore Hotel suite. He staggered ballplayers with offers of lucrative long-term contracts, and then accompanied them to the bank, where they could cash his checks on the spot for advances that often equaled an entire year's salary. "The señor is making no secret of his wealth," *Washington Post* columnist Shirley Povich noted. "His tie pin is a row of sparkling diamonds and his clasp is a diamond-studded miniature bat."[4]

Cuba was a choice market; over 40 percent of the men on Cuban winter league rosters had played in Mexico, including four who had managed there the previous summer. But Pasquel's shopping list differed from past years; this time he was seeking top major leaguers in addition to the best Cubans and Negro Leaguers. "American baseball owners are apparently up against a Mexican millionaire who has gone berserk with his dough," Povich observed. "It isn't sound business for Pasquel who can never hope to get his money back out of baseball in Mexico . . . but the fact remains that the big leagues are losing ballplayers to him and not only Cubans."[5]

The major leagues lashed back. Clark Griffith arrived in Havana with the Washington Senators and a proprietary attitude. The Senators were

there to play exhibitions against the Red Sox; Griffith, meanwhile, intended to preserve his pipeline of Cuban players. He had benefited more
from Cuban baseball than any other major league owner and was not
about to surrender his stranglehold of the island's talent, much of which
ended up in the Senators' organization. "Griffith," Povich wrote, "is spout-
ing maledictions at the rich Mexican Pasquel brothers who have set up
headquarters in Havana and are creating a dither with their fancy salary
offers." In a well-attended speech, Griffith denounced the men behind the
Mexican League as outlaws and "shady elements." He was taken to task
by Povich, who reminded his readers that Griffith had employed similar tactics back when he had raided National League players to create the
American League in 1900.[6]

Joining Griffith in Havana, Commissioner Happy Chandler commanded the players who had accepted Mexican contracts to return to
their teams before the major league season opened. Those who did not,
he warned, would be suspended for five years.[7] Pasquel's cash, however,
proved more persuasive than Chandler's threats, and the Mexican mogul easily picked off several Latinos who had been playing in the majors,
including the Senators' Roberto Ortiz, the White Sox's Alejandro Carrasquel, and the Athletics' Roberto Estalella. He also signed dozens of
Negro Leaguers and Cubans. It was an easy sell to players of color who
had been impressed by Pasquel's generosity and solicitude for their needs
in the past. They found his openness regarding race appealing and, if the
money was equal, preferred Mexico to the United States. Overall, they encountered even less discrimination in Mexico than in Cuba, where private
social clubs still maintained color lines. Many brought their families with
them, something they never did while playing in the United States.[8]

Pasquel's associates soon began tendering what were then unheard-of
contracts with generous signing bonuses (a rarity at the time) to bona fide
major league stars. Ted Williams, Hank Greenberg, Joe DiMaggio, and Bob
Feller were offered stupendous, multiyear deals that would have paid each
player over $100,000 per year in compensation. Williams, whose mother
was part Mexican, presented an especially enticing target. Like DiMaggio,
he made less than $50,000 in 1946. Although these men, as well as Phil
Rizzuto, Pete Reiser, and Stan Musial spurned Pasquel's entreaties, other

major leaguers gladly accepted. Vern Stephens, the 1945 American League home-run leader, signed a three-year contract for much more than he would have made that summer with the St. Louis Browns. Stephens bugged out after a few days of culture shock, but the Dodgers' Mickey Owen and Luis Olmo, the Giants' Sal Maglie, Danny Gardella, and Napoleon Reyes, and the Cardinals' Max Lanier and Lou Klein lasted longer. Some of these men were struggling to stay in the majors; others, like Lanier, who started the season 6–0 for St. Louis, were legitimate major leaguers. In all, eighteen major leaguers and several minor leaguers jumped to Mexico. They would become known as the Mexican jumping beans—a group of players willing to defy the moguls who ran professional baseball in the United States.

The 1946 Mexican season began with President Miguel Ávila Camacho throwing out the first ball and a capacity crowd of thirty-three thousand fans jamming Mexico City's Delta Park.[9] Crowds, larger than in previous seasons, roared their approval of the renegade major leaguers, most of whom played up to fan expectations. Two of them, Gardella and Olmo, homered in the opener.

Collier's Kyle Crichton went to Mexico in June to interview players who had forsaken the major leagues. "What is most immediately apparent," he wrote, "is that Pasquel would have had no luck whatever in his recruiting if the players had not been dissatisfied with conditions in the States." In Mexico, they received salaries that doubled what some of them had made in the majors, as well as signing bonuses, free apartments, and allowances for living expenses. Pasquel covered players' medical bills, gave gold bracelets to their wives, and bestowed cars, watches, and rings to the major league expats and some of their Cuban and African American teammates. "Pasquel treats the players with such prodigality that they go about with their eyes popping," Crichton exclaimed. "Without doubt, it is the most amazing thing ever known in the history of sports."[10]

There was something else radically different about the league: Pasquel was willing to share the wealth—both with players and among owners. Fifty-five percent of ticket revenues went into a pool that was divided equally among the eight clubs. And rather than monopolize the best players, Pasquel distributed them among the teams to promote greater competitive balance. He was more invested in the league's success than that of his own club, and he understood that its fate required the weaker teams to prosper. It would be decades before U.S. leagues adopted similar approaches to revenue sharing.

Both the *Washington Post's* Shirley Povich and the *New York Times's* Arthur Daley drew comparisons between Mexico and the Federal League, an independent major league that in 1913 and 1914 represented the last serious rival to National and American League domination. Povich reasoned that Mexico provided players with their first chance to negotiate higher salaries since the Federal League war had competed for their services in 1914. Daley noted that the owners who had once snickered condescendingly about Pasquel were laughing no longer. But, he countered: "Talk that the Mexican promotion is as much a threat to the two majors as was the Federal League is just so much poppycock. The parallel doesn't exist."

The difference was that the Federal League had contested for major league fans as well as major league players, while the Mexican League competed only for players in a "player-glutted market." Though Pasquel was willing to share the wealth, some doubted whether there was enough money to go around. Daley, the dean of the *Times's* sport department, considered the Mexican League economically suspect. He was correct. Mexico had too few cities where teams could make enough at the gate to sustain the league at the salaries they were paying. Several Mexican owners said as much. After Pasquel assigned former New York Giant Sal Maglie to the Puebla Pericos (Parrots), owner Castor Montoto complained that adding a $10,000 salary meant that the club could not possibly meet payroll on its own. It could, however, draw upon the league's treasury to make good on its obligations.[11]

These critiques of the league's business plan were of little comfort to major league owners as long as Pasquel was willing to lose money liberally to seduce their players. Even more alarming was the effect that Mexico was having on major leaguers who had no intention of playing there but were eager to use the possibility of being recruited away as a bargaining chip in salary negotiations.[12]

Pasquel spoke grandly of Mexican baseball's future. His plans called for investing $6 million to build new ballparks for the 1947 season, including a $2 million Baseball City in the capital, with apartments for players. Upgrading venues would put Mexican baseball on steadier financial footing. Indeed, its long-term viability depended on extracting more money from a greater number of fans. Nicer fields with locker rooms would also help Pasquel attract major leaguers.[13] After decades of turning a blind eye to their southern neighbor and acting as if they were the only game in town, U.S. owners anxiously watched these developments from afar.

• • •

During World War II, major league owners had dismissed the Mexican League as a serious rival. Though several notable Cuban major leaguers had opted to play in Mexico, those defections were likely spurred by the Selective Service Board ruling that foreign ballplayers living and working in the United States were eligible for conscription. But Pasquel's efforts to sign white major leaguers, together with the fallout from Jackie Robinson's signing and the renewed efforts by MLB's players to unionize cast Mexico in a different light.[14]

Because integration meant that dark-skinned ballplayers once beyond the major league's pale were now candidates for their rosters, Mexico was suddenly a competitor for their services. More importantly, the upstart American Baseball Guild had begun enlisting major leaguers in a union that spring. The labor movement had emerged from the war stronger than before and ballplayers sought an alternative to take-it-or-leave-it contract talks in which the owners held all the cards. A union and a collective-bargaining accord would reshuffle the deck. "Organized baseball no longer can rule with the iron hand of an absolute dictator," union organizer Robert Murphy declared. "Now it must deal with organized baseball players in the form of the American Baseball Guild." Leveraging Pasquel's challenge, Murphy argued that major league owners should ally themselves with their players in the fight against Mexico. "We have seen a lot of good players go over to the Mexican League. If they had been satisfied, they naturally would have remained in the United States."[15]

While the owners were not about to align with the union, they were savvy enough to recognize the connection between labor unrest and Mexico: both disputed their prerogatives over players. Since the merger of the National and American Leagues in 1903, MLB's owners had successfully rebuffed every challenge from rival leagues and players. Circling the wagons once again, the owners now redoubled efforts to squash Pasquel and the incipient revolt of players seeking to sell their services to the highest bidder.

Unlike Pasquel, major league owners were unwilling to share the wealth or ignore bottom-line considerations. They were accustomed to having things their way and saw compromise as a sign of weakness. They had never offered concessions to their players, resolutely sticking to a nonunion stance, and did not tolerate rival leagues that refused to accept their primacy. Nor were they keen on win-win solutions—the gutting of the Negro Leagues would be evidence of that. They were determined to destroy Pasquel because he jeopardized their monopoly over players. But they underestimated the man, who wielded his formidable wealth and political connections as a point of fierce nationalist pride.

"Most U.S. fans," *Life* magazine wrote, "visualize Jorge Pasquel, president and virtual dictator of the eight-team Mexican Baseball League, as a sinister, swarthy and unscrupulous man of limitless means whose widespread agents operate on a Fu-Manchulike scale."[16] Not Mexicans. They applauded him for unleashing what Fray Nano, the publisher of *La Afición*, called "a wave of hysteria in the land of the dollar." Milton Bracker, covering the conflict for the *New York Times* and *Saturday Evening Post*, wrote: "Pasquel is a patriot to the point of chauvinism. Nobody doubts he views his baseball triumphs over the MacPhails, the Rickeys . . . as over Uncle Sam himself."[17]

Excelsior, one of Mexico's leading newspapers, linked the raids to the centennial of the 1846 Mexican War, perhaps the sorest spot in U.S. relations with Mexico. It had been a century since President James K. Polk had ignited the war by falsely reporting to Congress that Mexican troops had crossed the border and shed American blood on American soil. The sordid invasion ended two years later, with Mexico surrendering almost a third of its territory, including California and what's now the American Southwest. Major league owners might have missed the relevance of these references to the war, but Mexicans remembered it as an unjustified land grab that still rankled.

Just as major league owners would never seriously entertain the idea of bringing black owners into the fold, they didn't consider the benefits of welcoming Pasquel and making him a respected partner. St. Louis Cardinals owner Sam Breadon, who had lost several ballplayers to Mexico because of the low salaries he paid, was the exception. Breadon visited Pasquel in Mexico City, where he likely broached selling his franchise to the Mexican magnate. "They think they're doing the honorable thing in building up baseball for Mexico," Breadon said afterward. "They believe they are merely retaliating in a big way for what American baseball scouts in the past have done to Mexican baseball in a small way." Pasquel embraced Breadon and said he would no longer go after St. Louis players. But the other owners were unwilling to treat Pasquel as anything but a pariah.[18]

Undaunted by his opposition, Pasquel pointed out that major league clubs, particularly the Senators, had often signed Mexican players despite their contractual obligations to Mexican teams. "Those days are gone forever," he swore. "Now, it's every man for himself and players looking for bigger salaries will come to the Mexican League, instead of shunning us for attractive major league offers of the past."[19]

Mexican League rosters proved his point. Of the 180 men who played in Mexico in 1946, over half were foreigners. Twenty were white U.S. citizens, including major and minor leaguers and two men who were not playing organized baseball in the States. Twenty-seven were African Americans and forty-nine were Cubans (almost evenly divided between darker- and lighter-skinned men and including many former major and minor leaguers). A few were Canadian, Puerto Rican, or Venezuelan. To make it easier for teams to abide by the limit of eight foreigners per team, Cubans were counted as if they were Mexican. The African American and Cuban contingents, led by Martín Dihigo, Ray Dandridge, Santos Amaro, Ray Brown, and hard-hitting outfielder Claro Duany, were superior to their major league counterparts. Several of these black and Cuban players were destined for Cooperstown; none of the white U.S. players who went to Mexico joined them there.[20]

While Mexicans savored the raids on U.S. baseball, Commissioner Chandler launched verbal salvos at Pasquel that splashed across the pages of newspapers throughout the United States, Mexico, and Cuba. Trying to shore up his league's stature while diminishing Mexican baseball's, Chandler came off as arrogant and petulant. He, Branch Rickey, and Clark Griffith lambasted the Mexican League owners as outlaws running a bush-league operation. Writer John Lardner chastised the Americans in turn for issuing "as reckless and vindictive a series of insults to the Pasquel brothers as you could expect to hear from a high-school sophomore with indigestion."[21] After Rickey impugned Mexican baseball's integrity for poaching Luis Olmo, his star Puerto Rican outfielder, Pasquel rejoined: "That hurt me; that hurt my pride. It hurt the pride of all Mexicans. If American baseball wants peace with us, I will not go to them. They will get peace only when Commissioner Chandler comes here to this office and sits in this chair and explains what he has meant by his words about Mexico."[22] To underscore his intentions, Pasquel announced that he had deposited another half a million dollars with U.S. bankers to purchase additional players.[23]

Realizing that Pasquel would not be intimidated, Chandler tried to expel Mexico from the baseball system that orbited the major leagues. After warning in March of 1946 that players who jumped to Mexico would be suspended for five years if not back by opening day, he imposed the bans in April. Chandler defined contractual obligations liberally, maintaining that even if a player had not yet signed a contract for the 1946 season, the reserve clause made him the property of the club he had played for in 1945. In all, Chandler banned eighteen men, including six Latino major leaguers, from joining any major league or minor league club under his jurisdiction, effectively blackballing these men from making a living playing baseball in the United States.

In addition, the Yankees, Dodgers, and Giants brought lawsuits against the Mexican League for tampering with players. Although these legal maneuvers failed, Major League Baseball was able to pressure U.S. sporting goods companies to halt shipments of balls and bats that Mexican teams had ordered.[24] The majors also recognized a rival Mexican circuit, which included a team in El Paso, Texas, as an official minor league. Pasquel was not so easily diverted; he raided the new league's players and managers and prevented its teams from using Delta Park in Mexico City. The Mexican press all but ignored the rival league and it folded before the end of May.[25]

Through it all, Pasquel relished the notoriety. He delighted reading in *Life* magazine that despite terrific attendance at American ball games, big league owners "went around with harried, haunted looks, worrying which might be the next of their players to tear up his contract and jump to the fabulous Mexican League."[26] He rebuked major league owners and sportswriters who claimed that he was throwing away money on a quixotic quest. "Those who manipulate the baseball monopoly in the United States are alarmed because they are paying their players slave wages," he countered. "We are paying them exactly what they are worth and this is why they are coming to Mexico." Expatriate major leaguers said much the same when asked why they had jumped.

Ballplayers told *Collier's* Kyle Crichton that major league contracts were harsh and inequitable. Players could be discharged on ten days' notice but were bound to a team for life because of the reserve clause. "It is plain from speaking to players on both sides of the border that the Pasquel threat is the finest thing that ever happened to them," Crichton wrote. "Even if they don't jump to the Mexican League, their salaries are being hiked here. Instead of being at the mercy of the American club owners, they now have a leverage that makes life infinitely sweeter." With great prescience Crichton concluded: "It seems inevitable that if Pasquel persists in his campaign, changes will be made in the American system that will greatly better the status of the players."[27]

Laughing off claims that baseball was bleeding his family's fortune, widely estimated at $50 million, Pasquel proposed a wager in which he and the major league owners would each deposit $2 million in a New York City bank. "The $4,000,000 will be given to the gentlemen who control the United States monopoly if the Mexican League collapses," he said, "and to the Mexican League, if the latter finishes its season as it has in the past twenty-two years."[28] The owners didn't respond.

In May 1946 Pasquel upped the ante and attacked the major leagues where they were the most vulnerable. The Mexican League filed suit in the New York State Supreme Court, charging that organized baseball's player contracts were monopolistic and held players "in peonage for life." Attorney Mark Hughes, representing the New York Yankees, countered that "the great American game as we know it" would be destroyed if the contracts were declared illegal.[29]

The owners believed their own rhetoric. Their great game, in which they maintained near feudal sway over the players, would crumble without the reserve clause. Crichton offered a sobering assessment. Even if Pasquel loses the war, he said, the Mexican may "yet blow up the whole structure of baseball by getting the present standard contract held invalid."[30] MLB had depended on its exemption from antitrust laws ever since the U.S. Supreme Court ruled in 1922 that it did not constitute interstate commerce. The exemption had granted MLB immunity from federal court action when it restricted player movement. The New York State Supreme Court, adhering to precedent, ruled against the Mexican challenge and preserved the exemption, but the case gave the owners considerable *agita*.

Pasquel was entertaining Babe Ruth in Mexico City when the judge's decision was announced. Ruth defended his host, saying that anyone who read a major league contract would see that it was one-sided and unfair. Pasquel, for his part, bristled: "I am not in the least interested in what things took place in New York. I disregard all the stupidities of the Americans."[31] Journalist Milton Bracker, who was covering Ruth's visit, described the gusto with which Mexicans enjoyed their defiance of the major leagues. "In fact it has even been said that not since the historic oil expropriation of March, 1938 has any circumstance so delighted the Mexican national ego as that of 'Saint Jorge' tilting with the 'dragon' of American baseball."[32] Pasquel's ego may have been outsized, Cuban sportswriter Eladio Secades argued, but there was more to the man than self-centered audacity. Pasquel, he said, was inspired by the greater cause of racial equality, determined to showcase darker-skinned Latino and African American ballplayers in competition with major leaguers.[33]

If major league owners did not understand the political fallout of their actions, the U.S. State Department did. "Baseball is making it tough on us," an unidentified official complained. "We try to build up good will and this sort of thing tears it down."[34] *Washington Post* columnist Shirley Povich wondered why it had taken the State Department so long to object to Major League Baseball damaging relations with a close ally. "It has been apparent for months that the organized baseball people were doing a disservice to what the statesmen like to call hemispheric solidarity." Mexicans, he argued, rightfully resented the "superior air of American owners" and their insulting accusations that they were running an outlaw operation.

Organized baseball's arrogance was also damaging relations with Cuba, where it was threatening to bar major leaguers from playing. "The cry of 'Intervention!' was raised," Povich wrote, "and that's next thing to a fighting word in Latin America." Tone-deaf and patronizing, Chandler kept casting aspersions on Mexican baseball, stating: "We will deal only with reliable and reputable men." When pressed, Chandler replied defensively, "The State Department has enough to do without meddling in baseball." To that, Povich uttered: "Brother, the war must be over." Povich recalled the moment after Pearl Harbor when the owners had prostrated themselves before the government, terrified that it would deem baseball unessential to the war effort and force suspension of play. "Nobody was ever more polite to the Government during the war than the baseball people," he pointed out. "Now Commissioner Chandler tells the State Department, in effect, not to concern itself with baseball's Mexican hayride and mind its own marbles."[35]

* * *

During the 1946 season, Commissioner Chandler confronted a many-headed hydra. What worried him more than Mexico or racial integration were efforts by his own players to unionize. With foes wherever they looked, the owners convened in July to plot strategy. Although unionization had lost momentum after a vote by players on the Pittsburgh Pirates fell short of the two-thirds majority needed to authorize a strike, owners' apprehensions had not been allayed. They created a steering committee that reported back a month later. "Today," the committee's report argued, "baseball faces the most critical period in all its history." Although the big leagues were enjoying a record season at the gate, Pasquel had tarred Major League Baseball as an illegal monopoly. The confluence of the Mexican raids and the union campaign had forced baseball's antitrust status and contracts before the scrutiny of the courts. Such scrutiny, the owners believed, put their very survival on the line.[36]

The owners viewed the reserve clause as the foundation upon which the entire structure of professional baseball rested. If the court declared MLB's contracts illegal, invalidating that key clause, players would stampede onto the market as free agents. Scrambling to look even-handed, the owners' committee report argued that the reserve clause made baseball profitable and thus was actually in the players' interests. But the report concluded that major league contracts were toothless. They would neither hold up in court nor allow owners to gain a restraining order to stop a man from playing elsewhere. Facing lawsuits and expecting Mexican raids to continue, they called for strengthening contracts so that they would pass legal muster.[37]

In the report, which was intended for internal circulation only, the owners acknowledged that there was widespread player dissatisfaction and unrest because of inequitable contracts. They lamented that their efforts regarding the union campaign and the Mexican raids had been "completely ineffectual" in getting their side of the story before the public and pushed for a proactive public relations strategy. They realized that the union campaign was a more pressing matter than Mexico. Their candor behind closed doors was unusual, as was the alacrity with which they acted, but they had not been challenged so strongly and on so many fronts in more than a generation. Sensing their own vulnerability, they speculated that the union would have succeeded if it had begun by organizing minor leaguers. "In that event we would probably have awakened to what is known as a *fait accompli.*" Saying it in French did not make the thought of a union any more palatable to them.

Reluctantly facing the distasteful reality that they could not ignore player unrest forever, the owners tried to approach unionization the same way they had handled other challenges: on their own terms. The committee ultimately argued for building better relations with players. This was an historic admission; Major League Baseball's owners had never sought to accommodate their players. They asked Chandler to begin a process by which players would be authorized to represent teammates in contract negotiations. Meetings with duly elected player representatives were held quickly thereafter.[38]

Chandler, cannily assuming the persona of the national pastime's steward, as opposed to the owners' top gun, backed concessions. "I told the owners," he said in early August 1946, "that they're going to make more money this year than at any time in the history of baseball and now's the time to give the men who play for them something which should have been granted long ago." With postwar attendance skyrocketing by over 70 percent to an all-time high of 18.5 million fans, teams were flush. Chandler argued that it was in the owners' self-interest to reward their players;

put plainly, he saw it as the only way to stop Pasquel. "You can't blame kids for grabbing the big money he's putting out, but he can't keep that up, and won't. However, it is our duty to help our players rise above such temptation by providing for them where they really want to play. Then we can talk to Pasquel and anybody like him on our terms." He proposed a minimum salary, per diems during spring training, and a pension plan, all long-standing player demands.[39]

By late August 1946, virtually all player demands had been granted: representation on a grievance committee; spring-training expense allowances (which players called "Murphy money" as a gesture to union leader Robert Murphy); modification of the universally hated ten-day release clause; a pension plan; and a $5,000 minimum salary. About fifty major league baseball players made less than that in 1946; the American Baseball Guild, which had collapsed after the Pittsburgh Pirates failed to authorize a strike that summer, had sought a $6,500 minimum. Players also gained representation on an executive council that set baseball policy, subject to the owners' approval. Though the players' new powers were limited, they finally had a seat at the table.[40]

The owners could now deal with their other concerns from a position of strength, even if it came at the cost of concessions to players. It was a price they gladly paid to more fully co-opt the players.[41] As more radical calls for unionization efforts abated, players across the league began falling into line.

• • •

Major League Baseball had been in a tizzy since March, but after blunting the union campaign in August, the tide turned. The Mexican League began losing momentum. Mickey Owen, who had been playing and managing the Veracruz Azules, quit and came home. Owen, a country boy from the Ozarks who had turned back at the border en route to Mexico that spring, had always been ambivalent about playing there. But the Dodger catcher, the scapegoat of the 1941 World Series after he dropped a third strike in the fourth game that led to a Yankees comeback, had decided to go after all because he feared that Branch Rickey would make him the whipping boy as an example to other players considering Mexico. Once there, Owen did not adjust well to Mexico's more egalitarian racial atmosphere. He was troubled by playing with men of color and humiliated after losing an on-field fistfight with Afro-Cuban player Claro Duany. By the time Pasquel removed him as manager and took over the position himself, Owen had reached his breaking point.[42]

Owen's return offered a propaganda coup for the major leagues. The Philadelphia Phillies, who at the suggestion of their manager Ben Chapman voted on whether they thought Commissioner Chandler should rescind his suspension, were unanimous that he should not. Player representative Phil Hughes said that his teammates felt that "it would be unfair to players who remained loyal to American baseball to have Owen come back and be allowed to play." The Dodgers' representative disagreed. "Owen did a lot to improve the players' position," outfielder Augie Galan pointed out. "No sooner had he jumped to Mexico than a lot of our players and New York Giant players, too, got good raises."[43]

The owners were relieved that some of the players were willing to cast out one of their own. On top of that, they delighted in the Mexican League's visible decline. Attendance, though strong early in the 1946 season, lagged as the novelty of major leaguers playing in Mexico wore off and torrential rains and power blackouts took their toll. Perhaps, major league owners fantasized, the Mexican League would fail of its own accord.

• • •

The Mexican League's stubborn affront to Major League Baseball had been especially troubling because of the prospect that such discontent could become infectious and spread around the Caribbean. Cuba loomed large in major league owners' consciousness, since it was already producing major league players. Uneasy about the prospect of black players and fans in the majors, owners had moved hesitantly toward integrating their organizations. Most of them probably hoped that Jackie Robinson would fail on the field, delaying a racial reckoning. But they were accustomed to fielding light-skinned Cuban ballplayers and familiar with Cuba as a spring-training venue. Some twenty Cubans had debuted in the majors since 1940, scores more stocked minor league squads, and teams were returning to Cuba to train after the war.

Cuban baseball had always been a win-win venue for major league owners and players of all races and nationalities. Everybody could play and profit there. The best players of color, who performed in Mexico in the summer of 1946, segued to Cuba afterward for the winter season. By participating in both circuits, these men earned more than many major leaguers and much more than minor leaguers did in the United States. The specter of a Mexican summer–Cuban winter league combination emerging as a viable alternative to the majors, especially at a time when integration was revamping the game, underscored the gravity of the challenge confronting the owners. Cuba was about to become a central battleground.

Arriving in Havana after the 1946 season, Chandler drew a line in the sand. Not only would any player who went to Mexico be blacklisted, anybody who played against a suspended player might suffer the same fate and become ineligible to play in either the major or minor leagues. The edict jeopardized Cubans playing in their own winter league because it included banned players.

Widening the ban instantly affected thousands of ballplayers in the United States and the Caribbean and cast a pall over barnstorming and winter play. For the first time in almost a century of baseball, the major leagues were telling Cubans how to play baseball in Cuba. Though the suspensions and secondary boycott were aimed primarily at white major leaguers, they affected African American and Latin ballplayers. Once Robinson and other Negro Leaguers signed with major league organizations, a growing number of players who previously could have safely ignored the ban were also subject to the expanding sanctions. Some Negro League teams canceled games with suspended barnstormers, fearful that they would be shut out of major league ballparks; players who had major league aspirations hesitated before playing against them.

But the owners' secondary blacklist hit Cuba's winter league—which was stacked with men who had played in Mexico—especially hard. It meant that any major or minor leaguer or any ballplayer who aspired to sign with a major league organization could damage his career by playing with or against blackballed players in Cuba. This was especially galling because it would prevent Cubans from playing in Cuba.[44]

Cuba's national director of sports, Luis Orlando Rodriguez, was indignant. "Baseball was perfectly willing to use our 100 Cuban players during the war, when there was a manpower shortage," he protested, "but now that the war is over they are through with us." It struck his compatriots as grossly unfair that Cubans who played summers in the United States could not return and play winters in their own country because of the Mexican connection. "Since baseball has turned its back on us here," Rodriguez warned, "there seems to be no alternative but for us to form a Latin American federation of baseball and compete as best we can against the American monopoly."[45]

During the war, Cuba had edged economically and politically closer to the United States, which bought its sugar crop and stationed troops there. U.S. influence was on the rise throughout the island, with American movies, cars, tourists, and products cementing ties with Cuban businesses. A similar trend emerged in baseball, which was in ferment as a new group of Cuban entrepreneurs took on the old baseball families. The new money, more directly associated with U.S. interests, had just built the Gran Stadium, which seated more than thirty thousand fans, twice what La Tropical accommodated.[46]

As the majors tried to cope with Mexico, integration, and union organizing by their own players, two competing leagues played in Cuba that 1946–47 winter season. The freshly formed Liga de la Federación included players who had signed contracts with major league organizations or did not want to foreclose that possibility. It played at La Tropical and was backed by traditional baseball interests. The rival Cuban League played at the new Gran Stadium and was backed by men who had more recently become team owners. Although these *arribistas* tried to curry favor with organized baseball in the United States, their winter league included the Mexican renegades, and they were willing to defy Commissioner Chandler. This group included banned major leaguers like Sal Maglie, Danny Gardella, and Max Lanier, aging Cubans like Martín Dihigo, Armando Marsans, and Adolfo Luque, and an array of African American, Cuban, and Caribbean stars—Santos Amaro, Buck O'Neil, Beto Ávila, Ray Dandridge, Orestes Miñoso, and Cocaína García. Overall, the Cuban League fielded far more accomplished players, but it had fewer promising young players because these prospects did not want to derail their major league careers before they had begun.

The major-league-compliant Liga de la Federación struggled, losing $100,000 and never catching on with fans. But the Cuban League flourished and its pennant race between "eternal rivals" Habana and Almendares captivated Cubans. Miguel Angel González and Adolfo Luque, two of the most respected men in Cuban baseball, managed the teams, which featured an international mix of players. After Almendares rallied late in the season, the championship came down to the final game in February. Several Brooklyn Dodgers, who had recently arrived for spring training, were on hand as Max Lanier, one of the most prominent major leaguers to have jumped to Mexico, pitched his Almendares squad to victory.

During the season Cuba's relationship to organized baseball had hung in the balance. It was resolved soon after. In January 1947 Almendares co-owner Dr. July Sanguily told the *Sporting News* that the Cuban League would forever ban the jumpers in return for amnesty for Cubans. "Much harm has been done unnecessarily," Sanguily said. "But we must heal the wounds. I realize that we must get into Organized Baseball for our own protection." To accomplish that, the Cuban League agreed to sacrifice the suspended major leaguers. "We will do anything else they demand but Americans must understand that Cubans will not take a slap in the face. They will be anxious to see what is done about [Miguel] González, who is a hero down here."[47]

By then, Major League Baseball had banned at least twenty Cubans, including González and Luque, two of the island's most revered players. With the threat of additional suspensions looming, the Cuban League reached an agreement with MLB on June 10, 1947. It would not risk rupturing relations with the majors.

By signing the pact, the Cuban League gave up its autonomy. The pact regulated the flow of players between major league organizations and the Cuban League, essentially making the latter a minor league for player development. It allowed the majors to determine who was eligible to play and left Luque, González, and others in the cold. Veteran major leaguers could no longer participate in the Cuban League, and any player who had signed a major league contract could be instructed to stop playing in Cuba at his club's request. The emphasis in Cuban baseball shifted from winning the league championship to preparing players to do well in the United States.

That set the tenor of their relationship for the next decade. It also generated greater turnover on Cuban rosters, as those who became successful in the majors no longer returned to play on the island.[48]

Not every Cuban rolled over for the major leagues. The winter season following the Cuban League's capitulation witnessed the creation of yet another rival, the Liga Nacional. The league was an option for Mexican jumpers, Cubans, and Negro Leaguers with no interest in or possibility of reaching the majors. Two leagues played that 1947 winter, with athletes taking advantage of the bidding for their services. But the competing leagues further destabilized the Cuban game and caused acrimony among players, owners, managers, and fans. Heated accusations, often cast in terms of fidelity to Cuban baseball, were made until the Liga Nacional folded after a season.

Major League Baseball subsequently signed deals with leagues in Puerto Rico, Panama, and Venezuela, normalizing relations á la the Cuban model. The Dominican Republic, still a baseball backwater, entered the fold a few years later. Dominican baseball was played in the winter and, as had happened in Cuba, the goal of the best Dominican players quickly became making the majors. An independent, three-team league in Maracaibo, Venezuela, where oil was booming, became an option for players banned because of their Mexican transgressions. These men played a few more years, outliers on the periphery of organized baseball's gravitational pull.

As MLB's international wheeling and dealing played out, Caribbean baseball's center of gravity moved steadily northward to the United States. As a consequence, the sport's role and meaning back in the Caribbean region changed. This global shift in power relations took place during an era in which Major League Baseball was also aggressively consolidating its control of the game at all levels stateside. Cuba, still the pearl of the baseball Antilles, was back in the orbit of the U.S. game. Soon, the rest of the world would be, too.

• • •

Jorge Pasquel returned to Cuba as the winter season ended in early 1947. He claimed that the Mexican League had broken even in 1946 after netting $400,000 the previous season. He chalked the difference up to salaries paid to the expatriate big leaguers. Pasquel said that almost all of them would be back in 1947, but his words lacked their usual bravado.[49] Problems had been evident since Mickey Owen had bolted back across the border the previous season. Nor did everyone accept Pasquel's claims about breaking even. By some accounts, the Mexican League had *lost* $400,000 in 1946, with Pasquel personally covering the deficit. More importantly, he shelved his ambitious $6 million plan for building new ballparks, the key to his vision of creating a legitimate rival to the major leagues.[50]

What had gone wrong?

If Jorge Pasquel was the unquestioned strength of Mexican baseball, he was also its biggest weakness. The Mexican League's viability depended on his willingness to invest in it as a vehicle for Mexican nationalism and his own ego. But the league was based on unsound economic fundamentals and could not survive, much less prosper, without Pasquel's subsidies.

Despite Pasquel's enormous equipoise and wealth, Mexican baseball faced huge hurdles. Some major leaguers had not handled the cultural adjustment of playing abroad. They were not as comfortable as Negro Leaguers and Cubans, who saw their Mexican experience through a different prism, adapted better, and enjoyed their time in Mexico more. Several of the white ex–major leaguers did not cope well with Mexico City's more than seven thousand feet of elevation, the lack of showers and dressing rooms at ballparks, dingy dugouts, Spanish language, bouts of dysentery, and unfamiliar food. Stories of their unhappiness rippled through major league locker rooms, just as word of their salaries had earlier grabbed players' attention.[51]

Of course, many of those who jumped to Mexico seemed satisfied with their lot. In June, *Collier's* Kyle Crichton wrote: "The players we interviewed in Mexico all felt they had landed in the middle of a gold mine and could easily put up with the hardships."[52] But that gold depended on Pasquel, and there were limits to his largesse. While he had paid the major leaguers fabulous salaries, he had not treated all players so well. That winter, many of the Cubans voiced their anger over the differential in pay between white and Cuban major leaguers. Mexican ballplayers, most of whom made only about $250 a month, were even more dissatisfied.[53]

Pasquel flew to Havana in 1947 because Cuban players, who comprised the core of his league, were threatening to hold out and not return to Mexico that spring. He also faced a rebellion by Mexican owners who resented the salaries paid to the Americans. These owners, despite what they gained from revenue sharing, considered the salary scale too high. The Nuevo Laredo club said that it would suspend play rather than pay the salaries foreign players demanded. Amid speculation that the league would stop recruiting Americans, it contracted from eight to six teams.[54]

The Dodgers and Montreal Royals, including Jackie Robinson, Roy Campanella, Don Newcombe, and pitcher Roy Partlow, were also in Havana in early 1947; both teams were avoiding the racial fallout they would have encountered at segregated spring-training facilities in Florida. The Sunshine State was beginning to lose a chunk of its spring-training industry. The Cleveland Indians and the New York Giants had already moved their spring camps to Arizona, in part because Cleveland owner Bill Veeck, who anticipated signing black players, hoped to find a more tolerant racial atmosphere. Arizona's Cactus League, as it came to be called, would eventually rival Florida's spring-training industry. Ironically, Branch Rickey housed the black players apart from their white teammates in Havana. As a result, they faced separate and unequal accommodations. While white Dodgers stayed at the exclusive Hotel Nacional and white minor leaguers at the Havana Military Academy, the four black players had rooms in a run-down hotel. The white players dined together on meals flown in from Florida; the black players were given money and told to make do on their own, a tall order given that only Campanella could speak Spanish and Robinson was weakened by dysentery.[55]

Pasquel met about forty Brooklyn players in the lobby of the Hotel Nacional late one night. As they surrounded him, Pasquel pitched his case for the Mexican League. Adamant that it would be stronger than ever, he told the players that they should talk to him if they didn't like their major league contracts. He had no takers. By now, players were dubious about the benefits and stability of Mexican baseball.[56]

The major leaguers who returned to Mexico in 1947 were men who had nowhere else to play. Salaries were lower than they had been the previous year and some players left before the season ended.[57] Pasquel's dream was crumbling. He began losing interest in baseball and turned to a new venture, publishing *Novedades*, a top Mexican newspaper. For sport, he hunted. Unable to put Happy Chandler or Clark Griffith's pelt on his office wall, he stalked black bears in Coahuila in northern Mexico and elephant in Africa.

By all accounts, the Mexican League lost several hundred thousand dollars in 1947, with Pasquel again covering its deficit. Even with reduced salaries, the gate was insufficient to allow owners to break even.[58] Pasquel was willing to incur losses to fulfill his vision, but those losses were mounting, as was opposition to his policies. Some owners threatened to quit the league unless it set a different course.

Following the season, the Mexican League capitulated. Pasquel stepped aside for a new president who said he would let major league owners know that the Mexican League, ready for rapprochement, would no longer go after their players.[59] To prevent bankruptcy, payrolls were slashed, and rosters shrunk to twenty players, with a sharp reduction in the number of foreign players. Major League Baseball exhaled in relief. Not only had Robinson's integration gone more smoothly and profitably than anticipated in 1947, the Mexican threat had finally subsided.

With Mexico waving the white flag, Chandler was magnanimous, ready to make peace with his chastened rival and consider reinstating the suspended players. An unidentified baseball source told the *New York Times* that the men who had been blacklisted for five years would have "paid their debt to baseball" by the time a deal was reached.[60] Peace talks temporarily collapsed when Pasquel proclaimed that he was still in control of Mexican baseball, but days later, he said that he, too, was "ready to make peace." Pasquel then flew to Cuba aboard President Miguel Alemán's plane to sign Cubans for the 1948 Mexican season. But he no longer hunted Major League Baseball's players.[61]

It was his last serious flirtation with baseball; the 1948 season was disastrous, and the league lost another $400,000 despite salary caps and roster cuts. Two clubs dissolved in July and players began drifting away. That fall, Pasquel left baseball for good amid plans to create the Mexican Baseball Federation.[62]

Mexico, unlike most of the Caribbean, did not become a conduit to the majors. In 1950, its league and U.S. organized baseball agreed to respect each other's contracts. A major league team that wanted to sign a player who had already signed with a Mexican team was required to pay that ball club to do so. Mexican baseball thus retained greater control of its players, slowing the flow of Mexicans to the majors and bolstering its own league.

As Pasquel's Mexican League disappeared as a credible rival, the eighteen men who had been suspended from organized baseball sought work where they could find it. Some played in Cuba, Venezuela, or Canada, where a few leagues survived on Major League Baseball's margins. Others tried barnstorming, but organized baseball blocked access to ballparks and scared away all but semipro opponents.[63] With Mexico fading as a concern, Major League Baseball sought to avoid catastrophe in the courts back home. Above all else, MLB sought to protect its reserve clause. That spring, in a bit of near-hysterical rhetoric, Branch Rickey had declared: "Those people who oppose the reserve system have avowed communist tendencies." Still facing lawsuits that might invalidate their antitrust status and the reserve clause, MLB executives settled with a group of blackballed players who had sued them and announced the end of the suspensions on June 5, 1949.[64]

Major League Baseball was now virtually the only game in town. It had faced its worst fears—rebellious players, racial integration, and a challenger who was wealthier and bolder than any major league owner—and emerged on top. Though it stumbled during the 1950s as it navigated television's terrain, it owned the future.

CHAPTER SEVEN

New Caribbean Currents

Between the time Jackie Robinson signed with the Dodgers in 1945 and his debut in Brooklyn almost two years later, his cleats slashed across ball fields throughout the Caribbean. Preoccupied with the challenges he soon would face as major league baseball's lone African American, Robinson had little sense of the dreams he was provoking abroad. But boys in the region fantasized about what the ebony-hued infielder's success might mean for them. "When I see Jackie Robinson play in my country," Cuban Edmundo "Sandy" Amoros recalled, "I say if he can do it, I can do it, too."[1] A few years after watching Robinson in Havana, Amoros became his teammate. In 1955 his desperate, lunging catch of a Yogi Berra drive in the seventh game of the World Series clinched Brooklyn's one and only title.

In Venezuela, where Robinson joined a squad of Negro League barnstormers in November 1945, soon after signing with Brooklyn, his teammates tutored him daily. Cool Papa Bell worked with him on his baserunning, William "Dizzy" Dismukes taught him how to move to his right when fielding ground balls, and outfielder Gene Benson massaged his psyche. "Jackie," Benson said late one night, "one thing I want you to know about playing in the major leagues. Where you're going ain't half as tough as where you been."[2]

By the time Robinson left South America in January 1946, his game refined and confidence boosted, Venezuela's winter league had begun its first season of play and ballplayers there began entertaining thoughts of playing in the United States. Maracaibo shortstop Luis Aparicio Sr. did not join Robinson in the majors, but in 1956, Jackie's last season in baseball, Aparicio's son, shortstop Luis Jr., would be named the American League Rookie of the Year.

In Havana, twenty-one-year-old Orestes Miñoso scrutinized Robinson when the Dodgers trained there in 1947. Miñoso, a rookie with the New York Cubans, realized that the Negro Leagues could serve as his steppingstone to the majors, as they had for Robinson. In Puerto Rico, twelve-year-old Roberto Clemente followed Robinson's exploits from afar, but nine-year-old Orlando Cepeda shook hands with him outside the ballpark in San Juan. Clemente's father was a foreman at the Victoria sugar mill in the town of Carolina; Cepeda was the son of "the great Peruchin Cepeda," who starred throughout the Caribbean but never joined the Negro Leagues because he couldn't stomach segregation. Orlando Cepeda's own career would take place at the major league level and surpass his father's, but he wouldn't stand for segregation, either. Roberto Clemente would become baseball's Latin icon, a fiery proponent of civil rights for darker-skinned players.[3]

In the Dominican Republic, twelve-year-old Felipe Alou and ten-year-olds Juan Marichal and Manuel Mota were thrilled when the Dodgers arrived in February 1948. Marichal listened to their games on the radio in Laguna Verde, his small hometown northwest of the capital. Alou and Mota were luckier; they saw Robinson play in person. "It was an incredible baseball game for a youngster who some day wanted to play the game," Alou reflected half a century later. Dominican baseball, he said, has never been the same since. "Neither have I." Mota, two years younger than Alou, instantly chose Robinson as his hero and the Dodgers as his favorite team.[4]

Within a decade, boys like Clemente, Aparicio, Cepeda, and Marichal were following Robinson's footsteps down major league base paths all the way to Cooperstown. Their exuberance for the game—learned on back alleys and diamonds carved out of cane fields—resonated in ballparks from New York to San Francisco. By virtue of their presence and passion, they would make major league baseball a truly international game, although never as free of racial barriers as baseball had long been in the islands.

Each winter, these men returned home to play in front of family, friends, and compatriots. Winter ball was more than a refuge from the racial and cultural scorn they bumped up against in the United States, or a chance to earn needed paychecks. It was a well-developed sporting life with its own traditions and ethos. The surrender of Caribbean baseball's autonomy in the wake of the Mexican League war had not led to its dissolution. Instead, Caribbean baseball entered a less independent but still robust age of peaceful coexistence with the major leagues. Latinos infused the majors with style and skill, while major leaguers journeyed south each winter, bringing their considerable talents and personalities to the islands. Both the United States and the Caribbean benefited from this cross-fertilization. Only Mexican baseball veered away from the major leagues and developed in isolation. The rest of the region enjoyed stellar winter play—for a time.

No longer competing with Major League Baseball, the winter leagues became a vehicle for major league player development. Though the focus of individual players shifted north, the leagues remained the center of popular sporting life in the Caribbean. Each winter, traditional rivalries played out before fans in Havana, San Juan, and Valencia, not thousands of miles away in the United States. For Latin fans, summer campaigns in the United States became the prelude to winter play, where their primary loyalties remained.

For the most part, Latin players slipped into major league baseball quietly, drawing less attention than the heavily scrutinized arrival of African Americans. For white fans accustomed to seeing race as binary—as either white or black—the varied hues and cultures that Latinos embodied were confusing. But soon, there were too many Latinos to ignore. While only fifty-five Latinos had played in the majors before 1950, sixty-five men from the Caribbean arrived during the 1950s and almost twice that number in the 1960s. By 1970, they constituted a tenth of all major leaguers; by the early twenty-first century, almost a quarter of all players were Latino.[5]

• • •

Every Latino who played in the majors before 1947 was either Caucasian or able to pass as such. Most were from Cuba, but the island's share of the Latin vanguard began shrinking after integration. Though still the largest single group of Latin ballplayers during the 1950s, Cubans were no longer a majority. After the 1959 revolution, the U.S. blockaded the island and tried to undermine, then topple, Fidel Castro's leftward-leaning regime. Cuban baseball soon spun out of its orbit around major league baseball, even though Cubans sought to prevent the rupture.

Puerto Ricans, Venezuelans, and Dominicans poured into the void created by the Cuban embargo. These men, many of whom were dark-skinned, faced greater challenges than the light-skinned Latinos who preceded them. Some lost or damaged careers because they could not make their way through the United States' daunting racial and linguistic terrain. Others accepted what they could not change, made accommodations, or adapted. A few, especially Roberto Clemente and Felipe Alou, actively resisted and became heroes along the way.

• • •

Two years after Jackie Robinson's rookie season, Orestes "Minnie" Miñoso broke the racial barrier for Latin players. The major leagues' first Afro-Latin player, he endured beanballs, brushbacks, and taunts, even jeering comparisons with Minnie Mouse. But at least Miñoso, who grew up playing baseball for a sugar-mill team, had three seasons in the Negro Leagues to figure out segregation before debuting with the Cleveland Indians in 1949. Clemente and Alou were far less equipped.

"We knew what was going on with Jackie Robinson to an extent," Alou recalled. A teacher had explained that the Dodgers moved their spring training to the Dominican Republic in 1948 to avoid the "race problem" in the South. "We heard these stories, but to us that really didn't have any relevance, because hey, I wasn't going to play baseball in Florida."

Clemente was a few months older than Alou. When he was a boy, Clemente carried Negro League star Monte Irvin's suit-bag into Sixto Escobar Stadium in San Juan to get in for free. By October 1952 Clemente no longer needed subterfuge to enter the ballpark named for the bantamweight fighter who became Puerto Rico's first world boxing champion. The seventeen-year-old was playing for the Santurce Cangrejeros when Dodger scout Al Campanis first spotted him there. Campanis, Jackie Robinson's teammate in Montreal, would never see a better prospect. By the time Clemente signed with Brooklyn in February 1954, he had played with Willie

Mays, Henry Aaron, Tetelo Vargas, Willard Brown, and scores of major leaguers and Negro Leaguers without ever leaving the island.

Because Clemente's $10,000 signing bonus made him a "bonus baby," Brooklyn had to place him on its major league roster or risk losing him in the postseason draft. The rule, adopted in 1947, was designed to prevent richer clubs from monopolizing talent. Although MLB had canceled the bonus-baby rule after three seasons, a committee chaired by Branch Rickey revived it in 1952. Rickey would soon become its greatest beneficiary. The Dodgers were reluctant to add another dark-skinned player, especially such a young one, to a club that already led the league in its number of black players. Taking a chance that they might lose Clemente, the Dodgers assigned him to Montreal.

Although a U.S. citizen, Clemente had never been to the North American mainland and did not speak English. It was a confusing season for the nineteen-year-old, who roomed with Cuban shortstop Chico Fernández in a French-speaking part of Montreal, ate ham and eggs every morning, and spent most games sitting on the bench. In a feeble effort to hide the young ballplayer from scouts and prevent him from being drafted away, Montreal rarely played him. When he was given a chance to play, Clemente was peremptorily taken out of the game if he did too well. "If I struck out I stay in the lineup. If I played well, I'm benched," he later said. "I didn't know what was going on, and I was confused and almost mad enough to go home." At the end of the season, Brooklyn's hopes of concealing Clemente were for naught, and the Pirates, baseball's worst team, drafted him away.[6]

Clemente returned home that fall to play for Santurce alongside Willie Mays, who was fresh off the New York Giants' sweep of Cleveland in the 1954 World Series. The Cangrejeros, which infielder Don Zimmer called the greatest winter team ever, were an eclectic crew.[7] Aging Negro Leaguer Bus Clarkson, Mexican League renegade Luis Olmo, and young infielders Junior Gilliam and Zimmer complemented an outfield of Mays, Bob Thurman, and Clemente. Orlando Cepeda was the team's batboy. In the morning, Clemente took classes to finish high school; in the evenings he hit well enough to finish third in the league in batting and help Santurce win the Puerto Rican and Caribbean Series titles.

Roberto Clemente at Forbes Field
(Carnegie Museum of Art, Pittsburgh; Heinz Family Fund copyright 2004, Carnegie Museum of Art, Charles "Teenie" Harris Archive). Date: Late 1950s. The son of a sugar-mill foreman in Puerto Rico, Roberto Clemente became the first great Latin player in the major leagues after they integrated. A thoughtful and proud man, he became an advocate for all Latin players.

Clemente arrived in Pittsburgh to begin his major league career in April 1955, three years before Alou debuted in San Francisco. While Alou would join a team with several black and Latin stars, Clemente was mostly on his own. The dark-skinned Puerto Rican was neither the first African American nor the first Latin player on the club. Negro League veterans Curtis Roberts and Luis Márquez had preceded him in Pittsburgh, but both departed before long. Clemente would stay his entire career.

Neither white nor black Pittsburgh knew what to make of Clemente. Though the city had once sustained two minority-owned and -run ball clubs, the Homestead Grays and the Pittsburgh Crawfords, few Latinos lived there. Clemente moved in with a black family on the Hill, still the city's principal black section. He listened to jazz at the nearby Crawford Grill, Gus Greenlee's old nightclub, where generations of ballplayers like Josh Gibson and Satchel Paige had congregated after games. Although hampered by injuries from a car crash the previous winter, Roberto played well his rookie season. But he never felt at home in the clubhouse or the city.

The Dominican Republic, where Felipe Alou grew up, was even more removed from U.S. culture than Puerto Rico in the 1950s. Alou was from the town of Haina, along the southern coast of the Dominican Republic, east of the capital. His father, a carpenter, was the grandson of African slaves, his mother of Spanish descent. As a boy, Felipe used bats his father crafted and played baseball in a uniform fashioned from flour sacks that drew derision from opposing players. For shoes, he wore army boots. "One time I slid and took all the skin off one boy's shin and they took me out of the game and I could not play for a long, long time."

By 1955, equipped with real gear, Alou played for the University of Santo Domingo and was selected for the Pan American Games in Mexico City. His four hits in the championship game against the United States led the DR to the gold medal. Afterward, every player on the team but Alou signed to play in the Dominican professional league, which began its first season as a winter circuit that October. Alou intended to study medicine and preserve his eligibility to throw the javelin, for which he held the national record, in the upcoming Olympics. But after his father lost his job and the Dominican Republic began questioning whether it could afford to send a delegation to Melbourne, Australia, where the games were being held, Alou became the first Dominican on the island to sign with a major league organization, the New York Giants.

Delayed by visa problems, Alou had missed more than a month of spring training by the time he arrived in Florida in April 1956. The Giants assigned him to their Lake Charles, Louisiana, club, which was beginning its season in the Evangeline League. "I have no idea why they sent me there," Alou said later. Although he had little knowledge of segregation or the tensions flaring in the Deep South, it didn't take him long to catch on. "Right away," he said, "I began to see the difference." Alou was held out of his first game. "I didn't know why. They find an interpreter and the interpreter told me I was on hold. They were going to try to play me in some city that was maybe more friendly to the black." When his Lake Charles club played in Baton Rouge, he started onto the field with his black teammates. "I was hoping they would respect the uniform. But they didn't let us pass. There was a policeman who singled us out who said: 'Not you!' *That* I understood perfectly. We were made to go back to the dressing room and take off the uniform and they put us with the black fans in left field." Soon Alou learned that the Louisiana legislature was debating whether to outlaw interracial play. The measure would pass later that summer. "I was shocked because we had always looked up to the United States. The word 'democracy' meant a lot to us because we were living at that time under a dictatorship."

Unable to play Alou in Louisiana, the Giants sent him back to Florida alone on a bus. He had $12 meal money for the two-and-a-half-day ride, but spent little of it. Every time the bus stopped and he tried to buy food, he encountered Jim Crow. Rather than accept such humiliation, he did without. "I more than once felt like continuing on to Miami and back to the Dominican Republic. But I thought about Horacio Martínez [the scout who signed him], not so much my mom and dad. I didn't want to let him down and I stayed. Thank God I stayed, but on that bus and that ride back to Florida, almost three days, many times I felt like continuing on to come back home."

It's questionable whether Clemente—or Jackie Robinson for that matter —would have made it to the majors if he had been sent first to the South, where the backlash to civil rights intensified after the Supreme Court's 1954 *Brown v. Board of Education* decision. This was a time, historian C. Vann Woodward troublingly observed, when "all over the South the lights of reason and tolerance and moderation began to go out."[8] Although some Latino players found greater tolerance accorded them because they spoke Spanish, many were threatened and abused. Called Spanish niggers, subjected to unfamiliar black-white segregation wherever they dined or slept, but further isolated by race, culture, and language, many became profoundly homesick.

Clemente may have been lonely in Pittsburgh, but he avoided the race-based hostility that darker-skinned ballplayers faced in the South. Alou, by contrast, was thrown at by opposing pitchers and undermined by some of his own teammates. Pitchers on his own club threw at him in batting practice; on one occasion, Felipe overheard teammates telling members of the opposing team how best to pitch to him. His education about race was brutal and ever-present. One evening in West Palm Beach, he and three black players sat in a car parked at a diner waiting for teammates to finish eating inside and bring them food. A sympathetic waitress came out and said she would take their orders. When the owner saw her, he exploded and yelled at the ballplayers to leave. "The Americans got out," Alou explained, "but I did not get out. I refused." Soon the police arrived and ordered Alou to leave. Just as they were about to forcibly remove Alou, his manager came out of the restaurant and drove the car, with Alou in it, from the lot.

"That, I say, was my first act of rebellion against racism," Alou recalled. "It brought out of me some things I didn't know about me. . . . I decided I was going to go the entire road, and I was going to fight whatever or whoever to do so." That summer, Alou fought hard on the field too, winning the Florida League batting championship, leading the league in stolen bases, and coming in third in home runs and RBIs.

By the time he arrived in San Francisco in 1958, clubs were scouting the Caribbean, with the Dodgers' Al Campanis, the Pirates' Howie Haak, and the Giants' Alex Pompez in the vanguard. Pompez, the lone Negro League owner to enter the majors in a front-office capacity, had begun working for the Giants after dissolving the New York Cubans in 1950. He hired Horacio Martínez to scout the Dominican Republic for him. Martínez, a former Negro League all-star who had been one of the Caribbean's greatest players, would sign not only Felipe Alou, but also his brothers Mateo ("Matty") and Jesús, Juan Marichal, and Manuel Mota. Meanwhile, older Latinos were rising to the game's upper ranks. Mexico's Beto "Bobby" Ávila won the 1954 American League batting title and Venezuelan Luis Aparicio Jr. was the AL's 1956 Rookie of the Year. He combined with Cubans Orestes Miñoso and Bert Campaneris to lead the AL in stolen bases nineteen of twenty-two times between 1951 and 1972. It was only the beginning.

● ● ●

Aparicio and Cepeda were the sons of ballplayers; Miñoso, Clemente, Marichal, Mota, and the Alou brothers products of the region's rich, grassroots network of local and company teams. Miñoso played for the Espana sugar mill, Clemente for the Sello Rojo rice company. Juan Marichal pitched for Bermúdez Rum and the Grenada Company before joining Mateo Alou and Manuel Mota on Aviación, the Dominican Air Force team. As boys, they played for fun, but each would soon have the rare chance to make a living from the game.

Mota grew up in a poor Santo Domingo neighborhood, one of eight children raised by a single mother. He played on a ball club organized by the Salesian Brothers, a Catholic order working in the barrios, until Ramfis Trujillo, son of President Rafael Trujillo, saw him in a game celebrating his father's birthday. President Trujillo had made Ramfis a brigadier general when he was nine and later the commander of the Dominican Air Force and its ball club. Mota, sixteen, was drafted the day after Ramfis saw him play. "We were soldiers," Mota chuckled. "The only thing, we have no guns."[9]

In 1955 Aviación journeyed to Manzanillo, along the Haitian border, to play Grenada, a team sponsored by the United Fruit Company's Dominican subsidiary. Juan Marichal worked for the company. He had never had it easier, living in a little bungalow and collecting pay for sitting idly on the dock checking the quality of bananas being loaded onto ships. Mostly, the skinny right-hander played ball, throwing underhand and sidearm. He pitched well against Aviación that afternoon. The next morning, Marichal was awakened by a lieutenant delivering a telegram from Ramfis Trujillo instructing him to report immediately for induction into the Air Force. He went to see his mother, who said nothing until a second telegram arrived. Then, she said: "Son, you cannot say no to those people."[10]

Marichal, like Mota and Mateo Alou, promptly became a full-time ballplayer. Drilling incessantly under the watchful eye of Francisco "Viruta" Pichardo, the best instructor in the country, Aviación rarely lost. The players had never worked harder or approached baseball with more discipline. When Aviación returned to Manzanillo for a doubleheader, Marichal lost the first game 1–0 and watched from the bench as Aviación lost the second game too. "Ramfis [Trujillo] didn't believe in that," he later laughed. Trujillo ordered an investigation, which accused the players of drinking. "The truth is not that we were drinking," Marichal said, "but that the water had made many of the players sick." Nonetheless, the players and Viruta spent five days in jail, the manager thirty.[11]

In 1956 Marichal, Mota, and Mateo Alou were on a team that beat Cuba and won a youth tournament in Mexico. On their return, the man-

Juan Marichal and Horacio Martínez *(Courtesy Juan Marichal). Date: 1957.* (Left to right: Epi Guerrero, Horacio Martínez, Juan Marichal, and Danilo Rivas). Juan Marichal's career stretched from his hometown of Laguna Verde, a small town in the Dominican Republic, to Cooperstown, where he became the first player from his nation to be elected to the Hall of Fame. Marichal was the winningest pitcher of the 1960s.

ager gave each of them a $10 reward from the president. "Ten dollars each!" Mota exclaimed. "In 1956, that was like ten million dollars." A year later, they signed with the Giants. "They offered me five hundred dollars," Marichal recalled. "Man, I was so happy when I got that offer. I told them yes right away. I was the happiest man on earth, knowing that I was going out, to the United States, to play at the next level."

But like Felipe Alou, the three newcomers were ill-prepared for what they stumbled against in the land of opportunity. "You were in a different country with a different language and different culture," Mota explained. "I didn't know any words, even how to say 'water.' I didn't even know what segregation was before I went to the States." [12] The young Latinos, especially those sent to the South, were bewildered. If they were lucky, there were other Latinos on the team. No matter where they played, all of them struggled to understand their demanding Anglo coaches.

Manuel Mota and Mateo Alou negotiated the hazardous social terrain surrounding the minors together. Once, in Michigan City, Indiana, they sat in a restaurant waiting for somebody to take their order until a woman who spoke Spanish told them not to waste their time—they would not be served. Another time, in Sanford, Florida, they were hauled before a police lineup because a white woman had complained that a black ballplayer had molested her. A mistaken identification could have derailed their careers.

In Danville, Virginia, where a restaurant awarded certificates for steak dinners to players who hit home runs, Mota clubbed two in a game. Not long afterward, when rain postponed a game, Mota and Alou decided to redeem their certificates. Unwilling to ruin their only shoes in the flooded streets, they walked barefoot to the restaurant. They could get their steaks, the manager said, but they could not eat in the dining room. They waited out back while a black cook prepared their meals. Barred from the kitchen, they found an old abandoned truck nearby and sat inside it eating their dinners as rain poured down.

But when they got to San Francisco, Mota and Alou were no longer isolated. By the early 1960s, the Giants had more Latin and black players than any team in major league history. Nor had any team ever fielded such a talented group of Latin and black players, four of whom became Hall of Famers—Willie Mays, Willie McCovey, Juan Marichal, and Orlando Cepeda. But San Francisco was no multiracial utopia. "The clubhouse, even in San Francisco," Felipe Alou pointed out, "was segregated." During his first years there, the lockers of white, black, and Latin players were clustered apart from each other. These cliques were even more evident away from the ballpark. The Latin Giants, though, had achieved critical mass: Cepeda, Felipe Alou, Marichal, Mateo Alou, Mota, and Puerto Rican shortstop José Pagán. Jesús Alou, the youngest of the three brothers, joined them in 1963. They stuck together on and off the field.

"It was like a family when they came over," Willie Mays marveled. "We were very, very close—myself, Felipe, José Pagán," Cepeda explained. "My second year," Felipe Alou laughed, "I lived in North Beach with the hippies. I didn't even know where I was moving; I wound up living with the hippies. Sometimes the team arrived home at four in the morning, and everybody was up like it was twelve noon. I was one of the guys there, on my way home. That was beautiful."[13] Though he enjoyed North Beach, Alou lived with his fellow Dominicans afterward.

The Latin Giants were inseparable, making music and meals in their apartments and listening to Cepeda's records. As a rookie, Marichal carried Orlando's record player on the road. "That thing was heavy," Marichal laughed, "but you couldn't refuse. As a rookie, you had to do it because otherwise you would have a problem with Orlando."

"We were more than friends," Marichal observed, "we were like brothers." He and Felipe Alou became *compadres*, godfathers for each other's daughters. Their friendships deepened during the winter when Felipe and Juan went skin diving together and Felipe was best man at Mota's wedding. They all played for Escogido in the Dominican winter league.[14]

So did some of their non-Latin teammates. Most major leaguers needed to make a living in the off-season and played winter ball if possible. While the North Americans handled the culture shock and linguistic challenges with varying degrees of success, they all appreciated the quality of the baseball played. "They put more pressure on you to win down there," Willie McCovey recalled. "If you don't get off to a good start down there, you're gone. They send you home." When McCovey played with Escogido, he was so homesick that Felipe Alou moved in with him to encourage him to stay. "They knew baseball very well," Willie Mays explained. "If you made bad plays, they let you know by whistling. Whistling meant: 'Hey, just because you're over here doesn't mean you don't have to go out there and play.' Sometimes, I played harder over there than I did in the States, where I could shag a little."[15]

But in the States, the Latinos felt like third-class citizens, warranting less consideration than Caucasians or African Americans. "It used to be white, black, and Latin," Orlando Cepeda said. "So we had two strikes against us." Felipe Alou concurred: "We came after the blacks because of the language barrier, because of the different customs." Sometimes it was difficult for the Latin players to distinguish whether the insults they faced were racial, cultural, or class-based. They stung just the same.

"We came from places that nobody had ever heard of. We don't go to Harvard or the Ivy League schools," Alou continued. "We were really a people who were doing the best that they could do under the circumstances." That meant standing up for themselves. In Cincinnati in 1961, Cepeda was on second base with José Pagan at the plate. "I was saying in Spanish 'come on, bring me in' to Pagan." Joey Jay, the Cincinnati pitcher, turned to him and snarled: "Speak English! Can't you speak English?" Cepeda replied: "Yes, I know how to speak English. Kiss my ass!" In another game, Cepeda rushed out of the dugout clutching a bat to defend his countryman Rubén Gomez. Willie Mays tackled him before he could use the bat, but Cepeda gave no ground in defending Latin teammates.

"We knew that in some eyes," Felipe Alou reflected, "we were not well-liked." It was a price they were willing to pay. "Hey," he emphasized, "it was Orlando, Juan Marichal, the Alous, José Pagan—they couldn't mess with that group."

The Latin Giants could laugh off other teams' jibes but not the Giants' hiring of the famously mercurial Alvin Dark as manager in 1961. Decades later, they remained ambivalent about their brilliant but temperamental manager. "He treated me with a great deal of respect," Mota explained. "That's the only thing I can say. He was a winner and he tried to win." Prone to outbursts after losses, Dark once tore off part of his little finger when he hurled a stool across the locker room. He also upset tables holding the postgame meal. Once, Felipe Alou slowly bent over, picked some food up off the floor, and stared at Dark as he ate it, letting the manager know that he disapproved of his tantrums. "In my heart," Marichal said, "I believe this is why Dark approved the trading of Felipe to another team." But in the spring of 1962, when political upheaval rocked the Dominican Republic, which had been turned topsy-turvy by Rafael Trujillo's assassination the previous year, Dark permitted Marichal to return home, marry his fiancée, Alma, and bring her back to the States. "Alvin Dark to me was one day the best man in the world and the next day, he was the worst. I love the guy, but I saw Alvin Dark do things that hurt me deeply." [16]

While Latinos had little choice but to become serious students of U.S. customs, few salty old baseball men like Dark bothered to learn much about their cultures. Orlando Cepeda viewed Dark as a product of his conservative Lake Charles, Louisiana, background. "So when he came to the Giants and saw so many Latinos going crazy in the dugout, laughing, having fun, young kids from the Dominican, from Puerto Rico, he cannot comprehend what's going on."

When Dark ordered players not to speak Spanish at the ballpark,

Cepeda and Felipe Alou balked. "I'm proud of being Puerto Rican," Cepeda said. "Why we can't speak our language?" Dark answered that white players had complained that they did not know what the Latinos were talking about. "Listen," Cepeda said, "when I came to America, I didn't know what you were talking about, but I tried to learn." He defied Dark; so did Alou. "I said there's no way I'm not going to talk Spanish to my brother, Matty Alou. No way! How could I explain that to my parents?"[17]

In Pittsburgh, Clemente had far fewer black and Latin teammates, but he began winning fans and some sportswriters to his side by 1960, his sixth season in the majors. Reaching career highs in batting, home runs, runs scored, and RBIs, he came through when it mattered the most. When he stepped up to bat, fans shouted "Arriba! Arriba!"—an exultation that Pirates announcer Bob Prince had popularized. The Pirates, coming from behind to win games all season long, captured the 1960 pennant. That set up a long-hungered-for rematch with the Yankees, who had swept them in the 1927 World Series.

The Pirates had not returned to the World Series since 1927 and few oddsmakers gave them better than a middling chance against the powerhouse Yankees, with a glittering roster that included Mickey Mantle, Roger Maris, Yogi Berra, and left-handed pitcher Whitey Ford. The teams split the first six games, even though New York outscored Pittsburgh in total runs 46–17. Clemente hit safely in every game and led the team in hits, but the hero of the series was second baseman Bill Mazeroski, whose walk-off home run in the bottom of the ninth inning of Game 7 gave Pittsburgh its first Series title in thirty-five years. Despite a breakout season, Clemente finished a distant eighth in voting for the league MVP, a slight that rankled him.

Clemente had an even better season statistically in 1961, winning his first batting championship with a .351 average. Compatriot Orlando Cepeda led the league in home runs and RBIs. They flew back to San Juan together, where a euphoric crowd at the airport delayed the conquering heroes for an hour as they made their way across the tarmac. When their motorcade arrived at Sixto Escobar Stadium, the owner of the Ponce ball club declared that it was "a day of glory for Puerto Rico."[18]

In 1962 the Giants hit their stride with the team's black and Latin players leading the way. Cepeda, Mays, Felipe Alou, and Marichal were selected to the All-Star Game that year. Cepeda, the National League Rookie of the Year in 1958, hit 35 home runs and drove in 114 runs; Mays did even better, hitting 49 home runs with 141 RBIs. Alou came close to scoring 100 runs and driving in 100 runs while hitting .316, and Marichal, in only his third season, made it clear that he was already on his way to a Hall of Fame career. The Giants, trailing the Dodgers by four games with seven left to play, rallied and tied them for first place on the final day of the regular season. After overcoming a 4–2 deficit in the ninth inning of the deciding playoff game, San Francisco celebrated the opportunity to face New York in the 1962 World Series.

The championship captivated the Dominican Republic. "Nobody slept," a fan explained. "Everybody had radios glued to their ears." This was the first time that Dominicans had appeared in the World Series, and no squad with as many Latinos and African Americans had ever contested for the championship. The streets emptied as if the nation was under a curfew, one Dominican reflected. "Everything shut down. Everyone everywhere was listening to the games, talking about the games, arguing about the games." [19]

After New York won two of the first three games, Marichal pitched Game 4 with a broken bone in his foot that had escaped diagnosis. "I think I was pitching the best game of my life," Marichal recalled. He struck out Mickey Mantle twice and San Francisco led 2–0 when Marichal came to bat in the fifth inning with a man on third. Dark ordered a suicide squeeze, but the pitch was in the dirt. Marichal tried to make contact to protect the runner coming from third, but the pitch hit the index finger on his pitching hand and tore the nail off. The young star's season was over.

Even without Marichal, the Giants won Game 4 as second baseman Chuck Hiller hit a grand slam and three Giant relief pitchers kept the Yankees in check. The two teams split the next two games to send the series to a seventh game. In the bottom of the ninth inning of the final game, New York led 1–0. Mateo Alou bunted for a single to lead off the inning but was stranded on third when second baseman Bobby Richardson snagged Willie McCovey's screaming line drive to end the game. "If that ball had been hit a little bit higher, I think it would have ended up in the ocean,"

Juan Marichal said. "But," he acknowledged, "when you play seven games, seven well-played games like we did in 1962, you say, well, the best team won. And we have to give the credit to the Yankees."

• • •

By then, the Dominican Republic was eclipsing Cuba in the baseball world. When Fidel Castro's revolution swept him into power in 1959, it did not immediately disrupt Cuban baseball. If anything, Castro gave baseball a revolutionary imprimatur. The Havana Sugar Kings won the 1959 Little World Series (played between the winners of the two top minor leagues) by beating the Minneapolis Millers, with Castro throwing out the first pitch in Havana and Che Guevara watching from the stands. Cuban play continued that winter, and the nation captured its fifth consecutive Caribbean Series in 1960. But, as Cuban-born Yale professor Roberto González Echevarría wrote, it was professional baseball's grand finale in Cuba.[20]

Soon, turmoil roiled the Caribbean. Relations between the United States and Cuba crumbled; so did those between organized baseball and the Cuban League. Cubans wanted to keep their team—Fidel Castro even offered to pitch for them—but the International League jerked the Sugar Kings out of Havana midway through the 1960 season, despite the protests of Cuban fans and the government. Then Major League Baseball commissioner Ford Frick, who had taken over at the game's helm after the owners failed to reappoint Happy Chandler for a second term in 1951, threatened to prohibit major leaguers from playing in Cuba's upcoming winter season. The Cuban League responded by playing with Cubans only and suspended play afterward. In March 1961 the Cuban government announced that professional sport would be abolished, replaced by amateur competitions.

The break with organized baseball meant that Cubans playing in the majors or gestating in the minors could continue their careers, but at the price of exile from their homeland. No new major leaguers would emerge from Cuba for some time. The Cuba–United States impasse also killed the Serie del Caribe (Caribbean Series). Beginning in 1949, the winners of the Cuban, Venezuelan, Panamanian, and Puerto Rican winter leagues had met each February in this contest. For many fans, the Caribbean Series mattered more than the World Series. After all, they had long judged their baseball in comparison to each other. Cuba, traditionally the touchstone of Caribbean base-ball, won seven of the twelve series played before their suspension in 1961.[21]

To the east in the Dominican Republic, three decades of ruthless autoc-racy ended in May 1961 when Rafael Trujillo was gunned down en route to visit his mistress in San Cristóbal. "It was a regime of torture and death," Felipe Alou reflected. "You had to keep your mouth shut." Alou might have kept his thoughts about Trujillo to himself, but he had followed U.S. policy in the Caribbean. "I believe at that time that the United States had the power to unseat him and he was allowed to tyrannize this country for thirty-two years. I lost friends and some relatives to the terror of the dictatorship."

Ironically, Alou played for Escogido, the team most closely associated with the Trujillos. Aviación was its farm club, producing half a dozen major leaguers and an even greater number of Escogidistas. Petán Trujillo, the dic-tator's brother, was an Escogido *fanático*. During the 1957 playoffs, he walked onto the field and slapped Andre Rodgers, after the Bahamian-born New York Giant playing shortstop for Escogido made an error. Petán's body-guards and other players prevented Rodgers from retaliating, and Rafael Trujillo made a rare appearance at the ballpark the next day to restore order.

"Even the air we breathed belonged to Trujillo," former major leaguer Winston Llenas recalled. "He had it all." Baseball, however, offered Domini-cans an outlet for their emotions. "The ballparks were the lungs that allowed us to breathe freely, if only for a few hours," Llenas said. "And even at the ballpark, you had to put up with his people shouting '*Viva Trujillo!*' after the national anthem. They say here '*Al pueblo hay que darle pan y circo.*' 'To the people you must give bread and circus.' Baseball has been the fucking circus! Trujillo used baseball to buy peace." But now Trujillo was gone.[22]

The twinned cataclysms in Cuba and the Dominican Republic rocked Caribbean baseball. As Cuba fell away from the major leagues, Puerto Rican and Dominican baseball edged closer. In the Dominican Republic, the 1961 season that began in October was suspended; the 1962–63 sea-son never got started. Juan Bosch, an intellectual of the left who had been elected president after Trujillo's death, took office in February 1963 only to be ousted by a coup seven months later. An April 1965 rebellion by demo-cratic forces, including constitutionally minded junior officers, was poised to return Bosch to power when the United States sent in the Marines to

Felipe Alou and Horacio Martínez
(Courtesy Emilio "Cuqui" Cordova). Date: approximately 1960. Former Dominican shortstop Horacio Martínez signed Felipe Alou, who became the first Dominican major league star. He was joined by Juan Marichal and his brothers Mateo and Jesús on the Giants, a club he later managed. Alou was a leader among Latin players.

crush it. President Lyndon Johnson charged that Bosch's movement had been taken over by communists. With U.S. support, an avowedly anticommunist regime, but hardly a democratic one, took over instead.

After Trujillo's assassination in May 1961, Dominicans could travel more freely to pursue professional careers, but the rupture of relations with the United States had left Cuban major leaguers in limbo. Felipe Alou reached out to Cincinnati Reds pitcher Orlando Peña, a Cuban, on the field before a game. Peña, he said, was "a man in need and I wanted to talk over things with him to see what could be done."[23] Through this compassionate gesture, Alou violated a rule against fraternizing with an opposing player on the field, and National League president Warren Giles fined him $10. On principle, Alou ignored telegrams ordering him to pay the fine. Giles let the matter go, but fined Alou again after he had been traded from the Giants after the 1963 season, this time for talking with his brother Mateo before a game. Alou flouted that fine too.

Ford Frick could not be so easily ignored. Though Frick was Major League Baseball's commissioner and had no authority over Caribbean baseball, he intervened in Dominican baseball with nary a second thought. With both Dominican and Cuban professional baseball suspended in 1962, the Dominican government organized a seven-game goodwill exhi-

bition series between Dominican and Cuban players. "Because of the political unrest in my land," Alou wrote, "the government felt that it had to
try something to calm down the people." Alou reasoned that the military
junta installed after Trujillo's death believed that "a few hours at the ballpark would divert the minds of the Dominican people from thoughts of
revolution, riot and mayhem."

Major League Baseball, however, had been itching to dictate who could
play winter baseball since the collapse of the Mexican challenge. Commissioner Frick learned of the exhibitions and imperiously commanded
Dominican and Cuban major leaguers not to participate. But the Cuban
players were already in Santo Domingo. "There was no way that Ford Frick
could scare us out of playing," Alou said. "If we didn't play there would have
been a revolution right on the spot, and we would have been the prime
targets." Besides, he added: "When the military junta 'asked' you to do
something, you did it." Frick neither understood Dominican culture nor
the pressures players felt. He fined several of the men who participated
$250 "for playing against ineligible players." Once again, Felipe refused to
pay. Frick then threatened to suspend Alou for the entire 1963 season if
he didn't obey. The standoff lingered through spring training; the Giants,
afraid of losing Alou, even offered to pay the fine for him. Felipe finally
relented, believing that he was acting more out of stubbornness than common sense. But he had made his point and would not be afraid to do so
again when *Sport* magazine called a few months later.[24]

The Giants brought Jesús Alou up that year and the three brothers played
alongside each other in the outfield for the first time in the United States.
At the end of the 1963 season, they joined with other Caribbean players to
stage a Latin all-star game at New York City's Polo Grounds. The exhibition
celebrated the creation of a Latin American Hall of Fame and raised money
for youth baseball. It reflected the growing identity that Latin players shared,
one transcending the different countries from which they hailed.[25]

Though the Giants had been a few inches from winning the 1962 World
Series, they regressed in 1963 and at the end of the season, their Latin core
was torn apart. Felipe Alou's cover story in *Sport* magazine that November
was one of the reasons why. Speaking not only for himself, but for all Latin
players, Alou recounted to journalist Arnold Hano why he had refused to

pay Commissioner Frick's fine for participating in the series against the Cubans. When he had received Frick's telegram, he said, "It made me so mad I balled it up and threw it away." What disturbed him the most was that he and other Latinos lacked representation to convey their concerns. "If I had not played," Alou declared, "it would have been a slap in the face of the people of my country." Cubans had played Dominicans since 1920. "It is a tradition sports fans in my country cherish, and it is unthinkable to many Dominicans that someone from a foreign country would tell other Dominicans who they can play with and who they can't."

Nor, Alou wrote, was it fair for Frick to deprive the men taking part from earning money. "We are ballplayers; it is the only thing we can do. Take away baseball from us in the winter, and you take money away from us." Though Alou made little by playing in the exhibition (he, Juan Marichal, and pitcher Diomedes Olivo had given most of their share of the gate to help pay for the cost of flying the Cubans—many of whom were poorly paid minor leaguers—back to Florida), he vowed: "I had to play." He was proud that he did, proud to have led all hitters in the series, and proud that the Dominican Republic won four games to three.

Alou argued that Latinos needed somebody to represent them within Major League Baseball. "He does not have to be Latin. He does not have to speak Spanish. He *does* have to see the conditions of these countries, face to face." Alou beseeched the commissioner to understand the pressures that Latinos faced, particularly the pervasive poverty of their Caribbean homelands.

Dissecting baseball's political economy with cool calculation, Alou cited the discriminatory burdens foreign players endured and baseball's indifference to their lives beyond the ball field. The Internal Revenue Service, he protested, taxed his salary as if he were single even though he had four dependents. Alou dismissed the suggestion that he could resolve this inequity by becoming a U.S. citizen. "I am a Dominican," Alou affirmed. "It is my country. And I love it."

He recounted his own difficulties in the South and assailed the cultural misunderstandings and ignorance of North Americans who cast Latinos as uncaring, lazy, unable to perform under pressure, or lacking guts. Alou pulled no punches, criticizing Alvin Dark and Ford Frick despite the power they held over him. But he also looked beyond his own situation to address broader collective issues affecting all Latinos. Nobody had ever spoken so eloquently or forcefully about Latin ballplayers, much less prescribed how baseball could and should address their unique concerns.[26]

"I was free minded," Alou reflected half a century later. "I'm still that way. You can't change the way you are and I said some things that the Giants didn't like, the commissioner of baseball didn't like." While the commissioner and the Giants didn't appreciate Alou's unvarnished comments, Latin players did. "He speaks freely about what he thinks," Manuel Mota observed, "and that, I believe, is one of the reasons that [Latino ballplayers] have a great deal of respect for Felipe. He does not hold back anything." Juan Marichal agreed: "Everybody respects Felipe Alou. He was the leader of most of the Latin players."[27]

A month after the *Sport* magazine story appeared, the Giants traded Alou to Milwaukee. "I played for Alvin [Dark] for two years," Alou explained, "and by the end of the second year, I knew I was going to be traded. There were some things I said that they did not like. There was no shouting, but it did not go very well. The first meeting that they had after the 1963 season, I was gone." His teammates were stunned. "To this day," Cepeda maintained, "I do not know why, because Felipe was a premier baseball player in the National League." Marichal lost his closest friend on the team. "Sometimes you make mistakes," he concluded, "and I think that was one of the biggest mistakes the Giants ever made." Alou was devastated. "It shocked me and really hurt me. I missed the city, I missed Cepeda, Juan Marichal, and my brothers. It was very difficult."

During the 1964 season, relations between Dark and his African American and Latin players cratered. In July, not long after a fifty-seven-day-long filibuster was defeated in the U.S. Senate to allow passage of the 1964 Civil Rights Act, *Newsday's* Stan Isaacs interviewed Dark. "We have trouble because we have so many Negro and Spanish-speaking players on this team," Dark was quoted as saying. "They are just not able to perform up to the white ballplayers when it comes to mental alertness. You can't make most Negro and Spanish players have the pride in their team that you get from white players."[28] His comments (he later claimed he was misquoted) reverberated on radio talk shows and in other print publications.

When the Giants came to New York, their black and Latin players found copies of the story in their lockers at Shea Stadium, and Dark encountered a horde of sportswriters.

Interestingly, Dark's rhetoric—or what was attributed to him in *Newsday*—conflicted with some of his actions as manager. He had replaced white starters with black and Latin players, often fielded lineups with seven non-Caucasian players, and appointed Willie Mays team captain. Dark confronted reporters and met with Commissioner Frick and his players to deny he was prejudiced. Jackie Robinson and others who had known the impulsive manager came to Dark's defense, but the damage with his players was beyond repair. At season's end, Dark's career with the Giants was over.[29]

But so were the careers of many of the Latin Giants. Felipe Alou and Manuel Mota had already been traded; José Pagan, Mateo Alou, and Orlando Cepeda were dealt away over the next two seasons. Only Marichal and Jesús Alou remained from the core of the club's once-vibrant Latin connection.

Marichal had his most difficult season in 1965. Until then, he had lived an almost charmed life in baseball, enjoying spectacular success from an early age and displaying an easygoing demeanor that led to his being nicknamed "the Laughing Boy" while he was in the minors. In his July 1960 debut, Marichal had no-hit the Philadelphia Phillies for seven and two-thirds innings before surrendering a single hit. He had led the majors in wins in 1963 and was pitching brilliantly that 1965 summer, with a 19–9 won-loss record and a 1.65 ERA, when the Giants and Dodgers met in a four-game series in San Francisco that August. Earlier that month, U.S. troops had occupied the Dominican Republic to prevent Juan Bosch's return to power. A week later, rioting broke out in Watts, a black neighborhood in Los Angeles, after a period of heightening racial tensions there. Ironically, the Voting Rights Act had passed only days before. Twenty thousand U.S. soldiers suppressed the Dominican rebellion, while in Watts, thirty-four people were killed in the rioting, some four thousand people were arrested, and over $40 million of property was destroyed in what proved to be the lid-lifter on several summers of civil disturbances that tore apart many cities.

The bitter Giants and Dodgers' rivalry was on full display. By the fourth game, with Marichal pitching against Sandy Koufax, batters had been decked and many more threats exchanged. In the first couple of innings, Marichal knocked down Dodgers shortstop Maury Wills and outfielder Ron Fairly while Koufax whistled a ball over Willie Mays's head. Dodger catcher John Roseboro, an African American, three-time All-Star, and former football player, told players on both squads that he was going to go after Marichal, who had beaten Los Angeles ten straight times at Candlestick Park.

In the third inning, with Marichal at bat, Roseboro returned a pitch to Koufax that either clipped Marichal's ear or came perilously close to doing so. Given what he had heard of Roseboro's intentions, Marichal whirled and confronted the burly catcher. Roseboro barked an epithet at Marichal and moved toward him. Marichal tried to push Roseboro back with a hand, then panicked and clubbed Roseboro with his bat, gashing his scalp. A brawl ensued before the umpires restored order. Marichal was subsequently fined $1,750 and suspended for nine games, probably costing the Giants the pennant.

The attack reinforced a rapidly spreading stereotype of Latinos as troublemakers. Television, which now could be found in almost every U.S. household and was amping up its sports coverage, created an echo chamber in which Marichal was denounced and his actions took on a second life. Prior incidents involving Latin players—from Adolfo Luque beating up Casey Stengel in 1923 to Cepeda leaving the dugout with a bat in hand to go after Pirates manager Danny Murtaugh during the 1958 season—were dredged up in the press. "These young Caribbean hotheads absolutely must be taught restraint," wrote writer Bob Broeg in the St. Louis Post-Dispatch.[30] Marichal, pilloried in print and on television, and abused by fans, was shaken by the ferocity of the verbal attacks. Few came to his defense and the confrontation would ultimately delay his election to the Hall of Fame. Years passed before he and Roseboro reconciled and became friends.

Sportswriter Dick Young noted baseball's double standard. A white player, Frank Thomas, had attacked African American teammate Richie Allen with a bat earlier in the season. Thomas was not penalized by the commissioner, on the grounds that the assault occurred before the game and was not subject to league discipline, although he was waived by the Phillies. Young also offered a troubling comment: "The true problem is that the American Negroes and the Latin Negroes do not like each other—not even a little bit."[31] The Dodgers included half a dozen African Americans but no Latinos that season; the Giants featured six Latinos and several African Americans. Young's piece helped spread the notion of deep-seated black-brown antagonisms among baseball players, a belief that many would continue to hold for years to come. In all likelihood, though, the Marichal-Roseboro blowup had more to do with long-standing Giants-Dodgers animosities than with Latino–African American ill will.

Not surprisingly, white fans, unaware of these intraracial tensions, continued to lump together African American and Latino players. Although they dealt with similar issues, African Americans and Latinos thought about race differently. Language was as big an obstacle in relations between blacks and Latinos as it was between whites and Latinos. For over half a century, African Americans and Latinos had joined ranks to create their own transnational baseball world, an alternative to the major leagues' segregated system. But after the color line was breached, their shared struggle became a more fractured fight. Most whites were blind to this social transformation, but not men like Clemente and Alou, who often spoke for all players of color but never lost sight of Latinos' particular problems or third-class status.

• • •

Despite the special hurdles to their success, Latinos had scaled major league baseball's heights by the mid-1960s. The 1964 All-Star Game fielded a record number of Latinos, while the Senators, renamed the Twins after moving to Minneapolis, returned to the World Series in 1965 with a quartet of Cubans—Tony Oliva, Camilo Pascual, Sandy Valdespino, and Zoilo Versalles—leading the way. Oliva, the 1964 Rookie of the Year, won back-to-back batting titles; shortstop Versalles was the 1965 American League MVP. Dominicans Mateo Alou, his brother Felipe, and Rico Carty were the top three batters in the National League in 1966. Juan Marichal was the NL's winningest pitcher in 1963 and 1968, and Orlando Cepeda the NL's 1967 MVP.

But no player better represented Latinos on the field than Roberto Clemente. During the 1960s, the enigmatic Puerto Rican became the game's best right fielder, won four batting titles, and began a string of twelve consecutive Gold Glove awards, a record for outfielders that he still shares only with Willie Mays.

Nor was any Latino ballplayer as misunderstood off the field. As a young player, Clemente had received little guidance in dealing with the media or coping with Major League Baseball. He compounded his naiveté by speaking from the heart, passionately and directly. Sportswriters often mistook his dignity and pride for aloofness and irascibility. They reduced his comments to a demeaning "Spanglish" when quoting him. "I no play so gut yet," the *Sporting News* reported him as saying. "Me like hot weather, veree hot. I no run fast cold weather."[32] Nor did they appreciate his panache; unsympathetic writers portrayed his sensitivity as a character fault. The ballplayers they knew were tobacco-chewing, plain-spoken Caucasians, men who deliberately lacked style and flair. Writers portrayed Clemente as an egocentric hot-dog, not a team player. Jim Brosnan, a former major leaguer previewing the 1960 World Series for *Life*, wrote that "Clemente features a Latin-American variety of showboating. 'Look at *número uno*,' he seems to be saying." Perhaps because of their collective dislike or inability to understand him, sportswriters also underplayed the injuries Clemente had sustained, including a 1955 car accident in which he damaged three spinal disks. In a 1966 *Sports Illustrated* profile, Myron Cope observed that "Roberto has acquired a reputation as baseball's champion hypochondriac."[33]

What U.S. sportswriters failed to understand was that when Clemente said, "For me, I am the best ballplayer in the world," he was not indulging in self-flattery or denigrating the talents of others. "It is a Spanish saying, an expression of self-respect," his friend, Puerto Rican engineer Libertario Avila, explained. "You are not to underestimate yourself, but that does not mean you are to underestimate anyone else's ability."[34]

Clemente, who had continued to feel isolated in Pittsburgh, often signed autographs for hours after games because he was lonely and had little else to do. But when he walked out of the clubhouse after the 1960 World Series and saw fans swarming the streets, he was overcome. "It was something you cannot describe. I did not feel like a player at the time. I felt like one of those persons, and I walked the streets among them." A few years later, Myron Cope called Clemente's relationship with Pittsburgh fans "one of the unwavering love stories of the national pastime."[35]

Clemente became ever more a man of the people in Pittsburgh and Puerto Rico, among Hispanic Americans throughout the United States, and in the Caribbean. The Hispanic share of the U.S. population was on the cusp of exploding late in his career. In 1970 the percentage of foreign-born Americans had reached a record low of 4.7 percent. But it would more than double over the next two decades, with Latin Americans constituting the bulk of all arrivals. Along with people of Hispanic descent who had lived in the United States for generations, even centuries, they formed growing enclaves on both coasts and in many major league cities. They identified with Clemente, who resonated among disparate groups sharing ties to Latin America.[36] "I grew up with people who really had to struggle to live," Clemente said.[37] He never forgot them. If not the first Latino to speak out, he was the most impassioned to decry racial and cultural discrimination. "Latin American Negro players," he told *Sport* magazine in 1961, "are treated today much like all Negroes were treated in baseball in the early days of the broken color barriers. They are subjected to prejudices and stamped with generalizations. . . . They bear the brunt of the sport's remaining racial prejudices."[38] He used the podium he had gained as one of the game's brightest stars to speak to larger questions. "Clemente was interested in more than sports," his biographer David Maraniss observed. "He was very political . . . and one of the people he admired the most in the world was Martin Luther King Jr."[39]

By 1966, Clemente was lobbying the Puerto Rican government to make land available to build Ciudad Deportiva (Sports City), offering opportunities for children of humble circumstances to grow into proud and productive citizens through the empowering discipline of sports. "I like to work with kids," he said. "I'd like to work with kids all the time, if I live long enough."[40]

In 1970 the Pittsburgh Pirates abandoned Forbes Field, their home since 1909, and began playing at Three Rivers Stadium near the confluence of the Allegheny and Monongahela rivers. Shortly after the move, the team held a "Roberto Clemente Night" to honor the longtime Pirates player. During the evening, Clemente was presented with a scroll signed by three hundred thousand of his native countryman, heralding the island's favorite son; it had taken a Puerto Rican businessman less than a month to collect the signatures. The festivities, attended by hundreds of people from Carolina, Clemente's hometown, were broadcast back to the island. Overwhelmed by the outpouring of support, Clemente declared that his triumph belonged to all Puerto Ricans and citizens of the Caribbean. "We are all brothers."[41]

Clemente's dedication to the Pirates and his commitment to Puerto Rico only increased as he entered his final seasons. He became a team leader, taking a particular interest in mentoring younger Latinos. He schooled them in ways that nobody had helped him, convincing Mateo Alou, for example, to hit to the opposite field, which led to Alou's batting title; he also offered warmth and kinship, inviting Manuel Mota and others into the home he shared with his wife, Vera, and their three sons, all of whom, in keeping with the Clementes' wishes, had been born in Puerto Rico.

In 1971 Clemente helped the Pirates return to the World Series. Their roster, by then almost half Latin and African American, included players from Cuba, Venezuela, Panama, and Puerto Rico. That season, the Pirates became the first club ever to field a team made up exclusively of black and Latino players. After Pittsburgh lost the first two games of the 1971 Series to Baltimore, Clemente almost single-handedly put the team back in contention. His twelve hits, two home runs, .414 batting average, aggressive baserunning, and spectacular fielding over the course of the series rallied Pittsburgh. In Game 3, Clemente dribbled a ball to pitcher Mike Cuellar. It was an easy out, but Clemente bolted pell-mell to first base, startling Cuellar and beating his throw to the bag. In the next at-bat, Willie Stargell walked, then Bob Robertson homered, and the Series' momentum reversed. Pittsburgh won in seven games, with Clemente leading the way in the final game. When interviewed by Pirates announcer Bob Prince in the clubhouse after the last out, Clemente said: "First, I would like to say something in Spanish to my mother and father in Puerto Rico." Breaking into Spanish, he continued: "On this, the proudest moment of my life, I ask for your blessing." He addressed Puerto Ricans on the island and in the United States before entertaining questions in English. "To have someone suddenly speak to you in Spanish," writer Juan Gonzalez recalled, "reinforced a pride in your own language and culture and in who Roberto was." The World Series made Clemente a Pan-Caribbean hero.[42]

The next season, Clemente collected his three thousandth hit in his final regular season at-bat; he was only the eleventh player to reach that plateau. That November, he managed Puerto Rico's team in the world amateur championship in Nicaragua. Clemente was showered with adulation in the baseball-crazy country. "When we went to Nicaragua," Vera Clemente remembered, "we found the people as we had been in Puerto Rico thirty years ago. Roberto saw himself in the boys in the streets—without shoes, living in a one-room house with ten people—much like it had been when his father worked for the sugar mill in Carolina." After they returned to Puerto Rico, an earthquake devastated Nicaragua. The Clementes organized efforts in Puerto Rico to send relief to the stricken country. When Nicaraguan dictator Anastasio Somoza's National Guard began looting aid shipments, Roberto decided to accompany the deliveries himself, to ensure that the supplies reached those in need. "He didn't want to go," Vera recalled, "but he felt he had to."[43]

On New Year's Eve 1972, Roberto Clemente and four other men took off from Puerto Rico in a small, overloaded charter plane. Minutes later, the plane disappeared into the waters off Boca de Cangrejo. Pirates teammate Manny Sanguillén, who was playing winter ball in San Juan, joined divers searching the waters where the plane went down, but Clemente's body was never recovered. "He was everything to the Latin ballplayers," the grieving Sanguillén, a Panamanian, said.

With Puerto Rico, Pittsburgh, and fans throughout the baseball world in mourning, tributes poured in. "Somehow, Roberto transcended superstardom," then Major League Baseball commissioner Bowie Kuhn said. "He had about him a touch of royalty." The Hall of Fame waived the five-year waiting period for former players to become eligible, and Clemente was enshrined as its first Latin member that summer. Vera Clemente subsequently took on her husband's dream of creating the Ciudad Deportiva complex for youth sport back home on the island. Despite the daunting task of raising the funds to build and maintain the ambitious effort, she and her sons have nurtured the complex ever since.

In the quarter century between Jackie Robinson's major league debut and Roberto Clemente's death, Latin players changed baseball indelibly. The careers of Clemente, Aparicio, Marichal, and Cepeda would all be capped with induction into the Hall of Fame. A score of other men would win recognition as All-Stars and league leaders. They would be the first of many to claim their place in baseball's firmament.

CHAPTER EIGHT

Whiteout

Seated behind home plate at the Houston Astrodome late on the evening of April 6, 1987, Al Campanis committed professional suicide in front of a national television audience. The veteran Los Angeles Dodgers general manager was on ABC's *Nightline* with Ted Koppel to commemorate the fortieth anniversary of Jackie Robinson crossing baseball's color line. Campanis, Robinson's minor league teammate, had not been the intended guest. But when former Negro League and Dodger pitcher Don Newcombe's flight to Texas was delayed, Campanis agreed to appear instead. The seventy-year-old Campanis had been traveling that day and was visibly tired, having sat through opening-day ceremonies and a drawn-out ballgame between the Dodgers and the Houston Astros, an expansion team that had entered the National League in 1962. He could not possibly have anticipated that his twenty-year career as the Dodgers' general manager was about to end, or that its demise would advance the long-delayed integration of baseball's front office.

Koppel, the British-born moderator who had achieved international prominence by hosting *Nightline* during the Iran hostage crisis a decade before, asked Campanis a blunt question: "Why is it that there are no black managers, no black general managers, no black owners?" Only three African Americans had ever managed a major league club, and just two had held front-office jobs. Campanis hesitated. "The only thing I can say is that you have to pay your dues when you become a manager. Generally, you have to go to the minor leagues. There's not very much pay involved, and some of the better-known black players have been able to get into other fields and make a pretty good living in that way."

There was some truth to that, but not enough to explain the near-total absence of African Americans from these positions for forty years. Koppel dismissed Campanis's response. "You know that that's a lot of baloney," he said. "I guess what I'm really asking you is to, you know, peel it away a little bit. Just tell me why you think it is. Is there still that much prejudice in baseball?" Rather than concede that some degree of racism plagued the game he'd spent his lifetime serving, Campanis replied: "No, I don't believe it's prejudice. I truly believe that they may not have some of the necessities to be, let's say, a field manager, or perhaps a general manager." Koppel paused, then gave Campanis the opportunity to extricate himself. Instead, Campanis buried himself deeper. Scrambling to defend his point of view, he argued that African Americans were well suited for some pursuits, but not others. "Why are black men, or black people, not good swimmers?" he asked by way of example, concluding: "Because they don't have buoyancy."[1]

Campanis was distraught after the *Nightline* interview, aware that his remarks would be perceived as racist. But it was too late; ABC switchboards were already lighting up with calls from angry viewers. The next day, Jackie Robinson's widow, Rachel, along with Henry Aaron and Peter Ueberroth, who was Major League Baseball's commissioner at the time, expressed their consternation. Campanis seemed to be saying that there were race-based differences in aptitude and skill—that African Americans did not have the drive and intellectual makeup to succeed off the field. The off-the-cuff interview quickly became a national scandal.

Those who knew Campanis, especially the African Americans and Latinos whose careers he had advanced, were just as upset, but not at Campanis. They felt their friend had inadvertently cast himself as a racist, which they maintained he was not. Don Newcombe, Maury Wills, and other African American ballplayers defended Campanis. "He will be my friend as long as he lives and as long as I live," Newcombe attested.[2]

Only three photos adorned the walls of Campanis's office at Dodger Stadium: shots of Roberto Clemente, Sandy Koufax, and Jackie Robinson—a

Puerto Rican, a Jew, and an African American. Campanis had signed Clemente and Koufax and stuck up for Robinson, his roommate on the road in the minors. When Jackie, constrained by Branch Rickey's orders, had been unable to fight back, Campanis offered to do it for him. After the season, Campanis joined a barnstorming team that Robinson put together.

The day after his *Nightline* appearance, Campanis apologized profusely. "This is the saddest day of my career," he said. But with African American groups calling for his ouster, the Dodgers forced the issue. After meeting with owner Peter O'Malley, Al Campanis resigned his position with the organization for which he had worked most of his life.[3]

"He just said what a lot of baseball people have been thinking for years," Frank Robinson remarked. Robinson, a former outfielder who won MVP awards in both leagues before becoming Major League Baseball's first black manager, added: "I'm glad it's finally out in the open, so we can address it."[4] The ill-advised comments, African American slugger Reggie Jackson wrote in *Sports Illustrated* the next month, were "the best thing to happen to minorities in baseball since Jackie Robinson." Campanis, he said, was neither a bad man nor a bigot, but somebody who had "brought the problem into a sharper focus than we could have ever asked for." Jackson, nearing the end of a Hall of Fame career, declared: "It's not only management that is at fault, either. Although some 25% of the players on the field are black, there isn't a black in the Players Association office."[5]

Koppel's questions may have been tough, but they were right on the mark. Forty years of integration had brought about radical changes on the field, but not among managerial ranks or in owner's boxes. By design, integration had driven African Americans out of positions of authority they once had held. Although the game's power structure had since evolved, it had not become more inclusive. No African Americans had managed in the major leagues until Frank Robinson took over in Cleveland in 1975, and he lasted fewer than three seasons. No African Americans had even managed in the minors until the Pirates hired their former second baseman Gene Baker to direct their Batavia, New York, farm club in 1961. Nor were there more than a handful who had coached in the big leagues. Emmett Ashford became the first African American umpire in the majors in 1966, while the Atlanta Braves' Bill Lucas was the first black general manager when he took over a decade later. There had not been a second.[6] Meanwhile, African American ownership had been absent and forgotten since the collapse of the Negro Leagues.

Baseball front offices—made up of the decision makers in finance, marketing, and administrative work—were also uniformly segregated. A survey of twenty-four franchises in 1982 revealed that African Americans held but 32 of 913 white-collar and 15 of 568 scouting positions. A study five years later found only 17 African Americans and 15 Hispanics among baseball's top 879 administrative positions. Four California teams—Los Angeles, San Francisco, Oakland, and California—accounted for two-thirds of these minority hires.

Because of the sharp attention that the Campanis interview brought to baseball's front offices, their monochromatic cast was about to change. Peter Ueberroth, the media-savvy executive who assumed the commissioner's job after his successful stewardship of the 1984 Los Angeles Olympics, had not addressed the issue during his two-year tenure. The only minority working in the National and American League offices was a black receptionist. But Ueberroth understood that baseball could not defend itself in the court of public opinion from criticism that it had failed to transform its off-the-field racial makeup. He quickly created a working group to bring minorities into front-office positions and hired Harry Edwards, the activist sociologist who had led the campaign for African Americans to boycott the 1968 Olympics, to advance employment for blacks and Latinos in baseball. He also hired Clifford Alexander, Lyndon Johnson's former Equal Employment Opportunity Commission chairman, to work on the issue. Ueberroth, Edwards, and Alexander together pressed teams to integrate front-office staffs, and most soon did.

Clubs made 180 new minority hires in front-office and field positions in 1988, albeit in relatively low-level positions with little authority.[7] These new men and women constituted 36 percent of all major league front-office and 30 percent of major league coaching hires. Within two years of the Campanis interview, 9 percent of front-office positions were held by African Americans and an additional 6 percent by other minorities. The most notable and surprising hire was that of former All-Star first baseman Bill White as the National League's new president. The outspoken White, who had protested discrimination during spring training as early as the late 1950s, was the first African American to head any sports league. "What baseball has done in these two years is really quite impressive," Clifford Alexander contended.[8]

After Campanis's appearance on *Nightline*, Major League Baseball also sought to make amends for its neglect of black communities and its tortured connections to black baseball history. It began by acknowledging the Negro Leagues as part of the sport's rich past. The Pittsburgh Pirates acted first, inviting former members of the Homestead Grays and the Pittsburgh Crawfords to the ballpark in the fall of 1988 to honor them before a game celebrating the fortieth anniversary of the 1948 Negro League World Series, the last one played. During a pregame ceremony, Pirates president Carl Barger apologized for his club's and baseball's discriminatory past. Major League Baseball commissioner A. Bartlett Giamatti, who had succeeded Ueberroth just days before the event, told the *New York Times's* Doron Levin that he would make matters of social justice a priority: "We must never lose sight of our history, insofar as it is ugly, never to repeat it, and insofar as it is glorious, to cherish it."[9]

Other clubs followed suit, working Negro League salutes into marketing campaigns. Teams began wearing Negro League uniforms for regular-season games and honoring former players; the Pirates built Legacy Square, a permanent exhibit on the Negro Leagues, at their ballpark. While these efforts were designed to attract African Americans to games, they also reflected Major League Baseball's increasing awareness of race and history. The men and women implementing these programs and tributes were often the same African Americans who had been hired in the wake of the *Nightline* interview.[10]

The commissioner's office also threw its support behind John Young, a former major league player and scout who in 1989 organized a new initiative called Reviving Baseball in Inner Cities. Young, who had grown up in Los Angeles, could see that its black neighborhoods were no longer a source of young baseball talent. He approached former White Sox general manager Roland Hemond, who was working in the commissioner's office, and sought backing for a community-based program promoting baseball among youth. With support from Major League Baseball, Los

Angeles mayor Tom Bradley, and the Amateur Athletic Foundation of Los Angeles, which had been created with the surplus from the 1984 Los Angeles Olympic Games, Young set up a baseball program for thirteen-to sixteen-year-olds in South Central Los Angeles. After Young convinced gang leaders to leave the boys participating in RBI alone, 180 youth took part in its first season. He added an academic component to the initiative the following year and began advising groups in other cities trying to emulate his program.

Despite MLB's better-late-than-never intentions, in 1997 only three African Americans—Dusty Baker in San Francisco, Cito Gaston in Toronto, and Don Baylor in Colorado—managed clubs; one served as a general manager—Bob Watson in Atlanta; and another—Leonard Coleman—was the National League president. Coleman, who had played football and baseball at Princeton, advanced Major League Baseball initiatives in black communities across the country. But Montreal's Felipe Alou, who had managed in the minors and coached in the majors since finishing his playing career in 1974, was the sole Latin manager. Nor had any minorities gained an ownership stake.[11]

By then, Campanis was more sanguine about his exit from the game. "It has turned out to be a plus for baseball," he contended. "When I said blacks lacked the 'necessities' to be managers or general managers, what I meant was the lack of necessary experience, not things like inherent intelligence or ability. I was dead tired after traveling when I went on the show. I got confused."[12]

Some progress, if limited and inadequate, had been made since 1987, but the focus on baseball's segregated front offices masked other ultimately more important trends. A widening gulf had emerged between baseball and the black community. Fewer African Americans were playing baseball professionally and hardly any black fans could be spotted at games. Even as the ranks of baseball's African American decision makers ticked upward, the game was becoming scarce at the grass-roots level in the black community.

• • •

In 1975 more than 27 percent of all major league ballplayers were African American, more than twice their share of the U.S. population. Sixteen

Reggie Jackson *(National Baseball Hall of Fame Library, Cooperstown, NY).* Reginald Martinez "Reggie" Jackson, whose father played in the Negro Leagues, was one of baseball's greatest sluggers. Never afraid to speak his mind, Jackson was on five World Series champion squads; he was nicknamed Mr. October for his performance in the postseason.

black players, including future Hall of Famers Henry Aaron, Lou Brock, Reggie Jackson, and Joe Morgan, appeared in the All-Star Game that year, where they made up about 40 percent of all nonpitching selections. Their presence in baseball and that of Latinos had steadily ramped up during the 1960s and 1970s. With the best black, white, and Latin players finally competing together, baseball realized its truest golden age. Yet at the height of the black players' prominence, their eclipse was imminent. By 1997, a decade after the Al Campanis *Nightline* interview, African Americans comprised just 17 percent of all major leaguers. Their numbers plummeted even lower in the twenty-first century, bottoming out at 8 percent in 2007, down over 70 percent from their 1975 high. What prompted African Americans to bolt for baseball's exit?

The exodus of African Americans from baseball began amid a radical makeover in sport's political economy that wiped out much of the black community's baseball infrastructure. After World War II, sport in the United States became ever more of a corporate affair. As television advertising, commercial sponsorships, and merchandizing pumped dizzying new revenue streams into baseball, corporate ownership prevailed. The traditional baseball families began selling out; by 1977, only the Griffiths in Minnesota and the O'Malleys in Los Angeles still controlled franchises and they, too, were not long for the game.

Corporate sport overwhelmed community-based sport. Commercially driven leagues—both at the professional and collegiate level—became more powerful, while independent, community-based sport fell apart. Television had shifted the balance from playing sport to watching it. TV had also lavishly lined professional sport's coffers by providing entertainment without directly charging those who watched, a stark departure from the days of carefully counted gate receipts.[13]

As television conquered most American homes during the 1950s, sport programming decimated attendance at events. Independent baseball, already thrown off its moorings by changing community patterns and suburbanization, was savaged, unable to compete. Enormous numbers of sandlot and semipro clubs disappeared. As a result, men had fewer opportunities to join the neighborhood and workplace teams that had been the mainstay of local baseball between the two world wars. Minor league baseball, meanwhile, contracted from fifty-nine to twenty-one leagues during the 1950s, and baseball's professional workforce shrunk by several thousand roster spots.[14]

Most sports, whether big league or sandlot, had difficulty coping with television. After the shaving company Gillette began sponsoring fight cards on television several nights a week, boxing won a large TV audience. But fans stopped patronizing the venues that sustained local boxing, and 250 of the nation's 300 fight clubs folded between 1952 and 1959. When the fight game bounced back up off the canvas, it did so as a televised (and increasingly cable and pay-per-view) affair. Major league baseball attendance similarly plunged after teams began televising home games, falling by a third from a 1948 high of 21 million fans at ballparks that season to 14.3 million five years later. The Cleveland Indians' home attendance collapsed by 67 percent, while the Boston Braves' dropped by 81 percent. National Collegiate Athletic Association football attendance fell, too, though not quite as drastically, and over seventy small colleges dropped football in the first half of the 1950s.[15]

Major League Baseball, the increasingly savvy NFL, and the NCAA slowly learned not just how to cope with television, but how to prosper from it. In time, their revenue streams swelled to a torrent few could have foreseen. But less commercialized levels of sport were more vulnerable. Sport in the black community was especially hard hit and the Negro Leagues, already reeling from integration, were soon extinct. Black players in organized baseball now worked for white owners; black fans became patrons of major league teams, at least for a while. Though the number of African American players in the majors increased steadily through the 1970s, black baseball's infrastructure of teams, leagues, and coaching was crumbling.

By the 1960s, black baseball's tributaries had all but dried up, stifling future generations of black ballplayers. The Negro Leagues no longer developed players, the semipro and sandlot clubs in the black community that had served as their farm clubs vanished, and historically black colleges and universities lost students, especially student-athletes, to previously segregated institutions. While Jackie Robinson had become an iconic figure, subsequent generations of black youth came of age in households with little attachment to baseball. These boys had not grown up watching their fathers, older brothers, and neighbors playing on the sandlots or hearing stories about legendary black ballplayers. They were no longer culturally rooted in baseball, and many of them turned to other sports.

Nor had the arrival of black players in the majors resolved organized baseball's deep-seated institutional racism. African Americans frequently faced virulent opposition when pursuing careers in baseball. Like the civil rights movement, where more battles were lost than won during the 1950s, more black athletes saw their careers end than flourish in the South, where most minor leagues were based. The first generations of African American ballplayers received little encouragement to endure the travails of minor league life. Hostile fans, hesitant teammates, and the absence of black scouts, coaches, and managers made it less likely that a black player would receive an offer to sign, much less a chance to succeed professionally.

In a piece for *Sports Illustrated* published one month after the infamous Campanis interview on *Nightline*, Reggie Jackson recalled his college coach cautioning him about dating non–African American women, and described an incident when he was playing in the minor leagues in Lewiston, Idaho, when after being hit in the head with a pitch, he was rushed to the hospital. "They wouldn't admit me because I was black," Jackson wrote.

Although Jackson's allegations were disputed by a local paper that investigated the incident, the effects of segregation were plain to see, including in locker rooms, where black players were often assigned lockers away from white members of the team as late as the 1980s.[16]

Black players were typecast as fast, athletic, and agile, but less than capable of handling the so-called thinking positions. The same stereotypes applied in football, where African Americans were overrepresented in positions emphasizing speed but underrepresented at quarterback, center, guard, and middle linebacker, the decision-making positions. Noting how few African Americans pitched or caught in the majors, Jackson asked: "Isn't this the black-quarterback syndrome all over again? Aren't blacks smart enough to be starting pitchers or to run games as catchers? The subtle message is that we have genetic talent, but we're just not intelligent. People have told me I have a gifted body. They always say that to black athletes. If I were white, they would say I was good because I was a diligent worker."[17]

These stereotypes encouraged pronounced stacking, the concentration of African Americans as outfielders and corner infielders, their absence as pitchers, catchers, and middle infielders. Because coaches and managers tended to be drawn from those who had caught or played second base and shortstop, African Americans were less likely to be considered managerial material. Overall, African Americans suffered from informal quotas, positional segregation, higher entry standards, and shorter careers. Until the 1980s, black athletes were generally excluded from the lucrative commercial endorsements that their white counterparts received. When African American athletes began to cash in, they tended to come from basketball, football, and track and field, but not baseball. Rod Carew, a dark-skinned Panamanian elected to the Hall of Fame in 1991, reflected that because of discrimination, "You had to be twice as good as a white player; if you weren't, you were going to sit on the bench."[18]

•   •   •

As Major League Baseball became more corporate in character and its bottom line dependent on broadcast and marketing revenues, the owners lost their ironclad grip on the players. In 1966, when Marvin Miller became executive director of the Major League Baseball Players Association, the average ballplayer made $19,000. The union's assets consisted of a filing cabinet and $4,500 in the bank; its collective-bargaining agreement was a lopsided deal favoring ownership. "Players were not only ignorant about unions," Miller later wrote, "they were positively hostile to the idea."[19] Miller, the most significant figure in baseball history not in the Hall of Fame, soon changed that. He used the acumen he had gained as chief economist and negotiator for the United Steelworkers of America to consistently outmaneuver baseball owners during his seventeen years at the union's helm. Miller forged solidarity among the players that few thought possible, and the players association prevailed over the owners in three strikes and two lockouts. *New York Times* sportswriter Ira Berkow contended that Miller crafted "the most successful union not just in sports, but in the history of American labor."[20]

Miller led the union to two critical victories: free agency and salary arbitration. Free agency replaced the reserve clause, which had bound a player to the team that first signed him in near perpetuity. Just what constituted free agency went through several iterations before assuming its current shape, in which players are free to bargain with any clubs seeking their services after six seasons in the majors. If free agency was a declaration of player rights, salary arbitration seemed less consequential. It offered players who were not yet free agents but who had spent more than two years in the majors a means to resolve salary disputes. Both the player and his team could propose a salary to an arbiter, who could pick either the player or team's submission as the player's salary for the next season.

The combination of free agency and salary arbitration, however, exploded old salary levels. The arbiter, who came from a pool of individuals who both the union and owners deemed acceptable, decided on the basis of how players of comparable production were paid. But free-agent signings had inflated these comparable salaries because some teams recklessly overpaid free agents whose statistical production did not warrant such amounts. Their salaries affected pay scales across the board and boosted the salaries of players who filed for arbitration. Teams began submitting salary figures in excess of what they thought was justified because of the inflated salaries paid to free agents of comparable production. As a result, players rarely lost in salary arbitration. Mediocrity was rewarded and few ever took pay cuts no matter how poor their statistics from the previous season. For example, Steve Avery won seven games but lost thirteen with a 4.67 ERA while pitching for the pennant-winning Atlanta Braves in 1995. Despite posting subpar numbers (by far the worst on the Braves' pitching staff), he went to salary arbitration and received a raise to $4.2 million, up from $4 million, because that was what players with comparable production were making.

As average pay soared, reaching $3.26 million in 2009, African American players finally shared in the bonanza.[21] Discrimination did not disappear, but it did ease, especially for top players. Race likely mattered more for marginal or bench players, where teams seemed inclined to stock white players instead of blacks or Latinos. Studies confirmed that minority players on average performed better than white players between 1968 and 1977. A follow-up analysis prior to the 1986 season showed that black players continued to outperform white players. The percentage of active African American players who had lifetime batting averages of .280 or better was twice that of white players, and almost four times as many black as white pitchers had career earned-run averages under 3.00. Whites, on the other hand, were disproportionately represented among lower-performing players.

But another report a few years later determined that the differences in black and white players' performance were diminishing. A study of 1991 opening-day rosters concluded that merit now mattered more than race in determining salaries. Economist Gerald Scully concluded that "racially-based pay discrimination had disappeared."[22]

The post–free agency salary explosion benefited the generation of African Americans already in the major leagues. But it altered the patterns of player procurement in ways that made it difficult for subsequent generations of African Americans to join them. Escalating salaries placed greater emphasis on player development as a way for teams to field affordable talent. Small-market teams recognized that they would not be able to keep their most talented players when they reached free agency, because deep-pocketed teams could offer them far more money. They also faced the discouraging reality that salary arbitration would drive up salaries for players in their third year in the majors. Finding fresh talent became ever more critical and influenced how organizations signed players. That placed a premium on collegiate athletes and the Latin free-agent market.

Since 1965, Major League Baseball has signed most of its prospective players out of an annual draft in which any U.S. player whose high school class had graduated was eligible for selection. Like the NFL, whose draft began in 1936, the team with the worst record picked first, the team with the best, last.[23] Once drafted, a player lost the right to negotiate with any team other than the one that drafted him. If a player signed with that organization, it owned his minor league rights for the next six seasons. If he made the majors, he would be beholden to that organization for another six years before free agency kicked in.

Undrafted players were able to negotiate with any club seeking their services. But most undrafted free agents in the United States were considered marginal prospects and received small signing bonuses. Players outside the United States, however, were not subject to the draft (Puerto Rico and Canada were later included) and began their careers as free agents.

Clubs found it much cheaper to sign Latin free agents than players taken in the draft, even though Latinos, as free agents, could bargain with more than one club. Their relative lack of sophistication about the inner workings of MLB coupled with their frequent poverty tended to make them vulnerable and hungry to sign, even when offered much less than drafted players. In the late 1980s, for example, Pedro Martínez and Sammy Sosa's bonuses were just a few thousand dollars, about average for a Latin prospect, but paltry in comparison to first-round draft picks, who were beginning to receive as much as a million dollars by 1990. Major league teams went on a feeding frenzy south of the border. Quick to take advantage of families bewildered by the baseball industry's economics, major league organizations began scouting the Caribbean more intensively, signing large numbers of players for small sums in hopes that a few would pan out to be major leaguers.

Meanwhile, college players supplanted high school players as the primary source of drafted talent. Scouts could more accurately evaluate collegiate players, who were older and more experienced, more likely to sign if drafted, and who needed less time in the minors to develop. Collegians also had fewer options than high school draftees. A high school player un-happy with the team that picked him or the signing bonus it offered could go to college instead and reenter the draft after his junior year.

In 1965, 56 percent of all players drafted were high school players, and about half of those drafted signed contracts. By 2005, only 35 percent of draftees were high school players, and only a quarter of them signed. By then, two-thirds of the players drafted came from college ranks and about 70 percent of them signed to play professionally. That was terrible news for black players, because far fewer of them played college baseball. There were many reasons for that.

For starters, college baseball was simply not as financially attractive an option as football or basketball for African American high school gradu-ates. Unlike football and basketball, where NCAA Division One teams allotted 85 and 12 scholarships respectively, a college baseball team offered only 11.7 scholarships. Most were partial awards split among the twenty-five to thirty players on a team. Black athletes who could not pay for the part of their education that baseball scholarships did not cover became more likely to turn to football or basketball, where the entire cost of their education was supplied. "If you're an African American kid and you need help to go to school, do the math," Jimmy Lee Solomon, Major League Baseball's vice president for operations, said in 2007.[24]

By the twenty-first century, few African Americans played college base-ball. In the 2003–04 academic year, only 4.5 percent of NCAA baseball players were black, compared to 42 percent of basketball and 32.3 percent of football players. In the powerful Southeastern Conference (SEC), no baseball squad had more than two black players. Hardly any black fans attended SEC baseball games and not one of the conference's twelve head coaches or any of their assistants was African American. Meanwhile, many of the historically black colleges and universities had begun recruiting white and Latin players to fill their baseball squads. On Bethune-Cook-man's 2007 baseball team, only seven of thirty-one players were African American.[25]

The dwindling number of black college baseball players reflected the shifting demographics of high school and youth sport. The day of the mul-tisport athlete was largely over by the late twentieth century. As most high

school athletes specialized in one sport to maximize their chances for success, African Americans all but abandoned baseball. In 2009, when baseball writer Allan Simpson compared elite prospects for college basketball,
football, and baseball, he saw stark racial differences. All but one of the
top thirty-two basketball recruits was black, as were eighty-five of the top
one hundred football recruits. But only fifteen African Americans could be
found among baseball's top one hundred prospects. Football and baseball,
Simpson concluded, were mirror opposites when it came to race. "There
is irony in all this," he wrote. "At a time when major league baseball—save
for the current economic crisis that is impacting society as a whole—is
undergoing a period of prosperity like none other in the game's long, rich
history, and is literally awash in cash, more and more African Americans
may indeed be turning to football and basketball because they can't afford
to play baseball." [26]

There was even greater historical irony. Baseball had dominated the
sporting landscape early on because of its economic accessibility. It was the
people's game, played with homemade equipment on streets and empty
lots. During the first half of the twentieth century, baseball was the most
widely embraced pastime in working-class, immigrant, and black neighborhoods. But by the twenty-first century, the organization and finances
of youth baseball in the United States had changed, skewing participation
by class. As fewer children played baseball on their own—particularly in
urban neighborhoods where open spaces were rare—the game gravitated
to more organized and expensive settings. As a result, even fewer African
American boys took it up. And most of those who did received less instruction and had fewer chances to play than children from more affluent
households.

Travel teams make up the top level of youth baseball competition in the
United States. But a study of two thousand twelve- to fourteen-year-old
boys who played on baseball travel teams between 1998 and 2000 revealed
that only 3 percent were African American, even though these teams were
selected from communities where young African Americans made up about
9 percent of the overall youth population. Another study of fourteen hundred players on Midwestern select teams identified fewer than 2 percent of
them as African American. The relative absence of black youth from these

elite teams reflected an economic gap with white youth, who generally could better afford the costs of travel, participation, and instruction.[27]

"Suburban kids who play baseball," *Sports Illustrated*'s Tom Verducci wrote in 2003, "are saturated with practice and games year-round. Parents are doling out up to $5,000 to have their sons play on travel teams with multiple sets of fancy uniforms, up to $500 to attend showcase camps in which they walk away with promotional CD-ROMs of their son and up to $60 an hour once or twice a week in the off-season to have Johnny take private lessons." These suburban youth were disproportionately drawn from white neighborhoods. Although they might have been indistinguishable from black boys in terms of athletic ability, they benefited from more exposure to private lessons, clinics, and coaching. As a result, they became more proficient. They learned how to throw a repertoire of pitches including breaking balls and changeups, lay down a bunt, and execute a double play or hit and run. By practicing these plays, they acquired the muscle memory required to perform them during games.

Baseball players were unlikely to receive this sort of instruction in high school, where baseball has always been a poor stepsister to football and basketball. Instead, baseball players developed in Little League and community-based programs, which depend on family and community support. These programs require adults to organize them and convey the nuances of the game to young players. In areas with less parental and community support for such programs, African American youth turned to football and basketball, where the schools usually covered the costs of play and taught the game.

Few black youth returned to baseball at a later age. Cleveland Indians scouting director DeJon Watson put it bluntly: "We've lost them by age 13."[28] Major League Baseball's Jimmy Lee Solomon agreed: "We basically have lost the connection of a generation where we had kids that not only don't come to our games, but they don't understand the game."[29]

Even black communities with exceptional baseball traditions have witnessed their baseball infrastructure deteriorate. During the 1970s, Belmont Heights in Tampa prepared half a dozen native sons to play in the majors, including Dwight Gooden and Gary Sheffield. Its Little League team reached the Little League World Series four times, multiple youth teams competed in each age group, and the best learned the intricacies of the game from Billy Reed, Hillsborough High School's treasured baseball manager. Daily life revolved around baseball. "We used to play all the time, not just Little League ball," Gooden recalled. Youth organized pickup games against other neighborhoods and watched or listened to ballgames when they weren't playing. "Nothing like that happens anymore," Gooden said. "Nobody's playing." Belmont Heights' leagues are smaller now, its facilities visibly weathered.[30]

Even more importantly, baseball's continuity as part of popular culture ruptured in black communities. "Like the folklore of an ancient tribe," Verducci wrote, "love of baseball is passed down from elders in the form of oral history. Such are the nuances of the game and the subtleties of its requisite hand-eye skills that children rarely come to it naturally and independently—not, say, as jauntily as they learn to fling a ball through a hoop or tuck a football under one arm and feel the wind whistle past their ears as their feet fly over the ground. Baseball needs its elders."

The black community, however, had lost many of these elders. Fewer fathers living with their sons meant less transmission of the game's lore and fundamentals to the next generation of would-be major leaguers. In 1960 three-fourths of all black children lived in households with two parents. By 1978, fewer than half still did. By the twenty-first century, African American children living with just one parent vastly outnumbered those living with both. In households headed by a single woman, median incomes were only a third as much as those of married black couples and lagged households headed by married white couples by even more.[31] While the number of white children living in single-parent households also grew, the increase was not as great. Baseball lost ground there, too, but it retained more of a grip in white communities.

•   •   •

At some point, a cultural divide emerged between African Americans and baseball. This was due not only to baseball's troubled racial past, but the fact that that past was still very much present.

When he took over the players union in 1966, Marvin Miller quickly realized that black and Latino players had no confidence in the organization, which had never had a black representative or pressed a grievance for a black player. Nevertheless, as Dodgers shortstop Maury Wills told him: "The black and Latino ballplayers are especially eager to support this union." They understood the role it could play in erasing discrimination in their industry despite its previous failures to have engaged these issues. So did Miller, who knew the importance of solidarity across racial lines from his experience in the steelworkers union. He pushed for greater minority representation, but it was slow going.[32]

A year before his death in 1971, Jackie Robinson called attention to baseball's tenuous connection to the black community. "Black players have saved baseball, kept baseball on top," he contended, "but I think football and basketball have moved beyond baseball in race relations. In many instances, they hire a man to do a job regardless of his skin color. Baseball is still wallowing around in the 19th century, saying a black can't manage, a black can't go into the front office." Robinson viewed the men running baseball as vindictive. A black player who accepted their dictates would do well. "But if you're a man and you stand on your own two feet, then look out."[33]

Robinson might have been referring to Curt Flood, who had challenged baseball's reserve clause in 1969 by refusing to accept a trade from the Cardinals to the Phillies. The twelve-year veteran was a product of West Oakland, the black neighborhood that had sent almost a score of its sons into the majors, including Frank Robinson and former Cincinnati Reds outfielder Vada Pinson. *Sports Illustrated* had featured Flood in a 1968 cover story titled "Baseball's Best Centerfielder." But Flood was willing to sacrifice the last years of his career and baseball earnings in an effort to gain free agency for major leaguers.

At the December 1969 Players Association meeting, Flood asked for the union's support. Tom Haller, the Giants' representative, noted the rise of black power consciousness and asked: "Are you doing this simply because you're black and you feel that baseball has been discriminatory?" Flood responded: "All the things you say are true and I'd be lying if I told you that as a black man in baseball I hadn't gone through worse times than my white teammates." The changes in consciousness then coursing through the black community had affected him deeply. "But," Flood said, "I want you to know that what I'm doing here I'm doing as a ballplayer, a major-league ballplayer." That was good enough for Haller and the union representatives, who were more aware of the value of organization than most of their teammates.

But baseball ostracized its rebels, particularly its black ones, and few current or former players spoke out for Flood. Jackie Robinson, who testified on Flood's behalf when the Cardinal outfielder's challenge to the reserve clause went to trial, was one exception.[34] Although Flood's efforts were on the behalf of all players, many white players could not separate out the question of race. Nor were most sportswriters outside the black press sympathetic. The *Pittsburgh Courier*'s Bill Nunn Jr., comparing Flood to Muhammad Ali, tennis star Arthur Ashe, and other outspoken black athletes, lauded him for putting principle above personal gain. *Ebony* magazine wrote: "It will be a bit of poetic justice should it turn out that a black man finally brings freedom and democracy to baseball." Flood's case reached the U.S. Supreme Court in 1972, and former Supreme Court justice Arthur Goldberg argued his brief. But Flood lost on a 5–3 decision that hinged largely on the majority's desire not to overturn precedent—earlier court rulings that declared MLB exempt from antitrust laws regarding certain labor practices.[35]

Flood's lawsuit against baseball came at a time when black athletes' political protests were peaking. Ali had been stripped of his heavyweight boxing title in 1967 after refusing induction into the military during the Vietnam War. The following year, baseball players Maury Wills, Roberto Clemente, Rusty Staub, and players of all racial backgrounds refused to compete on the day of Martin Luther King Jr.'s burial. Months later, runners Tommie Smith and John Carlos drew international attention when they raised their fists in the black power salute on the winners' stand after the 200 meters final at the 1968 Mexico City Olympics. But MLB owners resisted changing the sport's racial status quo and the players union had only two nonwhite representatives, Reggie Jackson and Roberto Clemente, when Flood sought its support. To most African Americans, baseball seemed stuck in its traditional, more conservative racial ways.

Despite the fanfare accorded Jackie Robinson decades earlier, baseball had not escaped "the stigma," the *New York Times*'s Brent Staples wrote in 1987, "of having the longest, most persevering history of discrimination" in professional sport.[36] Though Robinson was the most talked about athlete of his time, Major League Baseball had integrated more slowly than either the NFL or NBA. By 1950, thirty-three African Americans had played in the NFL, but only twelve in the majors. While every one of the NFL's twelve teams but the Washington Redskins had integrated by 1952, only six of baseball's sixteen clubs had brought an African American to the big leagues. Every NBA club had at least one black player during the 1955–56 season, something the majors would not achieve until 1959.

Throughout the 1950s, African Americans held a higher percentage of roster spots in the NFL and the NBA than they did in Major League Baseball.[37] What were at first relatively small differences grew exponentially. By 2008, when African Americans comprised 12.3 percent of the U.S. population, about 75 percent of all NBA and 66 percent of all NFL players were black, compared to just 8 percent of major league baseball players. Baseball became a "white" sport in young African Americans' consciousness because that was who they saw featured in the game. As these dynamics played out, black baseball stars faded while black football and especially basketball stars loomed ever larger in popular culture. Baseball continued to lag in its managerial and front-office hiring, too. Northeastern University's Center for the Study of Sport in Society began issuing racial report cards for professional team sports in 1990. In 1992 the NBA received a B- for its managerial hiring practices and the NFL a C, while MLB failed outright. All three leagues received higher grades by the late 1990s, but MLB, with a C, still trailed its peers. While the major leagues had made some amends for past discrimination in hiring, its racial history was difficult to overcome.[38]

It's perhaps little surprise, then, that black attendance trended downward after the excitement of Robinson's debut wore off. One survey of African American attendance at ballgames in the late 1980s estimated that it was below 7 percent. Bowie Kuhn, baseball's commissioner between 1969 and 1984, placed the proportion of black fans even lower, at under 5 percent. In 1987 the Dodgers counted only twenty-five to fifty African Americans among their twenty-seven thousand season-ticket holders. There is little evidence that things have changed since. Although MLB does not track the number of black fans at its games, the Scarborough Sports Marketing group estimates that African Americans make up 8 percent of total attendance. Fans of Latino heritage now outnumber them, comprising 13 percent of ballpark crowds.[39] Meanwhile, the percentages of black fans has been consistently higher in both the NFL and NBA. "It is clear," Brent Staples wrote in the *Times*, "that black fans, after a romance with baseball that began at the turn of the century and flourished throughout the early 1950s, have abandoned the national pastime."[40] Sadly, those words, written in 1987, still ring true today.

As black fans turned away from baseball and toward basketball and football, marketers began following their lead. When Nike and other shoe companies began using black athletes to market their products, they invariably focused on basketball or football players, who had greater visibility and marketing thump. The NBA's Michael Jordan became the new face of the black athlete. It was a nonpolitical visage. Fewer black athletes took unpopular stands. Jordan, for example, refused to endorse African American candidate Harvey Gantt in his tight 1990 North Carolina U.S. Senate race against race-baiting incumbent Jesse Helms. Although Jordan refrained from explaining his apolitical stance, friends and critics alike attributed it to his unwillingness to jeopardize commercial endorsements. Jordan was alleged to have said: "Republicans buy shoes, too."[41] Jordan, according to *Fortune* magazine in 1988, had been responsible for generating $10 billion worth of economic activity in the United States alone. He moved product but lacked the activist sensibilities of Muhammad Ali or Arthur Ashe. While African Americans became ever more visible on the field, they lost their political voice off it.[42]

•   •   •

Not all of the factors diverting African Americans from baseball were negative. African Americans had gained a wider range of sporting options when the nation's colleges and universities began admitting more than token numbers of black student-athletes in the 1950s. Integration was piecemeal and uneven, but even the last bastions of segregated college sport began falling during the 1970s. And as football and basketball at the Division 1 level leapt in popularity, scholarship opportunities for African Americans multiplied. So did the cultural cachet of football and basketball. The same could not be said of baseball.

As the NCAA grew in stature and popularity, it became a de facto farm system for the NFL and NBA. Almost all of the former's workforce and most of the latter's developed as budding pro players while on college scholarship. Though only a few college athletes reach the NFL or NBA, those who did were often highly marketable commodities by the time they arrived. Better yet, they had already appeared frequently in the media; minor league baseball players, on the other hand, lived in obscurity.[43]

As higher education integrated, the balance of athletic power shifted away from the nation's historically black colleges and universities. In the 1970 draft, NFL teams drafted 135 athletes from thirty-one black institutions. The Pittsburgh Steelers won four Super Bowls in the 1970s with major contributions from players from Southern University, Alabama A&M, South Carolina State, Florida A&M, and other black schools. But by the 1980s, many of the best African American prospects began eschewing the black colleges and universities they would have attended in the 1950s and '60s to play for teams in major football conferences. As college sport integrated, the same off-the-field power shift played out as in black baseball. Black schools still turn out pro prospects but fewer than before, and their infrastructure of administrative personnel and coaches has deteriorated. Few African Americans became assistant, associate, or athletic directors at Division 1 schools and even fewer became head football coaches.[44] Even MLB had done better integrating its leadership ranks than the NCAA.

•   •   •

In the twenty-first century, Major League Baseball has thrived as a business but hurt itself in other ways. Its failure to adopt a salary-cap agreement with players, inability to divide revenues among the teams in ways that encourage competitive balance, and foot dragging in addressing the use among players of performance-enhancing drugs have alienated many from the game. Even without these self-inflicted wounds, baseball would have lost its mantle as the national pastime.

Gallup Poll surveys underscore how far baseball has fallen with fans. More popular than football and basketball combined in 1960, baseball trailed football by a substantial margin by 1972 and fell into third place, behind basketball, in the 1990s. In 2009 four times as many Gallup Poll respondents chose football over baseball as their favorite sport to watch. While baseball has gained greater allegiance among women since the early 1950s, it has lost the interest of males, especially younger men who form the prime recruiting grounds for both players and spectators. Since the early 1990s, the number of Americans who said they were not baseball fans has substantially outnumbered those who said they were. According to Gallup's rival, the Harris Poll, pro football thrived among African Americans, with 47 percent calling it their favorite in 2005. Baseball, on the other hand, was an afterthought among African Americans, with only 6 percent naming it their favorite sport.[45]

The bald-faced truth is that baseball now faces too much competition from other team sports, as well as from tennis, golf, NASCAR, and even mixed martial arts, to ever regain its once unrivaled popularity. In a nation of increasingly fractionalized sporting passions, with more and more media outlets catering to those passions, it's safe to say that no sport will ever again exert the all-encompassing grip on the American people that baseball did in its heyday. While that's not necessarily a bad thing, it does signal a larger shift toward a society in which common ground is ever harder to find.

If there is hope for baseball as a vibrant people's game, it will likely be found in burgeoning Hispanic American communities and in the Caribbean, where baseball's humble, often rambunctious, character is still strong. The Hispanic American presence in the United States will continue to grow both in demographic heft and cultural clout. That augurs well for baseball. So does the helter-skelter growth of baseball academies in the Dominican Republic and Venezuela, where the next chapters of the game's history are already being written.

CHAPTER NINE

The Rise of the Academies

On January 6, 1987, a crowd of boys and girls stood outside the eight-foot-high walls of Alfredo Griffin's pastel-blue stucco compound in San Pedro de Macorís, chanting "Reyes! Griffin! Reyes!" It was Three Kings Day, the traditional day of holiday gift giving in the Dominican Republic. Most of the children had been there since dawn, hoping that Griffin, shortstop for the Oakland Athletics during the summer and the hometown Estrellas Orientales in the winter, would give them a glove, bat, or pair of cleated baseball shoes. He did not disappoint, but soon eased his BMW 635Csi down the driveway, taking most of his presents to Consuelo, the nearby sugarcane estate where he grew up.

The previous April, Griffin had been one of nine Dominicans who had played shortstop on the same night in the major leagues. Nobody made much of it at the time; Dominican ballplayers had become commonplace. But those games on April 27, 1986, reflected baseball's new movement to a swelling Dominican beat. Griffin, the American League's Rookie of the Year in 1979 and three-time World Series champion, was known as El Brujo (the magician) for his wizardry on the field and in San Pedro dance halls. His Consuelo compatriot, Cleveland's Julio César Franco, would win the 1991 American League batting title and play until he was forty-nine. And Toronto's Tony Fernández, arguably the most adept of all shortstops then in the majors, was a perennial All-Star and Gold Glove winner. They were the vanguard of a takeover at shortstop, where a dozen

Dominicans had played in the majors and threescore more in the minor leagues that season.

A few months after the 1986 World Series, Griffin, Franco, Fernández, and three other Dominican shortstops—Rafael Santana, Mariano Duncan, and José Uribe—met *Sports Illustrated* writer Steve Wulf on San Pedro's town square. Wulf was there to write about the greatest concentration of shortstops in major league history. Because his story appeared in the magazine's 1987 swimsuit issue—which was shot in the Dominican Republic—it drew an unusually large readership. In it, Wulf called Fernández the best shortstop in baseball and *Listin Diario* sports editor Félix Acosta-Núñez called the Dominican Republic *la Tierra de Mediocampistas* (the Land of Shortstops).[1]

The island republic was on the cusp of remaking major league baseball in its own image. In 1986, a tenth of all major leaguers were Latinos, and Dominicans made up half of the Latin contingent. But an even greater Dominican wave soon began crashing on to baseball America's shores. Twenty years later, when Latinos comprised over a quarter of all major leaguers and almost half of those playing in the minors, the Dominican presence was enormous. It encompassed a tenth of all major leaguers and a third of those in the minors. By the early years of the twenty-first century, they had become the best and best-known players in the game. Pedro Martínez, Vladimir Guerrero, Alex Rodriguez, Albert Pujols, Miguel Tejada, David Ortiz, Manny Ramirez, and Alfonso Soriano led a Dominican contingent that topped one hundred major leaguers and sent a remarkable twelve players to the 2005 All-Star Game.

Unbeknownst to anyone at the time, the 1986 season would come to represent a significant tipping point. Most Dominican major leaguers in 1986 were the byproducts of a rich baseball tradition. But those who arrived afterward were more likely to come out of a burgeoning academy system. The reason behind the shift came during the late 1980s, when Major League Baseball launched an ambitious effort to industrialize its operations on the island. The Dodgers, who decades before had led the way in scooping up black players, now took a similarly bold move in developing Dominican talent. In 1987 they opened Campo Las Palmas, the prototype of the academy system that would eventually restructure baseball's Dominican grass roots. They built it midway between San Pedro and Santo Domingo. While Haitian boys and men toiled in nearby cane fields, dozens of young Dominicans started to train at the Dodgers camp all day, every day in their quest to become major leaguers. Before long, Campo Las Palmas's graduates—Ramón and Pedro Martínez, Raúl Mondesi, Adrián Béltre and many others—were arriving in the United States, primed to play.

Other organizations noticed the Dodgers' strikingly talented new workforce and tried to replicate their mojo. A dozen teams soon opened academies, most also near San Pedro. By the twenty-first century, almost every major league organization and even one from Japan—the Hiroshima Toyo Carp—maintained year-round facilities to house and drill their youngest prospects.

The academies meant that Major League Baseball had established a permanent presence on the island for the first time. Teams could systematize player procurement and development while cultivating players at a fraction of the cost of securing comparable talent in the United States. Few major league investments have ever proved more efficient or productive.

The academies intervened in the physical maturation, training, and socialization of their young charges. Their teams competed in the Dominican Summer League, a rookie league that Major League Baseball initiated in 1985 as a way to evaluate players and avoid limits on the number of U.S. visas. It became baseball's largest professional league. Each spring, its most promising players departed for minor league camps in the United States. The rest saw their professional careers end before they ever left the island.

For their part, the Dominican boys who gathered at academy gates most mornings hoped for a tryout that would bring admission to the dormitory and a signing bonus. Even acceptance for a thirty-day evaluation period had tangible benefits. "Here you get to eat every day," a boy at one academy explained. "That's not always the case at home."[2] If signed, a boy could dream of mind-boggling rewards.

But the academies' viability and Dominican success in baseball were not simply functions of baseball's drive for profits and a country's hunger to survive. The academies and Dominican baseball rested on a deeper

Julio César Franco *(Rob Ruck).*
Date: 1988. Julio César Franco
grew up in Consuelo, a sugarcane mill
town outside San Pedro de Macorís.
During the height of his twenty-
three-year-long major league career,
the hard-hitting infielder and 1991
American League batting champ
returned to Consuelo each winter
and worked out with local boys.

set of sporting traditions. In San Pedro, they revolved around cricket, the black nationalist philosophy known as Garveyism, and collective action in the community and workplace. These practices—not Major League Base-ball's financial blandishments—had created an infrastructure of neighbor-hood and workplace teams where boys developed their talents long before the academies took over.

In 1986, *Sports Illustrated's* Steve Wulf was struck by more than the spectacular play or sheer number of big leaguers who came from the Do-minican Republic, a nation of fewer than 7 million people. He marveled that seven of the nine Dominicans who had played shortstop on that same April evening came from San Pedro de Macorís or a sugarcane mill town nearby. San Pedro was rapidly becoming the most remarkable town in baseball history. On a per capita basis, no other town in the world ever sent more native sons to the major leagues. Fewer than a quarter of a mil-lion people lived in or around San Pedro in 1986, but thirteen of them were major leaguers and many more played in the minors. Within a few years, those numbers had tripled. At one point, the city and its environs became so stacked with talent that if San Pedro could have fielded a major league team itself, it would have included the likes of Pedro Guerrero, César Cedeño, George Bell, Joaquín Andújar, Sammy Sosa, Alfonso Soriano, Robinson Cano, and a stellar batch of infielders.

But even more remarkable were the origins of these Macorísanos. Most were descended from the *cocolos*, the English-, French-, and Dutch-speaking immigrants from the Lesser Antilles who had come to the area to cut cane at the turn of the twentieth century. By creating a community and fashioning more dignified lives amid the bittersweet poverty of the cane fields, the *cocolos* had made San Pedro into a sporting stronghold before Major League Baseball ever invested in the academies. All four Dominicans selected to the 1987 All-Star Game were the grandsons of San Pedro *cocolos*. These boys had not magically stepped out of the cane fields and exchanged machetes for bats. They were the products of a microculture of sporting excellence, a local infrastructure of leagues, coaches, scouts, rivalries, and role models that had encouraged ever larger numbers of boys to join baseball's elite.

• • •

As sugar production driven by booming U.S. demand expanded around San Pedro in the early twentieth century, the mills (called *ingenios* or *centrales*) faced a major problem. With land readily available for subsistence agriculture, few Dominicans were willing to cut cane—backbreaking, low-paying work from dawn to dusk under a harsh tropical sun. Because they could not hire Dominicans, the mostly American-owned mills recruited immigrants from the Lesser Antilles. These seasonal laborers came to cut cane during the harvest and returned home to Nevis, St. Martin, St. Kitts, Tortola, and other small islands afterward. Eventually these workers settled in the *bateys*—clusters of shacks in the fields—and on San Pedro's half-dozen sugar estates. At Consuelo, Angelina, Porvenir, Quisqueya, Cristóbal Colón, and Santa Fe, they lived alongside the families of men who had gained the better jobs inside the grinding mills, where cane was reduced to sugar.

Dark-skinned, English-speaking Protestants, they encountered discrimination at work and in the community. They were disdained by Dominicans, who used the term *cocolos* disparagingly (the word is widely believed to have originated as a mispronunciation of "Tortola," the British Virgin Island from where many of the early migrants came). "They were brought to cut cane on the estates," Roberto Caines said about his parents and their peers, as he sat in the shadow of the *ingenio*'s smokestack in Consuelo in the late 1980s. "But they were scorned. It was a great trial to go to another country. We lived in barracks, four families to a house, with plenty bugs, plenty sickness, and vermin." [3]

But the *cocolos* created a new identity for themselves that emphasized discipline and self-organization, at work and at play. Sport would help them turn *cocolo* from an epithet into a badge of honor by forging an identity in opposition to a frequently hostile host society. Without these community-minded sojourners, Dominican baseball would never have become the best in the western hemisphere.

The sugar estates offered little by way of simple social amenities and almost no economic security. Until after World War II, malaria, dysentery, and leprosy struck frequently; so did accidents in the fields and at the factories. The underpaid laborers put in physically wrenching twelve-hour days during the harvest, when the mills worked around the clock to grind the cane as soon as it was cut in order to maximize its sugar content. But then came a six-month *tiempo muerto*, the dead season, when the cane cutters had no work at all and fell into debt they could not repay until the next harvest.

The *cocolos* were politically powerless, as was everybody else in dictator Rafael Trujillo's fiefdom. But they were doubly lashed by a deep-seated racial antagonism from Dominicans, who were—and still are—profoundly uneasy with their own racial makeup due to their nation's violent and intertwined history with Haiti. Slowly, the *cocolos* were able to advance, becoming mechanics and craftsmen inside the mills. They spoke English, the language of their North American supervisors, and were often better educated than most Dominican farmers and workers.

And they understood the efficacy of collective action. "The only protection they have," reasoned Caines, a veteran mechanic whose parents came from St. Kitts and St. Thomas, "was to unificate (*sic*) with each other." They did so politically, socially, and athletically. "The first school we had here," he explained, "was the one we make in the yard under a tree to teach our children to read and write. And we make societies to care for people when they're sick and make the ceremony and carry them to the burial when they die."[4]

Unlike many Dominicans, for whom blackness was associated with Haiti, these migrants did not denigrate their African heritage. Instead, they embraced their transatlantic past. Blending militant black nationalism with a decidedly British sense of organization and sport, they forged an identity as "the English." It was a Pan-Caribbean identity that transcended their particular islands of origin and helped them cope with their new surroundings.

The *cocolos* became ardent followers of Marcus Garvey, the charismatic Jamaican black nationalist whose emphasis on Pan-African racial pride and self-reliance swept through the western hemisphere during World War I. Like residents of Harlem in New York City and Kingston, Jamaica, thousands of *cocolos* joined Garvey's Universal Negro Improvement Association. The U.S. military targeted the Garveyites during its World War I occupation, arresting and deporting their organizers. Political and labor activism remained dicey during the Trujillo era and was often brutally repressed, but labor organizer Mauricio Báez led cane workers out on strike in 1946.[5]

Báez had worked at the Cristóbal Colón mill and then on San Pedro's docks, where he absorbed the militant politics of seamen and longshoremen. A mesmerizing speaker, the tall, ebony-skinned Báez was not a ballplayer, but his agitation for shorter hours created the conditions for sugar workers to partake more easily in sport. "We just could not play during the grinding season," former millworker Coleridge Mayers remembered on the Santa Fe estate. "A man would go to work at six in the morning and work until six at night. . . . That's why we played in the dead season exclusively."[6]

Báez took advantage of a democratic opening in the region after World War II when Trujillo, noting the demise of dictators in Guatemala and El Salvador, allowed independent voices to be heard. The opening was short-lived, but Báez used it to mobilize millworkers. He also exploited conflicts between Trujillo and sugar-mill owners to win government intervention in the 1946 strikes.[7] Wages were raised and a third shift added, replacing two twelve-hour shifts in the mills with three eight-hour shifts. "That gave us more time and energy to play baseball," Armando Carty, the chief of Consuelo's pattern shop, recalled forty years later. Báez was forced into exile and Trujillo's henchman gunned him down a few years later in Havana. But his legacy could be found in the freedom working people gained to reclaim part of their lives, a freedom they used to play ball.[8]

•   •   •

The *cocolos* were even more successful organizing life on the estates, where they formed benevolent and mutual aid societies. Modeled after British fraternal societies they knew from their own islands, the Excelsius, Energetic, and St. Gabriel associations provided sickness and burial benefits and organized festivities to celebrate holidays.

They also fashioned a sporting life that, in the early twentieth century, revolved around cricket. William Joseph worked as a blacksmith in the Consuelo mill for fifty-one years. "My father came from Antigua to cut cane," he said in the 1980s. "They brought cricket with them from the islands and I learned the game from him. In this estate, we had two cricket clubs, the Ever Jolly and the Energetic, that began—whoooo!—long time ago. . . . After a while, cricket was established in the Republic—wherever there were English to be found, wherever there were *ingenios*." These cricket clubs were similar to the sandlot baseball teams then being organized in the United States.[9]

The players paid dues so that they could send to India or England for cricket gear, made their own uniforms (all white), and played on holidays and during sugar's long dead season. Before the first match of the season, a cornet player and the young women selected as the "queens of the clubs" led a parade through the mill town as the players sang team hymns.

They played the game with propriety and discipline—good British discipline, the older men would make sure to say. They were proud of their play but didn't compare themselves to Barbados, Trinidad, or Jamaica, where cricket was played at a higher level. Nevertheless, former cricket arbiter Sebastían "Basilio" Ferdinand maintained, this was proper cricket.[10]

"We didn't have much then," Roberto Caines recalled. "But though we were not Catholics, we had our trinity. It was Garvey, benevolence, and cricket. The children had sport crafted in them. They were taught that they must not fail or that the color will fail, and the race will be beaten." That the *cocolos* had constructed this pastime on their own—building pitches and organizing teams—lent it more significance. Cricket tied the English on the sugar estates together.[11]

But it succumbed as the children of the immigrants came of age as Dominicans. Nor were new waves of immigrants from the Lesser Antilles arriving to refresh their traditional culture. Trujillo, in his effort to "whiten" the nation, had stifled immigration from darker-skinned locales in the 1930s. The second generation of *cocolos*, meanwhile, grew up with their feet planted in two worlds: they spoke English at home but Spanish at school and, for many, with Dominican in-laws. Although they still played cricket with their fathers, the *cocolos* born on the island also played a new sport—baseball—with their Dominican friends.

Many of the foreigners imported for the 1937 Dominican baseball championship spent time in San Pedro. Coleridge Mayers, then a worker at the Santa Fe sugar mill, caroused with Satchel Paige, Josh Gibson, and Cool Papa Bell at local dance halls, and cheered them on during games. "Gibson could hit that ball from here to the sky," he recalled with excitement decades later, "and nobody ran the base paths like Bell!" Baseball spread like a cane fire among the *cocolos*.[12]

"Baseball overpowered cricket in Consuelo and the other estates," William Joseph reflected. "It was a great loss," he argued. "For many of us, it was our sport. But baseball becomes the English sport here and it almost teaches the same things as cricket did. The English gained acceptance by playing baseball and we found more benefit in it because in cricket we never were paid." Nobody had ever imagined compensation for playing cricket. Winston Richards, who starred for the Golden Arrows, the Porvenir estate team, laughed at the thought: "In fact, we used to pay fifty cents a week to maintain the team ourselves. But by playing cricket, we were keeping our English culture."[13]

Cricket had helped the first generation forge an identity that brought together people from different islands while retaining aspects of the culture that they had carried with them to the Dominican Republic. Baseball, however, helped their children and grandchildren become Dominicans. It was a way into Dominican culture, where excellence in baseball brought acceptance and respect.

Cricket faded as the first generation left the pitch. The Energetic, Ever Jolly, Golden Arrow, and other cricket clubs ceased play, and men like Leopoldo Carty, Albert Reed, and Stanley Norman put away their cricket bats. But their sons, Rico Carty, Alfredo Griffin, Nelson Norman, would pick up bats—baseball bats—and make their way to the majors. By the time that Dominicans Felipe Alou, Juan Marichal, and Manuel Mota arrived in the major leagues, cricket was all but forgotten on the estates. Baseball, though, was expanding with company and government sponsorship. A critical mass of men in the mill towns began teaching it to the next generation with the same hallowed dedication and exacting pride that their father's generation had instructed them in cricket.

•   •   •

If labor activist Mauricio Báez helped create the opening for baseball to flourish by mobilizing cane workers to fight for shorter hours, men like Luis Carty, Roberto Caines, and Austin Jacobo filled in the coaching and infrastructure that would allow boys to develop their talents. A Canadian priest, Father Joseph Ainslie, also played a leading role. Padre José, as he was known in Consuelo, was a member of the social justice–oriented Scarboro Order.

He arrived in Consuelo in March 1947, soon after the consecration of Santa Ana, a white stucco church with a mahogany-beamed ceiling. It was a gift from Ana Rosa Santoni Kilbourne, the wife of the mill's U.S.-born superintendent, who had it built after surviving a plane crash in a nearby field. Ainslie appreciated the lovely new church but was appalled by his congregants' living conditions and discouraged by people's hesitancy to speak out. "I encountered deplorable housing, poor wages, work for only four or five months a year, and moneylending at 20 percent per week," he recalled. "There was absolutely nothing but suffering." Seeking to gain people's confidence, he sponsored a baseball team called Santa Ana. "I had to get a technique, to find a way to introduce myself to that melee . . . and saw the obvious—that they played baseball—that they loved the game. I thought that this would be how I would infiltrate the people." [14]

The ball club, made up mostly of *cocolos*, became the fulcrum for Ainslie's larger agenda: to mobilize for better housing, decent wages, and the formation of a credit union. But surprisingly, as Santa Ana became the best amateur squad in the land, it also elevated the *cocolos'* stature in baseball and boosted their collective self-image.

Padre José entrusted the team to second-generation *cocolos* like Luis Carty and Roberto Caines. As boys, they had formed their own baseball clubs, modeling them after their fathers' cricket teams, paying dues to buy equipment and playing teams from other estates. Santa Ana merged with Agua Dulce, the Consuelo mill's team, and represented Consuelo in the national tournaments that Trujillo's government organized in the 1950s. As its manager, Carty led the club to the regional championship and, after reinforcing its roster with *cocolos* from the Santa Fe and Porvenir estates, the 1957 national amateur title.

When Luis Carty surrendered managerial duties, Roberto Caines and then Pedro González, who had grown up on the Angelina estate and played for MLB's Yankees and Braves, took over. By then Luis's younger cousin, Rico Carty, had emerged as Consuelo's first major league star.

Rico Carty played for Santa Ana before joining the Dominican squad at the 1959 Pan American Games in Chicago. Former Negro League star Horacio Martínez, who had signed Felipe Alou, Juan Marichal, and Manuel Mota, managed the club. Carty handled opposing pitchers with aplomb but was confounded by the contracts that nine major league organizations offered him in Chicago. The naive eighteen-year-old signed them all. After his confused contractual status was resolved, Carty joined the Braves for spring training. Carty, who weighed two hundred pounds and stood well over six feet tall, was no shortstop, but he hit with authority and became the second Dominican to win a batting title, hitting .366 in 1970. Returning each winter to play in the Dominican league, Carty moved from Consuelo to San Pedro, where he anchored what became a ballplayer's enclave. Joaquín Andújar, Alfredo Griffin, George Bell, Mariano Duncan, and other players from the sugar estates eventually bought homes nearby.

By the 1960s, Santa Ana had emerged as a powerhouse. It later fielded a lineup with five young *cocolos* who would play in the majors: Alfredo Griffin, Rafael Ramírez, Rafael Santana, Nelson Norman, and Julio César Franco. All but Norman were among the shortstops that *Sports Illustrated* profiled in 1987.

Though not all of the ballplayers from San Pedro and its mill towns—Consuelo, Angelina, Porvenir, Quisqueya, and Santa Fe—had *cocolo* pedigrees, the best players were disproportionately from the sugar estates with the highest *cocolo* concentrations and the strongest cricket traditions. Alfredo Griffin paid homage to legendary sporting activists Roberto Caines and Austin Jacobo for having "worked and fought hard to have sport in Consuelo." For Griffin, an ethic of respect and a large measure of discipline were essential to the success of so many boys from Consuelo. "It comes from playing cricket," he concluded. In the words of former cricket arbiter Sebastían "Basilio" Ferdinand, "One could say that it is perhaps from the seed of cricket that baseball blossomed." [15]

• • •

San Pedro's long history of community-based sport had much to do with it becoming an unrivaled source of ballplayers during the 1980s. But the subsequent infusion of major league capital turned the harvest of ballplayers into a bumper crop, arguably the country's most important export. MLB's new academies tapped into the fertile baseball culture that had developed throughout the Dominican Republic. Its goal was to turn prospects into major leaguers and to do so as cheaply as possible. By any Major League Baseball metric, the academies have been a resounding success, sending thousands into the major and minor leagues at a fraction of the cost to sign and develop players in the United States.

Scout Epy Guerrero opened the first academy, a small complex north of Santo Domingo, in 1973, and later affiliated it with the Toronto Blue Jays. A spartan facility where boys could concentrate on improving their skills and physiques, Guerrero's academy soon began supplying players to Toronto. If his recruits needed additional motivation to work hard at honing their skills, it could be found nearby, at the Santo Domingo dump, where an army of men, women, and children with rags tied around their faces scavenged for bits of plastic, metal, and cardboard.

Fifteen years after Guerrero's facility opened, Campo Las Palmas elevated the academy system to a remarkable level of efficiency. Though the Dodgers had led the way in acquiring African Americans during the Jackie Robinson era, they lagged the Giants and Pirates in cultivating Caribbean talent. In the 1980s, however, they struck gold with Mexican Fernando Valenzuela.

Mexico had remained outside MLB's gravitational pull since it won agreement by MLB to respect the contracts of players that Mexican teams signed first. Because major league teams needed to purchase a Mexican player's contract before signing him, few Mexicans had appeared in the majors. Nor had teams done much to cultivate Mexican American fans. By 1979, however, the Mexican American community, especially in California, had exploded. Mexican Americans, by far the nation's largest Hispanic group, had been growing steadily since the 1940s and was about to get much bigger during the 1980s. The Dodgers took advantage of these changes after paying the Leones de Yucatán (Yucatán Lions) the relatively large sum of $120,000 for Fernando Valenzuela. The native of Etchohuaquila, a small town in the state of Sonora, was soon in Dodgers Stadium. The portly screwballer with the ungainly windup baffled major league hitters in 1981, winning his first ten decisions and becoming the only pitcher to be named Rookie of the Year and claim the Cy Young Award in the same season. He was also a box-office sensation. Valenzuela instantly converted millions of Mexican Americans into Dodger fans and drew huge crowds whenever he pitched. Latin players made the Dodgers a winner on the field and at the box office, just as African Americans had in the 1950s. By the 1990s, a fifth of all Dodger major and minor leaguers were Latinos, with more and more of them coming from Campo Las Palmas. In 1998 the Dodgers estimated that one out of every eight players from the academy had reached the majors, well above the average for players signed to minor league contracts.[16]

Las Palmas's godfather was an expatriate Cuban named Ralph Avila. Avila had marched toward Havana with Che Guevara during the 1959 Cuban Revolution, but broke with Fidel Castro afterward. He tried to return home with other disaffected Cubans in April 1961 at Playa Girón, the CIA's botched Bay of Pigs invasion that came a few months after John F. Kennedy's inauguration. Rather than topple Castro, the U.S.-backed attack solidified his regime and led to the Cuban missile crisis. In its wake, Avila left politics, returned to baseball, and began working for the Dodgers. Their general manager, Al Campanis, saw great potential in the Dominican Republic and asked Avila to relocate there in the early 1970s.[17]

Avila established a relationship with Licey, the country's oldest team, and sometimes managed the club, whose roster included Dominicans and North Americans from the Dodgers organization. But the Dodgers were signing few Dominican players, and Avila began pushing his club to build an "academy" on the island to cultivate players at younger ages. In the late 1980s he finally persuaded them to invest in his vision. That decision would pay off more than anybody could have expected.

•   •   •

From its opening in 1987, Campo Las Palmas seemed out of place, an expansive first-world, first-class facility sitting nearby the San Isidro Air Force Base, the very place where Juan Marichal and Manuel Mota once played for Ramfis Trujillo's Aviacíon ball club. The boys fortunate enough to gain golden tickets of admission slept in well-kept dormitory quarters with sheets on their bunk beds. Fans overhead cooled their high-ceilinged sleeping quarters; wooden blinds kept out the sun's penetrating rays. They took hot-water showers in the Roy Campanella locker room, played on the Manuel Mota field where balls bounced truly, studied English in the Al Campanis classroom, and ate in the dining hall named after longtime Dodgers manager Tommy Lasorda. All the buildings gleamed in Dodger blue and white, with palm trees scattered about the gated compound. Most of its young residents had never received comparable medical attention, eaten so well, or enjoyed nicer quarters. When not training at baseball, boys studied English and acquired skills that would enable them to adjust more easily to living in the United States while they negotiated the minor leagues. "There is nothing like it in all of the Caribbean," Juan Marichal attested when he visited the facility on July 4, 1987, soon after it opened.[18]

For better and worse, most teams have since emulated the Dodgers. A decade after Las Palmas opened, Pedro González, who directed the Atlanta Braves academy in San Pedro, gauged how much baseball had changed since the 1950s. "We did almost everything on our own when I was coming up," he reflected. No longer. Major League Baseball was ever-present on the estates by the late 1990s. In San Pedro, Estadio Tetelo Vargas was in use all day, every day. "Everywhere you look you find scouts," González said. "They don't miss a boy, and these boys are better prepared than we were. We don't only teach them how to play, we give them lessons in English and try to make the adjustment easier for them when they go to the United States." Though most Dominicans arriving in the late 1990s were neither fluent in English nor fully prepared to navigate a new land, they bore little resemblance to a wide-eyed Felipe Alou who had traveled alone and confused through the Jim Crow South.

The intervention of major league organizations and the chance to earn unthinkable financial rewards feverishly intensified interest in the game. "Every boy grows up with a bat and a ball," González said. "It's the first present a male baby gets in his crib. Everyone that wants the chance to play gets it."[19] The academies became magnets for families seeking to better their lives by sending their sons away so that they could pursue the game with monomaniacal focus and just maybe follow in Sammy Sosa's or Pedro Martínez's footsteps. Sosa, a *cocolo* from Consuelo, signed for $3,500 in 1985. In June 1997 he became the highest-paid Dominican player ever when the Chicago Cubs offered him a five-year, $42.5 million contract. He made more than his original $3,500 signing bonus every time he stepped to the plate. Martínez, from Manoguayabo, a small town on the outskirts of Santo Domingo, had received a $5,000 signing bonus when he joined his older brother Ramón at Campo Las Palmas in 1988. In December 1997, six months after Sosa's contract had broken ground for Dominican ballplayers, Martínez surpassed him by signing a six-year free-agent deal with the Red Sox for $75 million. To most Dominicans, who averaged a bit over $5,000 in annual income, Martínez's wealth was unfathomable.

A woman working as a cook at the St. Louis Cardinals' academy at the time of the Martínez contract announcement spoke candidly about her son, then in his second year of residence there. "Ever since he was seven years old, his entire formation has been shaped on the playing field," she explained. When her son left school after the sixth grade, she did not resist. "I've never been after him to get a job," she continued. "Baseball has been his entire upbringing."[20] The boy was one of many to want to be like Sammy or Pedro, to win the great lottery of baseball fame and fortune. And even if they washed out after two years at an academy, they still had made more money in that time than their parents earned in six or seven years. But they likely had already experienced the best years of their lives. Disappointed and perhaps embarrassed by their failure to make it in baseball, and with minimal education to fall back upon, their long-term prospects were, for the most part, grim.

As of 2010, the academies continued to operate in concert with the Dominican Summer League (DSL), which fielded thirty-seven teams with rosters of thirty-five players each. The academies, Northeastern University anthropologist Alan Klein noted, allowed teams to control every aspect of their young employees' training as well as monitor their lives off the field. The summer league offered an arena in which prospects could be evaluated in competition with each other. Major league teams could sign, develop, and determine a player's fate before he ever left the island, and at bargain prices to boot.[21]

That approach resonated as far away as Japan, where team executives have long studied Major League Baseball and sought every possible competitive and financial edge. In 1990 the Hiroshima Toyo Carp, a chronically underfunded team that could not afford to sign free agents from the United States, joined the prospecting rush for talent and opened an academy outside San Pedro. There, former Cincinnati Reds star César Geronimo trained young Dominicans to play in Japan. "We want to make a good ballplayer," Geronimo said, "but one who thinks like the Japanese." Although Japanese clubs had a long tradition going back to the 1950s of hiring ex–major leaguers, usually men whose careers had already peaked, they found these U.S. imports too expensive. Further, ex–major leaguers often struggled to adapt to the rigorous discipline and training methods of Japanese baseball, and their behavior sometimes affronted their hosts. Young Dominican players were cheaper to sign and could bring power and verve to the Japanese game without jeopardizing its emphasis on *wa*, team harmony.[22]

By 1998, about half of all major league clubs had also opened academies in Venezuela and joined the Venezuelan Summer League. "We're at the point where it's almost prohibitive to participate in the United States draft," explained Houston Astros general manager Gerry Hunsicker, whose team was the first to operate in Venezuela. Between 1989 and 1998, the average signing bonus for a first-round draft pick had increased sevenfold, to

$1.3 million. "For what we'll spend on one high draft pick here, we can run our academy and sign 10 to 12 players a year."[23]

Throughout the Caribbean, the academy system, in concert with the summer leagues, encouraged teams to keep boys for at least two years. The result was that players used that time to get bigger and stronger, and to acquire not only the baseball skills they would need to succeed, but some of the language and sociocultural tools that would ease their transition if they were lucky enough to get a visa to advance to the United States. "After six or seven months at the academy," Juan Marichal said, "they come back and you don't recognize them. They eat, train, and learn the language. When I went to the United States, I can't even say 'glass of water.'"[24]

But most boys don't make it off the island. Rejection is crushing, but at least these boys had received a longer look than many who had been sent to the U.S. minor leagues in earlier times. Before the emergence of the academies and summer leagues, many Latin American youth were signed and brought to the States at age seventeen, or even younger. Lonely, homesick, blitzed by a foreign culture, and competing with U.S. prospects whose physical development dwarfed their own, more than a few cried themselves to sleep. Most were soon released.

Tony Peña's generation did not have the opportunity to mature at an academy before heading northward. Peña was a scrawny teenaged boy from Palo Verde, a banana-plantation town in the Dominican Northwest, when he arrived in the United States in 1976. "I was worried about whether he could take the pounding," Branch B. Rickey, the Pirates' minor league director at the time and the legendary Branch Rickey's grandson, recalled about his young catching prospect. But he saw enough to let Peña stick around. "When God gave me that luck, I decided I was going to work till I break in two pieces," Peña reflected. "My dad always said that no matter how hard a man worked in the fields, he never saw one break in two." Peña's work ethic paid off. For many of Pena's contemporaries, it didn't work out as well.[25]

The academies not only began maximizing a boy's chances by buying him time to develop, they also offered major league organizations a way to circumvent the limited number of visas that the State Department granted for minor leaguers. In the recent past, a foreign player on a major league team's forty-man roster received a P-1 visa (given to individuals "outstanding" in their professions), but foreign-born minor leaguers needed H-2B visas. The H-2B visas permitted them to work on a seasonal basis in the United States before returning home. The number of visas, however, was severely restricted in order to prevent foreign workers from taking jobs that might theoretically go to U.S. citizens. Major League Baseball received about twelve hundred to fourteen hundred visas annually, and distributed them among thirty clubs. Because most organizations had more foreign-born minor leaguers than they had visas, they placed the overflow in leagues based in the Dominican Republic, Venezuela, or Canada, where visas weren't needed. The consequence of all this shuffling around was that major league clubs kept over one thousand players in the Dominican Republic and hundreds more in Venezuela. Pressure finally eased in 2007, when after heavy MLB lobbying, congressional legislation extended the P-1 status to minor leaguers. President George W. Bush, the Texas Rangers' former president and a friend to MLB, signed the bill into law. But by then, the academies had become wildly successful and deeply entrenched.[26]

• • •

Since creating the academies in the late 1980s, major league teams have had little trouble filling them with boys hungry to play professionally. And they cost little to sign and develop. In 1990, as the academy system was still taking shape, teams took on about three hundred Dominican boys, doling out a total of $750,000 in signing bonuses. Most boys received between $2,000 and $5,000, much less than draft picks in the United States, but a relative fortune for many poor Dominican families.[27] Within fifteen years, baseball's costs in the Dominican Republic had risen substantially. By then, about four hundred to five hundred Dominicans signed each year, swelling the ranks of those under contract. As the number of foreign-born players shot up to an all-time high of thirty-five hundred in 2009, so did the total bonus money paid. Signing bonuses for foreign players surpassed $70 million in 2009, with a majority of it going to Dominicans. Many bonuses were for $40,000 to $50,000, with a few standouts surpassing the million-dollar mark. It's no wonder then that an estimated eight hundred thousand boys participate in organized baseball in a nation where the passion for the game is as intense as its poverty.[28]

As the academies have become more advanced, Dominicans have become more sophisticated about the business of baseball. Increasingly, they are better positioned to take advantage of two factors in the player-procurement system. The first is that Latinos were excluded from the amateur draft when it began in 1965, which allowed them to begin their careers as free agents. Free agency provided leverage; boys might benefit from competitive bidding for their services.

The second factor involves the institution of a minimum signing age in 1984. Before then, major league clubs had signed players at younger and younger ages to prevent rivals from snapping up hot prospects. But when Toronto signed thirteen-year-old Jimy Kelly in 1984, the club was roundly criticized for robbing the cradle. Kelly became more famous as the poster boy for reform than for his playing abilities; he was out of baseball before he was twenty-one. But the majors, embarrassed by the incident, decided a minimum age was in order. Henceforth, a boy could only sign with an organization after his seventeenth birthday (or a bit earlier, provided he would turn seventeen during the summer league season).

The combination of free agency plus the seventeen-year-old age requirement encouraged an unfettered, laissez-faire market for players, and the Dominican Republic became baseball's Wild West. Scouts and teams routinely hid young players in order to be the first to sign them when they reached the legal signing age; others signed underaged players and falsified birth certificates because they feared that if they waited until the boys were seventeen they would lose them to competitors. Prospective players could play this game, too, and many older boys lied about their age, claiming that they were younger than they were. They knew that organizations saw less of an upside in older players and paid higher bonuses to younger prospects. As a result, many players, including established major leaguers, aged several years overnight in the wake of 9/11, when U.S. immigration officials began scrutinizing passports and other documents much more closely.

The most infamous case of age deception was that of seventeen-year-old Esmailyn González. The Washington Nationals, seeking to make a splash on the Latin market, signed González, whom they nicknamed Smiley, for $1.4 million in 2006. But Smiley, *Sports Illustrated*'s Melissa Segura revealed in February 2009, was not Esmailyn González; nor was he seventeen. He was twenty-one-year-old Carlos Alvarez Lugo. Esmailyn González was a physically challenged relative of Alvarez's, who seldom left his home in the poor rural village of Pizarrete, where he and Alvarez had been raised. The $1.4 million signing bonus substantially improved the lives of their extended families and others in Pizarette who were complicit in concealing Alvarez's true identity. In the wake of the González scandal, Major League Baseball investigators have found that teachers, principals, municipal officials, and neighbors often collude in identification fraud in the Latin baseball market. As a former investigator told Segura, "There is so much money [in signing bonuses] now that the entire town can be paid off." [29]

• • •

The academies and the Dominican Summer League represented a U.S. beachhead on the island, not a conquest, and intensified the competition for players, driving up bonuses. Meanwhile, the imposition of an age limit in 1984 created a vacuum into which a new breed of baseball entrepreneurs rushed.

Buscar means "to search" or "to look" in Spanish. In baseball parlance, a *buscon* was traditionally a bird dog, someone beating the bushes to flush out prospects for a major league scout. Many of these bird dogs have since evolved into independent operators, taking boys into their homes or housing them in private, non-MLB-affiliated academies. For some young Dominicans, the intervention of a *buscon* in their lives is the best thing that ever happened to them. These *buscones* become surrogate fathers and mentors, providing boys with food, shelter, medical care, and instruction until they reach age seventeen and are eligible to sign. The 10 to 30 percent of the signing bonus that ends up with the *buscon* seems a reasonable trade-off for the *buscon's* speculative investment in a boy's well-being and his efforts to bring the prospective ballplayer to the attention of major league teams. But for some boys, a *buscon* is more like a pimp than a trusted adviser. A *buscon* might steal heavily from the boy, enmesh him in fraud that derails his budding career, or even risk his health by administering "vitamins" that turn out to be veterinary steroids. The *buscones* run the gamut from unscrupulous hustlers to bona fide agents.

Austin Jacobo was a respected sporting activist and scout in Consuelo before he left the country to avoid political repression for his community organizing. His son, Astin Jacobo Jr. (who spells his first name differently than his father), attended college in the United States, but returned to the island in the mid-1990s to improve his own son's chances of playing professionally. He is one of a few hundred Dominicans who run for-profit baseball academies. Jacobo spends about $70,000 a year and employs a staff of coaches, cooks, and groundskeepers to supervise the forty boys who train at his camp in San Pedro de Macorís. Almost thirty of Jacobo's boys have signed contracts with major league organizations and turned over a quarter of their bonuses as compensation for his investment in them.[30]

Jacobo competes with Edgar Mercedes, Moreno Tejeda, Rob Plummer, and upward of a thousand other *buscones*. The Dominican Mercedes represented Miguel Inoa, the six-feet-seven-inch seventeen-year-old pitching prospect who received a record-setting $4.25 million bonus from Oakland in 2008. Mercedes made over a million dollars off Inoa, whom he had trained since Inoa was thirteen. Focusing on top prospects, he often buys players from less-well-connected *buscones* and takes them to his Born to Play Baseball Academy, where he guides their career in hopes of a future payday.

Tejeda and Plummer, meanwhile, represented 2009's richest bonus baby, shortstop Miguel Angel Sano, signed by Minnesota for $3.15 million. Tejeda, a Dominican, cared for Sano and nurtured his abilities. Plummer, a U.S. citizen and University of Virginia law school graduate who began building a Dominican clientele in the mid-1990s, helped create a market for Sano by encouraging different organizations to bid for his services. He steered Sano away from Pittsburgh, where the boy wanted to play because of long-standing ties to the organization, to the slightly-better-paying Minnesota. Dominican boys often find their *buscones* making the decisions that will shape their lives.

Each year, new and better-capitalized *buscones* appear on the scene. In 2009 ex–New York Yankees chairman Steve Swindal, former U.S. ambassador to the Dominican Republic Hans Hertell, and former Yankee vice president of international operations Abel Guerra entered the Dominican market. They opened La Academia de Beisbol Internacional in Boca Chica across from the Yankees' own academy and began hosting talent showcases for major league teams. A privately owned, for-profit academy, it differs from most of the 150 or so other *buscon* operations in two ways: its facilities are on the higher end and its owners are not Dominican nationals.[31] But like everybody else, they're selling island talent.

Critics of the *buscones* point to the all-too-frequent scandals that have plagued the largely unregulated system. They argue that the *buscones* take an unconscionable percentage from boys' signing bonuses and that a few of them have actually collaborated with major league scouts or employees to skim from bonuses.[32] Some *buscones* juice their charges with performance-enhancing drugs before tryouts. A regimen of steroids that allows a boy to throw faster or hit balls farther can result in a significantly higher signing bonus. Once signed, and the steroids' effects dissipate, the boy's velocity might suddenly drop several miles an hour and his fence-rattling line drives become easy outs. A majority of MLB players suspended for banned substances in 2008 and 2009 infamously came from the Dominican Summer League. For their part, many of the boys are often naive about the "vitamins" or "B-12 shots" they are given. Others willingly risk detection or harmful physiological consequences in order to boost their chances at a big payday.[33]

Juan Marichal, however, accepts the *buscones* as a legitimate part of player development. "They've replaced the scouting system and are more of a positive than a negative," he contends. Marichal cautions that excessive coverage of the scandals overlooks how important some *buscones* have been to many poor boys. "They give the boys shoes, bats, food, medicine, cab fare home every day, and pay for their *pensiones* [lodging]," he observes. "They help those kids and should get something back for that. But sometimes, they get nothing for it. Sometimes the *buscones* are the ones who are ripped off."[34]

In 2000 Major League Baseball opened its own office in the Dominican Republic and began requiring teams to upgrade their facilities. The academies built since then have featured major-league-caliber locker and weight rooms. But the major leagues have met resistance in their efforts to bring order to a free-for-all that bears greater resemblance to the chaotic local traffic patterns than an orderly system of rules and regulations. While some *buscones* have legitimized their operations, others continue to game the system.[35]

Major league teams, upset over rising signing bonuses in the Caribbean and eager to boot the business-savvy *buscones* out of the player-procurement system, have discussed expanding the draft. Foreign-born players would lose free-agent status and be able to negotiate only with clubs that draft them. Agents and *buscones*, of course, oppose such a move. They argue that a draft would reduce the financial incentive to develop players and ultimately shrink the supply. Even MLB employees acknowledge that *buscones* have become central to player development and are gatekeepers to the best talent. Some raise the specter of baseball's decline in Puerto Rico.

• • •

During the 1990s, the balance of power in Caribbean baseball shifted ever more toward the Dominican Republic and Venezuela, and away from Puerto Rico. After Puerto Rico was included in the major league draft in 1990, its players became more costly than those from elsewhere in the region. As U.S. citizens (albeit nonvoting ones), Puerto Ricans traveled freely to the United States, and teams didn't need to build academies in Puerto Rico to avoid visa limitations. Interestingly, player development soon lagged in Puerto Rico, while the Dominican and Venezuelan academies and summer leagues became hothouses for growing numbers of ballplayers. During the 2006 season, 146 Dominicans and 70 Venezuelans appeared in the majors, but only 42 Puerto Ricans. Just 21 Puerto Ricans began the 2010 season in the majors, the fewest in a quarter century.[36]

Venezuela, especially, came on strong during the 1990s, with Andrés Reiner leading the way. The Hungarian-born expatriate arrived in Venezuela as a boy in 1946. Although his father had played for the Hungarian national soccer squad, Andrés' soccer career was cut short when he lost a leg in a train accident. When he realized that his prosthetic device would allow him to pitch, he gravitated to baseball. Decades later, he began scouting for the Houston Astros. Reiner, like Cuban Ralph Avila in the Dominican Republic, won respect in his new homeland for his baseball acumen and how he treated players. Recognizing that the stunning downward mobility accompanying Venezuela's economic crisis in the 1980s would make baseball a far more attractive career, he convinced the Astros to invest in Venezuela. He created an academy that became Venezuela's answer to the Dominican Republic's Campo Las Palmas. Reiner's academy soon developed a cluster of major leaguers, including Cy Young–winner Johán Santana, outfielder Bobby Abreu, pitcher Freddy García, and infielder Carlos Guillén, each of whom would be named an All-Star on multiple occasions. By the twenty-first century, Venezuela lagged only the Dominican Republic and the United States in producing major leaguers.

When the Astros deemphasized their involvement in Venezuela in 2005, Reiner left the organization and began working for Tampa Bay, focusing on player development in the Caribbean. Then, relations between Venezuelan president Hugo Chávez and the United States government took a nosedive in the early twenty-first century. These tensions, amid growing instability in Venezuela, have given major league teams pause about their involvement in what baseball scholar Milton Jamail calls baseball's new frontier. Some have shifted resources to the Dominican Republic, sending Venezuelan players to academies there instead. But major league clubs have extracted too many outstanding ballplayers from Venezuela to turn their backs on the country altogether.[37]

Less than a thousand miles away from roiling Venezuela, Cuba has remained on the periphery of major league baseball. A few players who defected from the island have entered the major leagues, but their number remains small. Meanwhile, the U.S. embargo of the island—an artifact of the Cold War—and the unwillingness of politicians to challenge the still strong and angry anti-Castro Cuban lobby have limited sporting exchanges. An MLB-sponsored pair of games between Cubans and the Baltimore Orioles in 1999 did not spark ongoing ties. Though Cuban baseball has suffered from tougher economic conditions on the island since the end of Soviet assistance, the game remains a powerful force for cohesion and identity. Participation in the World Baseball Classic and other international tournaments still fires up the people of Cuba, for whom the game remains the undisputed national pastime. If Cubans were able to play in the United States and freely return to Cuba, their presence in the majors would grow enormously and change baseball on the island. That time may not be far off.

In the Dominican Republic, by contrast, where the business of baseball is the most advanced, the rise of the academies and the emergence of the *buscones* have already reconfigured the playing field. The academy system devastated amateur ball by eliminating many talented young players from its ranks at an early age. Once a *buscon* finds a boy, or the boy finds a *buscon*, he is removed from the pool of amateur players. Boys now train relentlessly to develop the skills they will display at tryouts. As a result, they have less game experience and understanding of how to think ahead of the play. Trevor Gooby, who directs the Pittsburgh Pirates' recently opened Dominican academy, has been impressed by the players' athleticism but surprised by their lack of knowledge, especially how to respond to game situations. But they certainly know how to run, throw, field, bat, and pitch in ways that grab major league scouts' attention.

Many promising young players now eschew amateur Dominican baseball entirely, seeing *buscones* as their fastest route to the pros. But most of them never graduate from the academies to the U.S. minor leagues, much less reach the majors. Upon their release from one organization, they might attempt to find another willing to give them a chance. But they are unlikely to return to the amateur leagues, even though the leagues have liberalized their policies in recent years to accommodate an island full of ex-professionals. The weakening of the amateur system, which had been a focal point of sport at both the community and national level, has paralleled the disastrous impact of Major League Baseball on the Caribbean winter leagues. It's a serious and profound shift in power.

•   •   •

As the grandsons of cane cutters and banana plantation workers triumphed in the major leagues, the baseball world that had created them was undermined by the major leagues. Though the Caribbean leagues would not be dismantled the way that black baseball was after integration, they have keenly felt Major League Baseball's impact since the 1980s. As free agency and salary arbitration fueled explosive salary growth, major league teams sought to protect their investments by contractually barring established players from the winter leagues. Clubs and players alike feared injury or exhaustion. "Perhaps our biggest problem," then Aguilas Cibaeñas general manager Winston Llenas said about Dominican baseball in 1989, "is the lack of desire on the part of the established players to play."[38] Some, like catcher Tony Peña and infielder Miguel Tejada, who were among MLB's better players, routinely defied their clubs. Not to play before his countrymen, Peña once said, would be like slapping them in the face.

Escalating major league salaries were a further disincentive to play winter ball; few Latin players needed to support themselves with two-season schedules. After a five-year-long hiatus, Carlos Beltrán returned to winter play in Puerto Rico in 2005 to ready himself for the inaugural World Baseball Classic. His salary for a full winter season was $29,210; the New York Mets were then paying him more than that for every at-bat.[39] The dearth of top players has undercut winter baseball's formerly unmatched appeal throughout the region. Their absence could not have come at a worse time, as the region has been wracked by several recessions over the last two decades.

By the mid-1990s, winter league fans were no longer seeing the caliber of players who had entertained them through the 1970s. The U.S. players sent to winter ball started coming primarily to develop a pitch, get at-bats, or learn a new position. Winning games for their teams became secondary and many were summoned home midseason. Latin fans, like African Americans before them, lost that feeling that their players were playing for them. Instead, they seemed to be performing for the gringos. Baseball became less about Dominicans or Venezuelans playing before Dominican or Venezuelan fans with a national or Caribbean championship on the line than about player development. The once-proud tradition of winter ball has become just one more batting cage for Major League Baseball to develop its next batch of players.

Winter baseball's slide in the late 1980s reflected a regional relapse as the Caribbean lost much of the ground it had gained since World War II. Its economic crisis resulted from poor exchange rates with the dollar, falling commodity prices, and a globalizing economy in which Caribbean basin countries have slipped backwards. Living standards collapsed and power blackouts in the Dominican Republic became daily affairs. Fans stayed home rather than navigate darkened streets to get to the ballpark, where they had already grown tired of seeing subpar play.

The Dominican Republic's eastern neighbor, Puerto Rico, suffered the greatest winter league reversal. During the 1980s, a new galaxy of Puerto Rican stars had emerged, including a cluster of All-Stars, catcher Benito Santiago, outfielder Ruben Sierra, catcher Sandy Alomar, and his brother, infielder Roberto Alomar. Many of these major leaguers had crafted their skills at Ciudad Deportiva, the sporting city that Roberto Clemente had envisioned before his death and that his widow, Vera, brought to fruition. But in the 1990s, crowds were sparse at winter games. "Shortly after free agency began to bloom," longtime Puerto Rican baseball man Luis Rodriguez-Mayoral said, "even journeymen players began to reap the monetary rewards, and then . . ." He stopped midsentence and threw up his hands in surrender over the declining quality of winter baseball's player pool. The league rebounded in 1996 when its top native players took part in the winter season and Puerto Rico won the Caribbean Series. Attendance set a record, surpassing a million fans. But the league plummeted afterward, and by 2005 attendance had fallen by almost 80 percent. After sixty-nine consecutive seasons, the league suspended play in 2007.[40]

Major League Baseball executives, most of whom had been wary of foreign play, created fall and instructional leagues in Arizona and Florida, and a winter league in Hawaii, as alternatives to the Caribbean. They believed that they could better control their prospects' development in these venues than in the islands or Mexico. U.S. minor leaguers also usually preferred the more familiar language and culture of a domestic league. With government subsidies, winter baseball resumed in Puerto Rico after a one-year absence, and continues uninterrupted in Mexico, Venezuela, and the Dominican Republic. Sadly, its future is not as bright as its past.

EPILOGUE

Estadio Quisqueya, the Dominican Republic's most hallowed ballpark, was nearly deserted and eerily subdued. Just three nights before, on January 12, it had held the biggest crowd in years as primordial foes Licey and Escogido battled for the last spot in the 2010 winter league championship. But earlier that same evening, the ground shook as tectonic plates slipped along the Enriquillo-Plantain Garden fault zone, one of two upon which the entire island of Hispaniola uneasily floats. Port-au-Prince, on the Haitian side of the island, was devastated.

Haiti casts long shadows over the Dominican Republic in the aftermath of the earthquake. The tremors of the Port-au-Prince catcaclysm were also felt in Santo Domingo, where buildings trembled and swayed. But they remained standing, unlike those in the Haitian capital, which collapsed into rubble, suffocating tens of thousands. Hall of Famer Juan Marichal was chatting with his sister and friends on his farm in Los Alcarrizos outside Santo Domingo when the earthquake hit. At first, he thought somebody was kicking his chair; when he stood up, he felt dizzy. "This could have happened to us," he said softly.[1] Nobody will ever be certain as to the death toll, but estimates range as high as 250,000 fatalities.

Despite their twisted and tortured history with Haiti, Dominicans have responded forcefully to the disaster. The refrain *Haití, pobre Haití* echoed frequently on television, in the press, and on the street in the days after the earthquake. For the time being, the earthquake's horrors have conquered Dominican fears of being overwhelmed—again—by Haitians. Hand-wringing over the long-term consequences of refugees pouring into the Dominican Republic, adding to the estimated 1 million Haitians already living there, will return in time. But for the moment, the better parts of the Dominican national character are ascendant.

Unable to contact Haitian president René Préval after the earthquake,

Dominican president Leonel Fernández commandeered a helicopter to fly to Port-au-Prince. Finding President Préval at a police station near the airport, Fernández pledged his nation's support and quickly dispatched rescue workers and medical personnel to Port-au-Prince. All official Dominican festivities were canceled and flags flown at half-mast. Government institutions, the private sector, and neighborhood groups mobilized overnight to save lives and aid survivors. Most Dominicans accepted that their country represented Haiti's lifeline, the only way in during a critical window for relief workers and supplies. Reconstructing Haiti in the long run will require building even stronger relations with the Dominican Republic.[2] Salvation for most Haitians on their side of Hispaniola is hard to conjure; it's too far gone, too ecologically and socially devastated by centuries of abuse by foreign and national elites.

Many years ago, Winston Llenas, then managing the Aguilas ball club, said to me, "Can you imagine what kind of hellhole Haiti must be that Haitians think the Dominican Republic is paradise?" In stark contrast to the now-decimated Port-au-Prince, the Dominican capital city of Santo Domingo has been transformed in the last decade, reflecting the great sophistication, wealth, and creativity that is flourishing there. Flocks of construction cranes crowd one another overhead. But urban squalor and rural privation have not gone away. The Dominican underclass is neither as large nor as desperate as in Haiti, where more than two-thirds of the country's 9 million people subsist on less than $2 a day. But still it numbers in the millions and its prospects are anything but bright.

The Dominican Republic has diverged more and more from Haiti since I first visited the country in 1980. Investments in education, transportation, infrastructure, tourism, and a more transparent democratic culture have paid compounding dividends. So has baseball. Haitians, on the other hand, hardly noticed baseball until U.S. sporting goods factories arrived in the 1970s. At their peak, Port-au-Prince's ten factories produced 20 million baseballs a year, stitched by hand by women making less than a quarter an hour for their labor. But baseball as a game did not catch on, much less displace soccer. In the late 1980s the sporting goods companies decamped for Costa Rica, citing chronic political instability. Baseball has scarcely been seen since. While Haitians growing up in the Dominican Republic play the game, many of them encounter difficulty in making it a career because they so often lack birth documents establishing age and citizenship.

Meanwhile, the Haitian diaspora in the United States, especially in Florida, has gravitated to football. A score of Haitian Americans play in the National Football League, hardly any in Major League Baseball.[3] In the aftermath of the earthquake, several of them spoke forcefully about the need to help the beleaguered country they had left behind. Indianapolis Colts receiver Pierre Garcon wrapped the American Football Conference championship trophy with a Haitian flag following his team's victory over the New York Jets on January 24, 2010, less than two weeks after the earthquake. "I felt like I had to represent Haiti," Garcon said. "There are people out there trapped and dying as we speak, children with legs being amputated. I had to play for them." Garcon not only set an AFC record in the championship game with eleven receptions, he raised several hundred thousand dollars for relief work on the island.[4]

But while baseball hardly matters in Haiti, it has emerged as a major wellspring of lifeblood for the Dominican economy, more so than in any other Caribbean nation. It has pumped billions of dollars into the Dominican Republic, strengthened its sense of national identity, and burnished its image abroad. In addition to hundreds of millions of dollars in salaries paid to Dominican ballplayers, Major League Baseball estimates that its academies annually inject $84 million into the economy and generate over two thousand nonplaying jobs. Several thousand other men and women work for *buscones* or the winter league.

Baseball's impact can be seen on an intimate level in Consuelo, where on a Sunday morning, boys clad in mismatched uniforms sit at attention in a dugout and listen wide-eyed as their manager tells them that Consuelo and neighboring San Pedro de Macorís are the true source of baseball in the republic. He stresses that Consuelo, home to about thirty thousand people, not Santo Domingo, whose population numbers over 2 million, is why Dominican baseball is the best in the world. He names local ballplayers—Julio Franco, Alfredo Griffin, Sammy Sosa, and former All-Star infielder Juan Samuel—and tells the boys that they can follow in the footsteps of such legends. The chances of that are slim, but still it's a better chance than the one they have of following their fathers into the nearby sugar mill. Consuelo's *ingenio* was shuttered several years ago and is unlikely to reopen, costing thousands their livelihood and much of their future.

In the vacuum created by the mill's closure, locals have turned to what remains: baseball. It's about all the town has left, and juvenile leagues fill Consuelo's ball fields, which exist in varying states of disrepair. Scores of Consuelo boys spend their weekdays at the academies. In addition, about ten *buscones* operate programs in Consuelo, recruiting prospects from the juvenile leagues. If sugar once defined Consuelo, now baseball is at the core of its evolving identity and battered economy.

Most Dominicans appreciate baseball for sport's sake or as a profession, but more and more are coming to see the game as a force for national development. Baseball figures in Dominican-sponsored tourist campaigns targeting North Americans as well as in efforts to create jobs and promote growth. President Fernández returned from a European junket in December 2009 with tentative Portuguese and Spanish commitments to build the Juan Marichal Sports Complex, the country's biggest baseball project yet. Whether financing ultimately materializes likely will depend on Europe's own troubled economy. The project's centerpiece is a major refurbishing of Estadio Quisqueya, which will allow the Dominican Republic to be considered as a host country for the World Baseball Classic in 2013. Plans call for several high-rise apartment buildings, a four-star hotel, and a baseball museum to surround the ballpark and rejuvenate adjacent neighborhoods.[5]

Marichal met Fernández in New York City after the president's trip to Europe. The two men rendezvoused at the Public Theater to watch Roger Guenveur Smith's one-man play *Juan and John*, which revolves around the notorious 1965 incident during a heated Giants-Dodgers game, when Marichal attacked John Roseboro. The two men later crafted a friendship far more enduring than their altercation, prompting Smith, who was a boy in Los Angeles that summer of '65, to write the play. When Fernández was a boy living in Manhattan at the same time that Smith was growing up in Los Angeles, his nickname was Marichal. After winning election to the presidency in 1996, he asked the real Marichal to serve as his minister of sport.

Marichal retains a country boy's down-to-earth demeanor despite being feted as a national icon since the 1960s. He was humbled when the president asked to name the complex for him. "What could I say but thank you," he explained. "I am so honored."[6] While a project of this magnitude is small when compared with the costs of developing a ballpark in the United States, where pricetags have routinely run upwards of a billion dollars, it is a significant undertaking for the Dominican Republic.

The Marichal complex reflects a push by Dominicans to gain greater influence over baseball on the island. In the last decade, they have clashed with U.S. interests over the game's ownership, just as Venezuelans and Mexicans have contested for control of baseball in their countries. While the *buscones* tangle with U.S. sports agents over who will represent players, and the Dominican government negotiates the terms of Major League Baseball's engagement in the country, some Dominicans are focusing on reclaiming the island's baseball infrastructure. Among them, Junior Noboa has led the way.

Thirty years ago, Noboa joined the Cleveland Indians organization as a seventeen-year-old. Despite hitting only one home run during his eight major league seasons, Noboa has since had as much impact on Dominican baseball as any league-leading slugger. "When I signed with Cleveland in 1981, there was nothing here," Noboa said. "Major league facilities at that time were really bad."[7] Noboa reasoned that if his country could develop so many players with a mediocre infrastructure, a better system would produce even more. After observing what the Dodgers had achieved at Campo Las Palmas, Noboa resolved to build his own academy.

These days, many in baseball regard Noboa as a visionary. In the mid-1990s he had a hard time finding people to take him seriously, much less bankroll his dream. But after securing a partner willing to invest in his venture, Noboa became the first Dominican to construct an academy and rent it to a major league club. The Arizona Diamondbacks began using the facility he built in Boca Chica in 1997.[8]

A few other Dominican ex–big leaguers—José Rijo, Salomon Torres, and Balvino Galvez—subsequently built their own academies, but Noboa didn't stop with the Diamondbacks complex. Since then, Noboa has built facilities that he rents to the Rockies, Cubs, Twins, Reds, Orioles, Indians, White Sox, and Phillies. The New York Yankees employed him to design and build their complex. So did the Academy, the private, for-profit complex run by ex–New York Yankees vice president Steve Swindal and former U.S. ambassador Hans Hertell. A third of the thirty major league organizations operate their academies at complexes Noboa built, and several more compounds are in the planning stages.

Because of Noboa, a majority of Dominican academies are now tightly clustered outside Boca Chica, a small coastal town near the airport close to both Santo Domingo and San Pedro de Macorís. Their location allows visiting major league scouting directors, coaches, and executives to fly in, evaluate their prospects, stay near the airport or in Santo Domingo, and leave without absorbing much culture shock. The academies' proximity to each other also cuts down on travel time for Dominican Summer League games.

Noboa, who also directs Latin American operations for the Diamond-backs and is the assistant general manager for Escogido in the winter league, leads a company of one hundred employees who maintain and manage the complexes for their major league tenants. He mentors his employees, like Luis Felipe Urueta. After signing when he was seventeen, the Colombian-born Urueta played for a decade in the minor leagues and in Italy. Noboa hired him when he retired, and Urueta has since managed in the Dominican Summer League and worked as the Diamondbacks' Boca Chica field coordinator. Like Noboa, Urueta acquired the bilingual, cosmopolitan facility to tutor the young men who live at the academy and help them succeed beyond the ball field. At the same time, he works with Diamondback executives who are counting on the academy to stock their minor league system and contribute to the major league roster. He personifies what writer Tim Wendel calls the "new face of baseball." [9]

Urueta nods dismissively at the *buscones* who hover near the backstop during a January 2010 tryout. He distrusts most of them, yet acknowledges that the number of prospects who have taken performance-enhancing drugs or lied about their age has been declining. Still, the perception that steroid use and age falsification are endemic has been difficult to overcome. The long-term hope is that the much-battered Dominican brand rebounds.

Major league teams now scrutinize the boys they sign much more carefully, investigating their age and identity and administering physicals to test for drug use. Signing bonuses are not disbursed until a boy has passed these examinations, and the *buscones* who hope to stay in business for long are cleaning up their acts. The reform message is mixed. Dominican third baseman Duanel Jones, for example, signed with the San Francisco Giants in December 2009 and was due a $1.3 million bonus until he failed the club's drug test. The seventeen-year-old's contract was voided and his career was over. But not for long; a few months later, the San Diego Padres and Jones agreed to terms that included a $900,000 bonus. After serving a fifty-game suspension, Jones will receive almost $1 million.[10]

Taking ownership of baseball on the island will require Dominicans to lead the effort to stop abuses in player procurement and development. They can ill afford to wait for Major League Baseball, whose dilatory style of confronting problems allowed age and drug quandaries to fester. But MLB has recently become more proactive, forcing Dominicans to react to their increasingly aggressive posturing. Upset over the growing number of incidents, which cost teams money and embarrassed them greatly, especially when team employees were proven to be complicit in skimming bonuses, MLB commissioner Bud Selig tasked longtime baseball executive Sandy Alderson with revamping its operations in the Dominican Republic.

After Alderson completed a preliminary investigation, MLB floated plans in February 2010 to organize its own youth leagues in the Dominican Republic as an alternative to *buscone* operations. A boy's participation would be contingent on submitting to fingerprinting.[11] Major League Baseball would then have a database to verify the identities and ages of boys its teams might sign. In May 2010 Alderson said that prospects as young as fifteen would be fingerprinted and tested for performance-enhancing drugs before they would be permitted to sign with teams. "Fingerprinting technology will help us [resolve age questions] and lock in their identities," he said. Alderson, who had studied Dominican operations before advocating the new policies, said that the problems were greater than he had realized. "It will require time and hands-on commitment to effect these changes."

Before MLB issued its new policies, Alderson met with a group of Dominican baseball men at the Ministry of Sports in an effort to allay their anxieties. "Everyone's really afraid of him," Edgar Mercedes said afterward. Mercedes, one of the more successful *buscones*, argues that most Dominicans welcomed stiffer drug testing and greater legal enforcement to stop criminal activity that exploits boys and dupes teams. But, he added, "everyone's in a panic mode. People are just saying he's using us to bring in the draft."

Redolent of the British Empire fingerprinting its Indian subjects in the nineteenth century, the identity program will likely affront Dominican sensibilities and could hit stiff resistance as it is implemented. But the draft is a greater worry. When Alderson met with major league scouts at the Embajador Hotel, where parts of *The Godfather* were filmed, hundreds of *buscones* and their young charges protested outside, shouting, "No to the draft!" They understand that a draft would eliminate their leverage to shop their clients to multiple teams in order to extract larger signing bonuses. Alderson acknowledges that expanding the player draft might be his trump card. "If we don't clean up the abuses, I think there's a very strong likelihood there will be a draft," he warned. "But that's not why we're here. I am not a precursor to the draft." [12]

"A draft would kill baseball here," Junior Noboa countered. "Fewer kids would be signed and it would hurt the country." [13] He argued that the *buscones* have become central to player development, and that maintaining good relationships with them is critical to gaining access to the best talent.

Expanding the draft abroad would require MLB to reach agreement with the MLB Players Association—never an easy matter—but many expect it to be a part of negotiations for the next contract, that will begin in December 2011. Whether the Dominican government would cooperate is also unclear, and extending the draft to Venezuela, Mexico, or Nicaragua seems even more problematic. Venezuelan president Hugo Chávez and Nicaraguan president Daniel Ortega, both ardent *fanaticos*, surely will defend their national prerogatives, while Mexico has tightly controlled the destiny of its players ever since the Mexican baseball war ended. Mexicans are unlikely to surrender that hard-won advantage. [14]

Dominicans are not in denial about age and drug problems. Juan Marichal, for one, readily acknowledges that deceit plagues the system. But he is wary of MLB efforts to cut Dominicans out of baseball operations and exert more direct control of young island prospects. "Major League Baseball," Marichal declares, "should do better for baseball in Latin America.

They make so much money here; they should do more and hire good people in each country to advance the good name of baseball." But Marichal is not counting on Major League Baseball to resolve the problems afflicting the Caribbean game. Dominicans, he believes, need to act first. Still, for the time being, MLB has seized the initiative.

Marichal cares the most about the young, often extremely vulnerable, boys seeking to launch careers. He was one of them once and reminisces about Buddy Kerr, his minor league manager for the Michigan City White Caps, who accompanied him and other Latinos and African Americans on a four-day bus ride through the Jim Crow South in 1958. Kerr went with them to the back doors of restaurants to make sure they were fed. "I never forget Buddy Kerr," Marichal says. "He was like our father." Baseball must put the boys first, he argues, like Buddy Kerr did. "If you treat a kid nice, he gives one hundred percent for you on the field and off of it, too. If not . . ."

Marichal understands that he, Felipe Alou, Manuel Mota, and their peers have roles to play in restoring Dominican baseball's integrity. He mentions a younger generation of men—former major leaguers who manage and operate Dominican teams, including Winston Llenas, Junior Noboa, Stanley Javier, and Felix Fermin—who can shape its future. "These are people not just trying to make money but trying to help," he emphasizes.[15]

Marichal believes that the Dominican Republic will produce ever-greater numbers of quality players. He's probably right. The academies are home to over a thousand players enjoying improved nutrition, training, and coaching. Teams are also engaging more seriously in academic efforts. For some, the effort is superficial. But elsewhere, clubs have worked with foundations and nonprofit groups to educate their Dominican players. At the Pittsburgh Pirates' new complex in La Gina, most of the boys in residence enter the academy with an education level anywhere between second and tenth grade. Working with a government-affiliated educational program, the organization seeks to help each attain an eighth- or twelfth-grade diploma before leaving. To that end, the boys attend classes four hours a day, four days a week.

Such efforts make sense from Major League Baseball's perspective. Better-educated boys who can communicate in English will adapt more readily to professional baseball in the United States. But as Trevor Gooby, who directs Pittsburgh's academy, points out, few of them will become major leaguers. The organization, he says, bears a responsibility to help those who will not make the majors better themselves, too.[16]

Educational efforts and regulating the *buscones*, Marichal contends, are crucial. But so is coming to terms with the past. "You don't know how hard I took it when Alex [Rodriguez] and Sammy [Sosa] admitted what they had done." He had believed their denials of steroid use. "When I found out I was wrong about them, it was very hard for me."[17] Everyone, he argues, should speak honestly and completely about what they have done. Major League Baseball, however, has dallied too long to easily overcome the damage it has inflicted upon itself and the game by its head-in-the-sand approach to performance-enhancing drugs. A commission to get at the truth, à la South Africa after apartheid or in Argentina after the end of its military dictatorship, would have helped make amends. But it's probably too late for that now.

• • •

On April 15 each season, every player in the majors wears a uniform with the number 42 to honor Jackie Robinson. In 2010 Gary Matthews Jr. found himself the lone African American on the Mets on Jackie Robinson Day. His teammates included six white Americans, one Hispanic American, three Puerto Ricans, one Cuban, two Japanese, two Mexicans, four Venezuelans, and five Dominicans. "It makes me sad," Matthews said as he reflected on his own experience growing up at the ballpark, the son of major leaguer Gary Matthews, at a time when black players were commonplace. Ironically, the just-released annual study conducted by Central Florida University's Institute for Diversity and Ethics in Sport awarded MLB an A for racial diversity based on the previous season. The Mets' last two managers were African American, and Matthews said that he doubted that his organization intentionally sought to discourage black players from making the roster. But neither have the Mets been especially proactive in cultivating black players and fans. The atrophy of their connection to the black community stands in marked contrast to their efforts to grow their

Latin fan base. After Dominican-born Omar Minaya became their general manager in 2005, he revamped the Mets roster by signing high-profile Latinos like Pedro Martínez and Carlos Beltran. At the same time, the club intensified marketing in the metropolitan region's Hispanic American neighborhoods. As a result, the Mets now estimate that more than 20 percent of their fans are Hispanic.[18]

The Mets are not alone in fielding few black players. African Americans comprised only 9 percent of all major leaguers in 2009. "All cultures bring something different to the game of baseball," Matthews offered. "The African American player, there is a charisma that he brings from his culture. That ingredient adds a little spice to the game. That little spice is missing when we're not participating."[19] Black zest is not about to return anytime soon. Nor is Matthews, who was released by the Mets two months after the event honoring Jackie Robinson.[20] Boosting African American participation in major league baseball would require high-energy efforts of a sort never seen before. The best MLB has going for it in this regard is RBI (Reviving Baseball in Inner Cities).

John Young's major league career lasted only two games, but his impact on the game in recent years has been profound. Since Young, who became a scout after he stopped playing, persuaded gang chieftains in Los Angeles to let him organize RBI in 1989, well over two hundred RBI programs have taken shape in the U.S. and abroad, with about two hundred thousand boys and girls participating. While Young built his first program in a black neighborhood, RBI welcomes youth of all racial backgrounds. More than one hundred RBI participants have been drafted by major league teams; forty or so of them were playing major league or minor league baseball in 2007, including Jimmy Rollins, Dontrelle Willis, C. C. Sabathia, Carl Crawford, B. J. and Justin Upton, and Coco Crisp.

But RBI's goal is more to rebuild the community than refurbish baseball's grass roots. Richard Berlin directs the Harlem RBI program, a community-based organization that seeks to repair the social fabric of black communities by capitalizing on a sense of nostalgia for when that community was healthier and baseball was part of the reason why. Berlin sees baseball's decline as a reflection of many aspects of life that have withered in black communities. In its Harlem neighborhood, an area five blocks

wide by twenty-five blocks long, RBI targets education and social development more than it does the acquisition of baseball skills. But these efforts
might be much too little and much too late.[21]

Back in the Caribbean, community life and parts of the economy still
revolve around baseball. Increasingly proactive Dominican efforts to gain
control of baseball's agenda there illustrate why the fates of African Americans and Latinos, once linked inextricably by the major leagues' color line,
subsequently diverged. After integration, baseball's center of gravity moved
from black communities and the Caribbean to the major leagues. But by
dint of geography and sovereignty, the Caribbean was better able to resist
Major League Baseball's takeover than black America. The region was too
far away for the major leagues to consider building stadiums or operating
leagues there. Nor were major league clubs easily able to comprehend and
deal with its tricky political landscape, hinging as it so often did on complex layers of foreign laws and the machinations of imperious leaders. As
a result, Latinos always owned their venues and teams. Their leagues, unlike the Negro Leagues, did not collapse after integration. Nor did the
all-important wellspring of amateur and semipro baseball in the region dry
up as it did in black neighborhoods in the 1950s and '60s. On the contrary,
Latin baseball prospered in integration's wake. Latin control of teams,
leagues, ballparks, and academies might even expand in coming years. That
sort of ownership in black America, absent for more than half a century, is
unlikely ever to return.

•   •   •

Mercifully, since Jackie Robinson shattered the color line in 1947, baseball
has neither witnessed a push to resegregate nor a xenophobic backlash
against foreign players. Perhaps that's because as players of color spread to
all corners of the majors, fans throughout baseball America began having
black and Latin stars of their own to cheer on to their club's greater glory.
But surely it's also due to the deeply held belief that baseball, at its foundation, is a democratic game, a meritocracy open to all. Racist and nativistic
comments are often heard at ballparks. At the same time, Jackie Robinson
remains baseball's greatest hero and Roberto Clemente, for many, is close
behind. Even amid the current crescendo of intense anti-immigrant at-

tacks in the broader U.S. culture, no voices have called to ban or limit Latinos in major league baseball. Nor is that likely to happen.

For their part, any number of African American and Latino ballplayers have engaged in good works, backed candidates, and supported socially progressive causes in recent years. Some, like Los Angeles Angels outfielder Torii Hunter and Mets general manager Omar Minaya, have done so thoughtfully and with great respect for the past. But ballplayers today rarely take stands that resonate beyond the ballpark. Baseball has no angry men today, no Robinson or Clemente to roar against, for example, the noxious anti-immigrant laws that Arizona passed in April of 2010.

Anger, of course, is harder to summon, much less express, when the average major league salary now tops $3 million. Black and Latino ballplayers no longer burn with the blatant indignities of segregated lodgings on the road and racial disparities in pay. They are among the best-paid players in the game, in fact, accounting for fifteen of the twenty highest salaries in 2010.[22] As a result, most ballplayers are well insulated from social injustice. That these men encounter so few issues in baseball demanding their attention explains some of their political quietude. If anti-immigrant sentiments in the United States, or MLB efforts to control baseball in the Caribbean, become even more contentious, Latin players might join the resistance to these trends. But for African Americans, sport simply does not matter as much socially and politically as it did when baseball was a high-stakes arena for symbolic struggle. One broken link—a relatively new phenomenon in baseball's long history—is that, today, black athletes can find themselves largely cut off from black neighborhoods after they achieve success. In stark contrast, Dominican ballplayers can always go home to the open arms of communities banded together across income levels by the great equalizer of baseball.

The hard truth is that black Americans no longer look to their ballplayers as reverently as Dominicans, Venezuelans, and Puerto Ricans regard their diamond heroes. In Venezuela, the 2005 death of Alfonso "Chico" Carrasquel, a shortstop who became the first Hispanic to appear in an All-Star Game, was remembered with two days of national mourning; Johán Santana's Cy Young Award affirmed the entire country. Dominicans see their ballplayers as treasures, their cherished ambassadors to the world. They still play and watch with infectious joy. It's not the same in black America. Black Americans resurrected baseball's spirit and remade the very way the game was played, but their turn center-stage is over. It's Latino time now.

For the moment, the Great Recession that began in 2008 has put the brakes on the radical corporate makeover of the baseball universe. A deep and prolonged slump in the business of sport might actually free Caribbean baseball to remain truer to its sandlot roots. At the least it's given the Caribbean a small reprieve from baseball's *yanqui* colonizers. Perhaps the Caribbean will avoid the fate endured by baseball in the black community, which lost control of its own sporting life. For over a century, Caribbean players have found renewal in a baseball world of their own, with its own constellation of leagues, teams and trainers, coaches, sports writers and broadcasters, vendors, and—most importantly—fans. It's a rich but fragile world, one where the very kinds of communities that first embraced baseball can still prevail. And if it's lost, the last, best piece of baseball's soul may well go with it.

ACKNOWLEDGMENTS

Raceball began in the spring of 2008 when Beacon Press editor Allison Trzop asked if I would consider bringing together the histories of African Americans and Latinos in baseball in a book focusing on the impact of integration. A few months later, while heading to Sydney, Australia, for the second international Sport, Race, and Ethnicity Conference, I began working on a proposal that Allison shepherded through Beacon. She was the catalyst for this project, and her enthusiasm, deft editing, and provocative analysis have made it a far better book than it would have been otherwise. Like most writers, I had become reconciled to less and less editorial assistance from publishers over the years; Beacon Press was a wonderful counterpoint to these trends.

When I began studying sport thirty years ago, a book like this one would have been impossible to write. The field of sport history was in its infancy. But the work of a cohort of pioneering scholars has changed the realm of possibility. *Raceball* builds on their work as well as earlier projects and collaborations of mine. Daniel Manatt and Bret Granato were my partners on *The Republic of Baseball: Dominican Giants of the American Game*, a PBS documentary about the first generation of Dominicans in the majors. About the time that we were finishing the film, I began working with the Hall of Fame on *¡Viva Baseball!*, a permanent exhibit on the role of Latinos in the game. I joined a group of advisers that included Milton Jamail, Alan Klein, Tim Wendel, and Adrian Burgos, all exceptional scholars. We worked with John Odell, Ted Spencer, Erik Strohl, Jeff Idelson, Tom Schieber, Brad Horn, Lenny DiFranza, Pat Kelly, and Mary Quinn from the Hall of Fame. I was also lucky to work with Bernardo Ruiz and Caroline Waterlow on their *American Experience* documentary *Roberto Clemente*. My great hope is to work again with such talented and simpatico people and have as much fun as I did collaborating with them.

Mark Cohen and Dave Bear, the first to read *Raceball* in draft form, discussed it and much else with me on trips that ranged from the Youghiogheny River to Yosemite. Several colleagues shared their work, thoughts, and passion for sport with me, including Roberto González Echevarría, Neil Lanctot, Michael Lomax, Sean Lahman, Roger Guenveur Smith, Winston Llenas, Juan Marichal, and Rafael Emilio Yunén, the executive director of the Centro Cultural Eduardo León Jimenes, whose 2008 exhibit on Dominican baseball was breathtaking in its historical and aesthetic impact. Kelsey Babik and Hilary Nykwest researched a range of questions for me under the auspices of the University of Pittsburgh's First Experience in Research program. Their work was enormously helpful and provided solid research to back up my analysis.

The History Department at the University of Pittsburgh has been my base camp since I entered its graduate program many years ago. An oasis of camaraderie and intellectual ferment, the department is a place where almost any question can be considered with the help of world-class scholars and graduate students. Its strongest suit might be the study of race, especially in Latin America and the Caribbean, and Reid Andrews, Alejandro de la Fuente, Lara Putnam, Larry Glasco, Rebecca Shumway, and Sy Drescher contributed their insight. Sport draws almost as much attention in the History Department as any other pursuit, and Dick Smethurst, Bernie Hagerty, Janelle Greenberg, and Bill Chase continue to school me on its intricacies. Ted Muller gave the manuscript a penetrating read and conveyed his thoughts over coffee many a morning during the semester with an indefatigable enthusiasm that even allows for the possibility of the Pirates reaching .500. Marcus Rediker championed this book whenever he paused from his life's work, getting Pitt into the Final Four. Marcus made the season's highlight film when the Oakland Zoo turned toward him en masse and chanted for him to stay at Pitt during a win over Villanova. The students in my history of sport classes and my graduate student-teaching assistants (Niklas Frykman, Julien Comte, Dan Bisbee, Johnathan White, and Matt Peterson) grounded my interpretation of these questions. Grace Tomcho, Molly Dennis-Estes, Patty Landon, and Kathy Gibson, the gang of four whose good cheer and grip on reality anchors the History Department, were indispensable.

Most of all, I want to express my gratitude and deep respect to the men and women, some who are no longer alive, who have thoughtfully and patiently answered my questions over the years—individuals like Harold Tinker, Roberto Caines, Mal Goode, Manuel Báez Vargas, Pedro Julio Santana, Cuqui Córdova, Winston Llenas, Felipe Alou, Juan Marichal, Manuel Mota, and Vera Clemente. They helped me understand the story of sport in their communities and why it mattered so much.

Finally, my thanks to Alex Ruck and Maggie Patterson, my son and wife, who make the sun come up each morning.

NOTES

Introduction

1. Tony Anderson, "CC Sabathia Works to Bring More Blacks to Baseball," The Grio, September 1, 2009, www.thegrio.com/2009/09/yankee-pitcher-unhappy-with-number-of-blacks-in-mlb-1 .php. Although over 180 RBI participants have been drafted by major league clubs, the program is unlikely to reverse the larger trends in sport that have pushed African Americans away from baseball.

2. Major League Baseball (MLB) is the corporate entity that resulted from the joining of the National and American Leagues in 1903. It is often referred to as "organized baseball"; "major league baseball" (lowercased) refers to the sport that MLB controls.

3. Determining a player's racial identity is not always a simple matter. The Yankees' Jerry Hairston Jr., for example, was considered an African American in calculating these demographic patterns. But his mother is Mexican, and Hairston competed for Mexico in the World Baseball Classic. Alex Rodriguez and Manny Ramirez were transnational citizens as children, spending part of their lives in the Dominican Republic, the rest in the United States.

4. Marc J. Spears, "NBA on Top of Diversity Game," Black Voices, May 17, 2007, www.blackvoices .com/black_sports/special/_a/nba-on-top-of-diversity-game/20070330152409990002; Travis Reed, "Study: NFL Has Slightly More Latino, Asian Players," August 27, 2008, www.usatoday .com/sports/football/2008-08-27-1555250552_x.htm.

5. ESPN.com, "Sheffield Says Latin Players Easier to Control Than Blacks," June 3, 2007, http:// sports.espn.go.com/mlb/news/story?id=2891875.

6. Nate Penn, "Whack!ipedia," GQ, June 2007; Perez on Sheffield's comments: "That's going to hurt a lot of people," ESPN.com, June 6, 2007, http://sports.espn.go.com/mlb/news /story?id=2893756.

7. Marcus Vanderberg, "Torii Hunter Is Right about Blacks in Baseball," The Grio, March 11, 2010, www.thegrio.com/opinion/why-torii-hunter-was-right-about-blacks-in-baseball.php. Disturbed by the reaction to his comments, Hunter later said that he had chosen his words poorly and that "on the field, we're all brothers." SI.com, March 10, 2010, http://m.si.com/news/to/to/detail /2438783;jsessionid=11419856A17F0031A9F76AE05B062FF0.cnnsi2.

Chapter One: The Gospel of Baseball

1. Quoted in Geoffrey C. Ward, Baseball: An Illustrated History (New York: Knopf: 1994), pp. xvii, 3.

2. Quoted in Harold Seymour, Baseball: The Early Years (New York: Oxford University Press, 1960), pp. 83, 345. As an interesting aside, Dorothy Jane Mills has recently been given credit for coauthoring her husband Harold Seymour's pioneering books on baseball's history. See Alan Schwarz, "Straightening the Record," New York Times, March 6, 2010.

3. Louis A. Pérez Jr., "Between Baseball and Bullfighting: The Quest for Nationality in Cuba, 1868–1898," *Journal of American History* 81, no. 2 (September 1994), pp. 494–95.

4. Roberto González Echevarría, *The Pride of Havana: A History of Cuban Baseball* (New York: Oxford University Press, 1999), p. 90.

5. Pérez, "Between Baseball and Bullfighting," p. 500.

6. Quoted in Pérez, "Between Baseball and Bullfighting," pp. 505–6.

7. Ibid., p. 509.

8. Ibid., pp. 511–12; Adrian Burgos Jr., *Playing America's Game: Baseball, Latinos, and the Color Line* (Berkeley: University of California Press, 2007), p. 31 (cites January 2, 1897, *Sporting Life* article written years after the incident in which this interpretation was raised).

9. Pérez, "Between Baseball and Bullfighting," p. 515.

10. Alejandro de la Fuente, *A Nation For All: Race, Inequality, and Politics in Twentieth-century Cuba* (Chapel Hill: University of North Carolina Press, 2001), p. 23.

11. Louis A. Pérez Jr., *On Becoming Cuban: Identity, Nationality, and Culture* (Chapel Hill: University of North Carolina Press, 1999), pp. 79–80.

12. González Echevarría, *The Pride of Havana*, p. 117.

13. John T. Bethell, "'A Splendid Little War': Harvard and the Commencement of a New World Order," *Harvard Magazine*, November–December 1998, http://harvardmagazine.com/1998/11/war.html.

14. Pérez, *On Becoming Cuban*, p. 248.

15. These efforts abroad anticipated those in the U.S. after World War I, when sport was used to Americanize immigrant laborers and win the hearts and minds of recalcitrant factory workers.

16. González Echevarría, *The Pride of Havana*, p. 127.

17. Ibid., pp. 129–30.

18. Ibid.

19. Organized by Afro-Cuban veterans of the independence struggle in 1908, the Partido Independiente de Color (Independent Party of Color) focused on resolving the new nation's racial inequities. It was banned by the government in 1910. When party activists protested in May 1912, it was savagely repressed. Fuente, *A Nation for All*, pp. 71–77.

20. Cuba's racial paradox, Alejandro de la Fuente argues, was that "under Cuba's racial democracy, blackness was frequently denigrated as atavistic and savage, yet this ideology also called for all Cubans to be equal members of an ideal republic with all and for all." Many Cubans struggled with the contradictions between the ideals of their new republic and its racial realities. Fuente, *A Nation for All*, pp. 14, 52.

21. Fuente, *A Nation for All*, pp. 14, 52.

22. Burgos, *Playing America's Game*, p. 90.

23. Ibid., pp. 96–98.

24. González Echevarría, *The Pride of Havana*, pp. 100, 138.

25. Pedro Julio Santana, interview, June 25, 1988, Santo Domingo.

26. Pérez, "Between Baseball and Bullfighting," p. 514; Gilbert M. Joseph, "Forging the Regional Pastime: Baseball and Class in Yucatán," in Joseph L. Arbena, ed., *Sport and Society in Latin America: Diffusion, Dependency, and the Rise of Mass Culture* (New York: Greenwood Press, 1988), p. 34.

27. Juan Bosch, interview, June 19, 1988, Santo Domingo.

28. Pérez, *On Becoming Cuban*, p. 258.

29. Quoted in Rob Ruck, *The Tropic of Baseball: Baseball in the Dominican Republic*, rev. ed. (Lincoln: University of Nebraska Press, 1998), pp. 27–28.

30. Frederick Douglass, *Narrative of the Life of Frederick Douglass, An American Slave* (New York: New American Library, 1968), pp. 83–84.

31. Michael E. Lomax, *Black Baseball Entrepreneurs, 1860–1901* (Syracuse, NY: Syracuse University Press, 2003), p. xix.

32. Ibid., pp. 23–24.

33. Ibid., pp. 29–30.

34. David L. Fleitz, *Cap Anson: The Grand Old Man of Baseball* (Jefferson, NC: McFarland, 2005), p. 112.

35. Burgos, *Playing America's Game*, p. 61.

36. *Harrisburg Patriot*, June 29, 1989, quoted in Lomax, *Black Baseball Entrepreneurs*, p. 99.

37. Quoted in Harold Seymour, *The People's Game* (New York: Oxford University Press, 1990), p. 15.

38. *Atlanta Constitution*, July 18, 1919; *Pittsburgh Post*, April 4, 1920.

39. Seymour, *The People's Game*, p. 95.

40. Dean Cromwell, *Championship Techniques in Track and Field* (New York: Whittlesey House, 1949), p. 6.

Chapter Two: Blackball's Heyday

1. From the *Freeman*, January 27, 1917, quoted in Janet Bruce, *The Kansas City Monarchs: Champions of Black Baseball* (Lawrence: University Press of Kansas, 1985), p. 13.

2. Bruce, *The Kansas City Monarchs*, pp. 15–24.

3. Quoted in Donn Rogosin, *Invisible Men: Life in Baseball's Negro Leagues* (New York: Atheneum, 1983), p. 33.

4. Rogosin, *Invisible Men*, pp. 12–13.

5. Bruce, *The Kansas City Monarchs*, pp. 62–63; Rogosin, *Invisible Men*, pp. 183–84.

6. Salary figures are sketchy and incomes were skewed in both the Negro Leagues and the major league because star players made much more than other players. Black players were more likely than white players to play ball during the fall and winter to augment their incomes. John B. Holway, *Blackball Stars: Negro League Pioneers* (Westport, CT: Meckler, 1988), p. 6; Robert Gardner and Dennis Shortelle, *The Forgotten Players: The Story of Black Baseball in America* (New York: Walker, 1993), p. 45.

7. Rogosin, *Invisible Men*, pp. 4, 33–35.

8. Laurence Glasco, "The Double Burden: The Black Experience in Pittsburgh," in Samuel P. Hays, ed., *City at the Point: Essays on the Social History of Pittsburgh* (Pittsburgh: University of Pittsburgh Press, 1989), pp. 69–109.

9. Harold Tinker, interview, August 31, 1990, Pittsburgh.

10. Quoted in Glasco, "The Double Burden," p. 76.

11. Monte Irvin, interview, November 4, 1991, Pittsburgh.

12. Mal Goode, interview, February 23, 1991, Pittsburgh.

13. Quoted in Rogosin, *Invisible Men*, p. 104.

14. Gabe Patterson, interview, July 12, 1980, Pittsburgh; Joe "Showboat" Ware, interview, June 28, 1980, Pittsburgh.

15. Ted Page, interview, June 24, 1980, Ashland, KY.

16. Adrian Burgos Jr., *Playing America's Game: Baseball, Latinos, and the Color Line* (Berkeley: University of California Press, 2007), pp. 110–12.

17. *Pittsburgh Courier*, "Posey's Points," April 10, 1937.

18. Burgos, *Playing America's Game*, pp. 112–16, 129–34; Rogosin, *Invisible Men*, pp. 105–6.

19. Ken Belson, "Apples for a Nickel and Plenty of Empty Seats," *New York Times*, January 6, 2009, www.nytimes.com/2009/01/07/sports/baseball/07depression.html.

20. *Life*, June 2, 1941, "Satchel Paige, Negro Ballplayer, Is One of the Best Pitchers in Game."

21. August Wilson, interview, March 19, 1991, Pittsburgh.

22. Goode interview.

23. Clarence Bruce, interview, August 8, 1989, Pittsburgh.

24. John Edgar Wideman, interview, May 9, 1991, Pittsburgh.

25. Bruce, *The Kansas City Monarchs*, p. 45.

26. Ibid., pp. 44–45.

27. Irvin interview.

Chapter Three: A Latin Challenge

1. Manuel Joaquín Báez Vargas, *Pasion Deportiva* (Santo Domingo: Editora Corripio, 1985), pp. 17–25.

2. Manuel Joaquín Báez Vargas, interview, June 26, 1988, Santo Domingo; Rob Ruck, *The Tropic of Baseball: Baseball in the Dominican Republic*, rev. ed. (Lincoln: University of Nebraska Press, 1998), pp. 6–10.

3. Báez Vargas interview; Ruck, *The Tropic of Baseball*, pp. 25–26.

4. Ruck, *The Tropic of Baseball*, p. 27.

5. Pedro Julio Santana, interview, June 25, 1988, Santo Domingo; Báez Vargas interview; Ruck, *The Tropic of Baseball*, pp. 7, 8, 28.

6. Ruck, *The Tropic of Baseball*, p. 12.

7. Santana interview; Ruck, *The Tropic of Baseball*, pp. 13, 18.

8. Satchel Paige, as told to David Lipman, *Maybe I'll Pitch Forever* (New York: Doubleday, 1962), p. 117.

9. Báez Vargas interview.

10. Santana interview.

11. Roberto González Echevarría, *The Pride of Havana: A History of Cuban Baseball* (New York: Oxford University Press, 1999), pp. 204–7, 219–21.

12. González Echevarría, *The Pride of Havana*, pp. 233–34; Milton H. Jamail, *Venezuelan Bust, Baseball Boom: Andres Reiner and Scouting on the New Frontier* (Lincoln: University of Nebraska Press, 2008), pp. 13–15.

13. Ruck, *The Tropic of Baseball*, pp. 41–44. Just days before ordering the execution of rebel leader Augusto César Sandino in 1934, Somoza attended a ball game in Managua with the U.S. am-

bassador, who he later said had agreed to the murder. When Somoza visited Trujillo in 1952, he tossed out the ceremonial first ball at a game in Ciudad Trujillo. Trujillo, wearing a crescent-shaped hat adorned with ostrich plumes, retired to the presidential box. After a few innings, Somoza left him there for a seat behind the dugout, the better to see the game.

14. Ruck, *The Tropic of Baseball*, pp. 45–46.

15. Cuqui Córdova, *Historia de los Leones Rojos del Escogido* (Santo Domingo: Editorial Cañabrava, 1999), pp. 41–48.

16. Ruck, *The Tropic of Baseball*, pp. 38–39; *Pittsburgh Courier*, May 15, 1937.

17. *Pittsburgh Courier*, May 15 and 29, 1937.

18. Donn Rogosin, *Invisible Men: Life in Baseball's Negro Leagues* (New York: Atheneum, 1983), pp. 167; Paige, as told to Lipman, *Maybe I'll Pitch Forever*, pp. 117–20.

19. Ruck, *The Tropic of Baseball*, p. 36.

20. Ibid., pp. 39–40.

21. Layton Revel and Luis Muñoz, "On the Move with Lázaro Salazar," *Black Ball* 2, no. 1 (spring 2009), pp. 68–77.

22. Ruck, *The Tropic of Baseball*, pp. 42–43.

23. *Pittsburgh Courier*, February 25, 1939.

24. For a discussion of Trujillo and the massacre, see Michele Wucker, *Why Cocks Fight: Dominicans, Haitians, and the Struggle for Hispaniola* (New York: Hill and Wang, 1999).

25. Santana interview.

26. González Echevarría, *The Pride of Havana*, p. 145.

27. *Diario de la Marina*, October 1, 1923, quoted in González Echevarría, *The Pride of Havana*, pp. 144–45, 173–74.

28. Revel and Muñoz, "On the Move with Lázaro Salazar," pp. 68–77.

29. González Echevarría, *The Pride of Havana*, pp. 180–84.

30. Ibid., p. 187.

31. John Virtue, *South of the Color Barrier: How Jorge Pasquel and the Mexican League Pushed Baseball toward Racial Integration* (Jefferson, NC: McFarland, 2008), pp. 38, 60–62.

32. Thomas Skidmore and Peter Smith, *Modern Latin America* (New York: Oxford University Press, 1992), p. 236; Virtue, *South of the Color Barrier*, p. 61.

33. Virtue, *South of the Color Barrier*, pp. 74–78, 94.

34. Ibid., p. 95.

35. Ibid., p. 1.

36. Ibid., pp. 1, 86–88.

37. *Pittsburgh Courier*, May 6, 1944.

38. González Echevarría, *The Pride of Havana*, p. 22.

39. Orlando Cepeda, with Herb Fagen, *Baby Bull: From Hardball to Hard Time and Back* (Dallas, TX: Taylor, 1998), p. 2.

40. Luis Tiant and Joe Fitzgerald, *El Tiante: The Luis Tiant Story* (Garden City, NY: Doubleday, 1976), p. 12. Tiant Sr., quoted in Adrian Burgos Jr., *Playing America's Game: Baseball, Latinos, and the Color Line* (Berkeley: University of California Press, 2007), p. 221.

41. Rogosin, *Invisible Men*, p. 174; Virtue, *South of the Color Barrier*, pp. 112–19.

Chapter Four: The Winds of War

1. Brad Snyder's *Beyond the Shadow of the Senators: The Untold Story of the Homestead Grays and the Integration of Baseball* (Chicago: Contemporary Books, 2003) is the best account of Washington, D.C., black baseball.

2. Roberto González Echevarría, *The Pride of Havana: A History of Cuban Baseball* (New York: Oxford University Press, 1999), pp. 46, 268–70; Red Smith (*Philadelphia Record*) is quoted in the *Pittsburgh Courier*, November 3, 1945.

3. Steven A. Reich, ed., *Encyclopedia of the Great Black Migration*, vol. 2 (Westport, CT: Greenwood Press, 2006), p. 551.

4. William Chafe, *The Unfinished Journey: America Since World War II* (New York: Oxford University Press, 1995), pp. 17–22.

5. Reich, ed., *Encyclopedia of the Great Black Migration*, vol. 2, pp. 551–52; Brian Knowlton, "Forgotten Battalion's Last Returns to Beachhead," *New York Times*, June 6, 2009; Chafe, *The Unfinished Journey*, p. 19.

6. Reich, ed., *Encyclopedia of the Great Black Migration*, vol. 2, pp. 551–52; Andrew Wiese, *Places of Their Own: African American Suburbanization in the Twentieth Century* (Chicago: University of Chicago Press, 2004), p. 171.

7. Reich, ed., *Encyclopedia of the Great Black Migration*, vol. 2, p. 880; Constance McLaughlin Green, *The Secret City: A History of Race Relations in the Nation's Capital* (Princeton, NJ: Princeton University Press, 1967), p. 200.

8. August Wilson, interview, March 19, 1991, Pittsburgh.

9. Donn Rogosin, *Invisible Men: Life in Baseball's Negro Leagues* (New York: Atheneum, 1983), p. 100.

10. Snyder, *Beyond the Shadow of the Senators*, pp. 113–47; Rogosin, *Invisible Men*, p. 100.

11. "Negro Leaguers Who Served with the Armed Forces in WWII," Gary Bedingfield's Baseball in Wartime, www.baseballinwartime.com/negro.htm, accessed June 8, 2009; Snyder, *Beyond the Shadow of the Senators*, pp. 155–66.

12. Snyder, *Beyond the Shadow of the Senators*, p. 147.

13. Cum Posey, "Posey's Points," *Pittsburgh Courier*, October 31, 1942, and March 27, 1943.

14. Jules Tygiel, "Black Ball," in John Thorn et al., eds., *Total Baseball* (New York: Total Sports, 1999), p. 501.

15. These critiques can be found on the pages of the black press. Neil Lanctot, in his remarkable study *Negro League Baseball: The Rise and Ruin of a Black Institution* (Philadelphia: University of Pennsylvania Press, 2004), offers the best survey of black baseball's internal problems.

16. Charles D. Chamberlain, *Victory at Home: Manpower and Race in the American South during World War II* (Athens: University of Georgia Press, 2003), p. 155; White quoted in Chafe, *The Unfinished Journey*, p. 29.

17. George Schuyler, "Keeping the Negro in His Place," *American Mercury* 17 (August 1929), pp. 469–76.

18. Green, *The Secret City*, pp. 248–49.

19. Chafe, *The Unfinished Journey*, p. 181.

20. Reich, ed., *Encyclopedia of the Great Black Migration*, vol. 2, pp. 509–11; Green, *The Secret City*, pp. 254–56.

21. *Pittsburgh Courier*, December 20, 1938.

22. Ches Washington, *Pittsburgh Courier*, December 11, 1937.

23. Wendell Smith, *Pittsburgh Courier*, September 2, 1939.

24. Gunnar Myrdal, *An American Dilemma: The Negro Problem and Modern Democracy* (New York: Harper and Row, 1944), p. 1004.

25. Lanctot, *Negro League Baseball*, pp. 232–33.

26. *Pittsburgh Courier*, February 12, 1938, February 19, 1938, October 28, 1939, and August 29, 1942. Benswanger said that Cum Posey had dissuaded him from going through with the tryouts.

27. *Pittsburgh Courier*, July 25, 1942.

28. Ibid.

29. Quoted in Lanctot, *Negro League Baseball*, pp. 240–41.

30. *Pittsburgh Courier*, August 15, 1952, August 22, 1942.

31. Quoted in Lanctot, *Negro League Baseball*, pp. 238–39.

32. Buck Leonard, interview, February 5, 1993, Rocky Mount, NC.

33. *Pittsburgh Courier*, July 25, 1942.

34. "Catholics Call for Fair Play in Major Leagues," *Pittsburgh Courier*, August 15, 1942; *Pittsburgh Courier*, "Pirates' Chief Scout to Handle Epochal Try-outs," August 22, 1942.

35. Lanctot, *Negro League Baseball*, p. 241.

36. Ibid., pp. 245–46.

37. Joe Bostic, *People's Voice*, July 11, 1944, quoted in Jim Reisler, *Black Writers/Black Baseball: An Anthology of Articles from Black Sportswriters Who Covered the Negro Leagues* (Jefferson, NC: McFarland, 1994), pp. 80–81.

38. Wilson quoted in Lanctot, *Negro League Baseball*, p. 253.

39. Rob Ruck, "Sandlot Seasons: Sport in Black Pittsburgh" (PhD thesis, University of Pittsburgh, 1983), pp. 559–62; Simon Gerson, *Pete: The Story of Peter V. Cacchione, New York's First Communist Councilman* (New York: International Publishers, 1976), p. 129.

40. Peter Golenbock, "Men of Conscience," in Joseph Dorinson and Joram Warmund, eds., *Jackie Robinson: Race, Sports, and the American Dream* (Armonk, NY: M. E. Sharpe, 1998), p. 14. Golenbock cites his own conversation with Chandler in 1983. See also Murray Polner, *Branch Rickey: A Biography* (New York: Atheneum, 1982), p. 174. I have not been able to find coverage of this in the *Pittsburgh Courier*.

41. Rob Ruck, *Sandlot Seasons: Sport in Black Pittsburgh* (Champaign: University of Illinois Press, 1987), pp. 174–79.

42. Lanctot, *Negro League Baseball*, pp. 266–70.

43. *Pittsburgh Courier*, May 19, 1945.

44. Ruck, *Sandlot Seasons*, pp. 174–79.

45. *Pittsburgh Courier*, December 29, 1945; Bill Weaver, "The Black Press and the Assault on Professional Baseball's Color Line," *Phylon* 40, no. 4 (winter 1979), p. 307. Racine is quoted in William Simons, "Jackie Robinson and the American Mind," *Journal of Sport History* 12, no. 1 (spring 1985), p. 43; Ferguson is quoted in the *Pittsburgh Courier*, November 3, 1945.

46. Rob Ruck, "Crossing the Color Line," in Lawrence Hogan, ed., *Shades of Glory* (Washington, DC: National Geographic, 2006), p. 338.

47. Jules Tygiel, "The Court-Martial of Jackie Robinson," *American Heritage* 35, no. 5 (August–September 1984), available at www.americanheritage.com/articles/magazine/ah/1984/5/1984_5_34.shtml.

48. Quoted in Lanctot, *Negro League Baseball*, p. 279.

49. Ibid., p. 275.

50. *Pittsburgh Courier*, April 6, 1946.

51. Wendell Smith, *Pittsburgh Courier*, April 27, 1946; Joe Bostic, *People's Voice*, April 27, 1946; Joseph Sheehan, *New York Times*, April 19, 1946.

52. Lanctot, *Negro League Baseball*, pp. 292–93.

53. See *Study of Monopoly Power: Hearings before the Subcommittee on the Study of Monopoly Power of the Committee on the Judiciary*, serial no. 1, part 6, Organized Baseball, 82nd Congress, 1st Session (Washington, DC: Government Printing Office, 1952). The section of the committee report focusing on race is included in Jules Tygiel, ed., *The Jackie Robinson Reader* (New York: Dutton, 1997), pp. 128–33.

54. Buck Leonard, interview, February 5, 1993, Rocky Mount, NC.

55. Lanctot, *Negro League Baseball*, p. 346.

56. Ruck, *Sandlot Seasons*, pp. 182–86; *Pittsburgh Courier*, October 16, 1948.

Chapter Five: Integration's Curse

1. William Nack, *Sports Illustrated*, May 5, 1997; Wendell Smith, *Pittsburgh Courier*, May 24, 1947; Jonathan Eig, *Opening Day: The Story of Jackie Robinson's First Season* (New York: Simon & Schuster, 2007), pp. 166–67. Nineteen of Robinson's steals were during the regular season; the other was during the 1955 World Series.

2. National League teams averaged sixty stolen bases in 1946; that number was up to seventy-four per team in 1966, after the league had been substantially integrated. Martin Johnson, "The Speed to Steal," The Root, June 12, 2009, www.theroot.com/views/speed-steal; Jackie Robinson, as told to Alfred Duckett, *I Never Had It Made: An Autobiography* (Hopewell, NJ: Ecco, 1995), p. 67.

3. Mal Goode, interview, February 23, 1991, Pittsburgh.

4. The *New York Sun* article ran May 1, 1947; Jimmy Cannon, *New York Post*, May 10, 1947, quoted in Jules Tygiel, "Jackie Robinson," in Patrick B. Miller and David K. Wiggins, eds., *Sport and the Color Line: Black Athletes and Race Relations in Twentieth-Century America* (New York: Routledge, 2004), p. 173.

5. John Crosby, *Syracuse Herald*, November 12, 1972; Durocher quoted in Tygiel, "Jackie Robinson," p. 174; Roger Kahn, *The Boys of Summer* (New York: Harper & Row, 1972), p. 358; William Nack, "17 Days in May," *Sports Illustrated*, May 5, 1997.

6. Goode interview.

7. Jules Tygiel, *Baseball's Great Experiment: Jackie Robinson and His Legacy* (New York: Oxford University Press, 1983).

8. Harold Parrott, *The Lords of Baseball* (New York: Praeger, 1976), p. 194, quoted in Jules Tygiel, "Jackie Robinson," p. 168.

9. Jackie Robinson, *I Never Had It Made*, quoted in Tygiel, "Jackie Robinson," p. 169.

10. Harold Parrott, "The Betrayal of Robinson," in Jules Tygiel, ed. *The Jackie Robinson Reader* (New York: Dutton, 1997), p. 138.

11. David Falkner, *Great Time Coming: The Life of Jackie Robinson, from Baseball to Birmingham* (New York: Simon & Schuster, 1995), p. 175, places this meeting later in the season.

12. Wendell Smith, *Pittsburgh Courier*, May 24, 1947; Associated Press, *New York Times*, May 18, 1947; Jackie Robinson, "Why I'm Quitting Baseball," in Tygiel, ed., *The Jackie Robinson Reader*, p. 217.

13. Tygiel, "Jackie Robinson," p. 185.

14. Joseph Dorinson and Joram Warmund, eds., *Jackie Robinson: Race, Sports, and the American Dream* (Armonk, NY: M. E. Sharpe, 1988), pp. 184–85.

15. Jenkins was born in Chatham, Ontario, a Canadian town largely populated by African Americans fleeing the United States after the imposition of the Fugitive Slave Act in 1850.

16. *New York World-Telegram and Sun*, July 25, 1949, quoted in Jules Tygiel, *Baseball's Great Experiment: Jackie Robinson and His Legacy*, rev. ed. (New York: Oxford University Press, 1997), p. 335.

17. Quoted in Geoffrey C. Ward, *Baseball: An Illustrated History* (New York: Knopf, 1994), p. 293.

18. Monte Irvin, interview, November 4, 1991, Pittsburgh.

19. Harold Tinker, interview, August 31, 1990, Pittsburgh.

20. Irvin interview.

21. George Vecsey, "Ray Dandridge, the Hall of Fame and Fences," *New York Times*, May 10, 1987.

22. Rob Ruck, "Raymond Dandridge," in David L. Porter, ed., *Biographical Dictionary of American Sports: Baseball* (New York: Greenwood Press, 1987), pp. 132–33.

23. Tygiel, *Baseball's Great Experiment*, p. 232.

24. The Campanis incident is discussed in chapter 8.

25. *Boston Chronicle*, quoted in Tygiel, *Baseball's Great Experiment*, p. 178.

26. Will quoted in Sol Gittleman, "The Fuse That Lit the Fire," *Tufts Journal*, June 10, 2009, http://tuftsjournal.tufts.edu/2009/06_1/corner/01/. Gaston quoted in Howie Rumberg, "Now Honoring No. 42: Jackie Robinson Saluted on Anniversary of Breaking MLB's Color Barrier," *Sports News*, April 15, 2010, http://blog.taragana.com/sports/2010/04/15/now-honoring-no -42-jackie-robinson-saluted-on-anniversary-of-breaking-mlbs-color-barrier-94050/.

27. George Will, *Bunts: Curt Flood, Camden Yards, Pete Rose, and Other Reflections on Baseball* (New York: Scribner, 1998), p. 87.

28. Roy Wilkins, *Michigan Chronicle*, November 3, 1945, quoted in Bill Weaver, "The Black Press and the Assault on Professional Baseball's Color Line," *Phylon* 40, no. 4 (winter 1979), p. 307.

29. Manning Marable, *Race, Reform and Rebellion: The Second Reconstruction in Black America, 1945–1982* (Jackson: University Press of Mississippi, 1984), pp. 13–25.

30. Goode interview.

31. *Pittsburgh Courier*, October 1, 1955.

32. Dr. Jake Milliones, interview, November 18, 1991, Pittsburgh; Robert Curvin, "Remembering Jackie Robinson," *New York Times Magazine*, April 4, 1982, p. 46.

33. Quoted in Arnold Rampersad, *Jackie Robinson: A Biography* (New York: Alfred A. Knopf, 1997), p. 179.

34. John Edgar Wideman, interview, May 9, 1991, Pittsburgh.

35. Goode interview.

36. August Wilson, interview, March 19, 1991, Pittsburgh.

37. Wideman interview.

38. Wilson interview.

39. Neil Lanctot, *Negro League Baseball: The Rise and Ruin of a Black Institution* (Philadelphia: University of Pennsylvania Press, 2004), p. 392.

40. John Holway, interview, September 1, 1991, Pittsburgh.

Chapter Six: *¡Viva México!*

1. Quincy Trouppe, *20 Years Too Soon* (Los Angeles: S and S Enterprises, 1977), pp. 143–45; Donn Rogosin, *Invisible Men: Life in Baseball's Negro Leagues* (New York: Atheneum, 1983), p. 174; John Virtue, *South of the Color Barrier: How Jorge Pasquel and the Mexican League Pushed Baseball toward Racial Integration* (Jefferson, NC: McFarland, 2008), pp. 112–19; *Pittsburgh Courier*, July 17, 1943, July 31, 1943.

2. Virtue, *South of the Color Barrier*, pp. 131–33.

3. To avenge the first attack on U.S. territory since 1812, General John "Black Jack" Pershing led thousands of troops in pursuit of Villa, chasing him into the Sierra Nevada. Eleven months later, they came back empty-handed.

4. Shirley Povich, *Washington Post*, March 10, 1946.

5. Ibid. See also Roberto González Echevarría, *The Pride of Havana: A History of Cuban Baseball* (New York: Oxford University Press, 1999), pp. 293–98.

6. Shirley Povich, *Washington Post*, March 12 and March 18, 1946.

7. *New York Times*, April 17, 1946.

8. González Echevarría, *The Pride of Havana*, p. 22.

9. *New York Times*, March 22, 1946.

10. Kyle Crichton, "Hot Tamale Circuit," part 1, *Collier's*, June 22, 1946, pp. 17, 62.

11. Jerry Hannifin, *Washington Post*, April 14, 1946.

12. Shirley Povich, *Washington Post*, April 3, 1946; Arthur Daley, *New York Times*, April 3, 1946.

13. Crichton, "Hot Tamale Circuit," pp. 62–63.

14. Virtue, *South of the Color Barrier*, p. 118.

15. *New York Times*, April 18, 1946; *Washington Post*, April 20, 1946.

16. *Life*, June 24, 1946, p. 121.

17. Milton Bracker, *Saturday Evening Post*, March 8, 1947, p. 145.

18. *New York Times*, June 22, 1946.

19. Ray Gillespie, "'O. B. Getting Dose of Own Medicine'—Pasquel," the *Sporting News*, February 28, 1946, quoted in Virtue, *South of the Color Barrier*, p. 134.

20. Virtue, *South of the Color Barrier*, pp. 162–63.

21. Shirley Povich, *Washington Post*, April 13, 1946; John Lardner, "Baseball's Big Bamboozle," *Sport*, May 1967, p. 79.

22. Crichton, "Hot Tamale Circuit," pp. 17, 63.

23. Povich, *Washington Post*, April 13, 1946. Ironically, Rickey and Griffith, who themselves shamelessly exploited the Negro Leagues and Cuba for profits and players, were among the owners goading Chandler to come down hard on jumpers.

24. *New York Times*, March 10, 1946.

25. Crichton, "Hot Tamale Circuit," p. 71.

26. *Life*, June 24, 1946.
27. Crichton, "Hot Tamale Circuit," pp. 17, 63.
28. *New York Times*, April 4, 1946.
29. *New York Times*, May 17, 1946.
30. Crichton, "Hot Tamale Circuit," p. 70.
31. *New York Times*, May 17 and May 22, 1946.
32. Milton Bracker, *New York Times*, May 16, 1946.
33. Téodulo Manuel Agundis, *El verdadero Jorge Pasquel* (México: Atenea Gráfica, 1956), p. 170, quoted in Virtue, *South of the Color Barrier*, p. 145.
34. Bus Ham, *Washington Post*, April 12, 1946.
35. Shirley Povich, *Washington Post*, April 13, 1946.
36. *Study of Monopoly Power: Hearings before the Subcommittee on the Study of Monopoly Power of the Committee on the Judiciary*, serial no. 1, part 6, Organized Baseball, 82nd Congress, 1st Session (Washington DC: Government Printing Office, 1952), p. 475.
37. *Study of Monopoly Power*, pp. 479–83.
38. *Study of Monopoly Power*, pp. 480–81.
39. *New York Times*, August 3, 1946.
40. *New York Times*, December 13, 1946.
41. *Study of Monopoly Power*, pp. 480–81.
42. *Washington Post*, April 15, 1946; Virtue, *South of the Color Barrier*, pp. 150–51.
43. *New York Times*, August 11, 1946.
44. Adrian Burgos Jr., *Playing America's Game: Baseball, Latinos, and the Color Line* (Berkeley: University of California Press, 2007), p. 175.
45. *New York Times*, August 5 and August 29, 1946.
46. González Echevarría, *The Pride of Havana*, pp. 14–18.
47. *Sporting News*, January 27, 1947.
48. This policy would be revised in the early 1950s, to the delight of Cuban fans.
49. Milton Bracker, *New York Times*, December 16, 1946.
50. Virtue, *South of the Color Barrier*, pp. 183–84.
51. Ibid., p. 162.
52. Crichton, "Hot Tamale Circuit," p. 71.
53. Frank Graham Jr., "The Great Mexican War of 1946," *Sports Illustrated*, September 19, 1966, p. 126.
54. *Washington Post*, February 24, 1947; *New York Times*, February 20, 1947; *New York Times*, March 12, 1947.
55. Jules Tygiel, *Baseball's Great Experiment: Jackie Robinson and His Legacy* (New York: Oxford University Press, 1997), pp. 165–66.
56. Roscoe McGovern, *New York Times*, February 26, 1947.
57. Virtue, *South of the Color Barrier*, pp. 183–95.
58. Ibid., pp. 186.
59. *New York Times*, October 29, 1947.
60. *New York Times*, January 22, 1948.

61. *New York Times*, January 28, 1948, and February 3 and February 4, 1948.

62. *New York Times*, September 21, 1948, and October 30, 1948.

63. Graham, "The Great Mexican War of 1946," p. 129.

64. Virtue, *South of the Color Barrier*, pp. 188–90; Rickey quoted in Lee Lowenfish, *Branch Rickey: Baseball's Ferocious Gentleman* (Lincoln: University of Nebraska Press, 2007), p. 488.

Chapter Seven: New Caribbean Currents

1. *New York Daily News*, July 20, 1972, quoted in Jules Tygiel, *Baseball's Great Experiment: Jackie Robinson and His Legacy* (New York: Oxford University Press, 1997), p. 343.

2. David Falkner, *Great Time Coming: The Life of Jackie Robinson, from Baseball to Birmingham* (New York: Simon & Schuster, 1995), pp. 120–21; John Holway, *Black Diamonds: Life in the Negro Leagues from the Men Who Lived It* (Westport, CT: Meckler, 1989), p. 73.

3. Orlando Cepeda with Herb Fagen, *Baby Bull: From Hardball to Hard Time and Back* (Dallas, TX: Taylor, 1998), pp. 11–12.

4. *The Republic of Baseball: Dominican Giants of the American Game*, documentary film directed by Dan Manatt, written by Manatt and Rob Ruck (Manatt Media LLC, 2006). Quotes in this chapter attributed to Felipe Alou are from this source unless stated otherwise.

5. Samuel Regalado, *Viva Baseball: Latin Major Leaguers and Their Special Hunger* (Urbana: University of Illinois Press, 1998), pp. 7, 40, 117. The statistics tracking the changing demographics of major league baseball are not very precise. They gauge the number of players of a particular grouping who appeared in the majors that season but do not differentiate between those who played briefly and those who were with a club the entire season.

6. Myron Cope, *Sports Illustrated*, March 7, 1966.

7. David Maraniss, *Clemente: The Passion and Grace of Baseball's Last Hero* (New York: Simon & Schuster, 2006), p. 57.

8. C. Vann Woodward, *The Strange Career of Jim Crow*, rev. ed. (New York: Oxford University Press, 1979), pp. 165–66.

9. Manuel Mota, interview, January 14, 2001, Santo Domingo.

10. Rob Ruck, *The Tropic of Baseball: Baseball in the Dominican Republic*, rev. ed. (Lincoln: University of Nebraska Press, 1998).

11. Ruck, *The Tropic of Baseball*, p. 73.

12. Mota interview.

13. Mays, Cepeda, and Alou quoted in Manatt and Ruck, *The Republic of Baseball*.

14. Manatt and Ruck, *The Republic of Baseball*. Quotes in this chapter attributed to Juan Marichal are from this source unless stated otherwise.

15. Quoted in Manatt and Ruck, *The Republic of Baseball*.

16. Juan Marichal, with Charles Einstein, *A Pitcher's Story* (Garden City, NY: Doubleday, 1967), pp. 62–63; Ruck, *The Tropic of Baseball*, p. 82.

17. Manatt and Ruck, *The Republic of Baseball*.

18. David Maraniss, *Clemente*, pp. 160–62.

19. Manatt and Ruck, *The Republic of Baseball*.

20. Roberto González Echevarría, *The Pride of Havana: A History of Cuban Baseball* (New York: Oxford University Press, 1999), p. 345.

21. Ibid., pp. 346–47.

22. Ruck, *The Tropic of Baseball*, pp. 108–9.

23. Felipe Alou, with Herm Weiskopf, *Felipe Alou: My Life and Baseball* (Waco, TX: World Books, 1967), pp. 59–60.

24. Alou, with Weiskopf, *Felipe Alou*, pp. 119–20; Felipe Alou, with Arnold Hano, "Latin-American Ballplayers Need a Bill of Rights," *Sport*, November 1963, pp. 21, 76–79.

25. *New York Times*, "Big-League Stars Play Here," October 12, 1963; William J. Biordy, "Latin All-Stars Paced by McBean," *New York Times*, October 13, 1963.

26. Alou, with Hano, "Latin-American Ballplayers Need a Bill of Rights."

27. Manatt and Ruck, *The Republic of Baseball*.

28. Stan Isaacs, *Newsday*, July 23, 1964.

29. *New York Times*, August 4, 5, 6, 1964; *Time*, August 14, 1964.

30. Bob Broeg, *St. Louis Post-Dispatch*, quoted in Larry R. Gerlach, "Crime and Punishment: The Marichal-Roseboro Incident," *Nine: A Journal of Baseball History and Culture* 12, no. 2 (spring 2004), p. 12. Gerlach's judiciously analyzed and well-researched article is the best account of the incident and its consequences.

31. Dick Young, *New York Daily News*, August 26, 1965, quoted in Gerlach, "Crime and Punishment," pp. 11–12.

32. *Sporting News* quoted in Adrian Burgos Jr., *Playing America's Game: Baseball, Latinos, and the Color Line* (Berkeley: University of California Press, 2007), p. 225.

33. Jim Brosnan, *Life*, October 10, 1960, p. 174; Myron Cope, *Sports Illustrated*, March 7, 1966.

34. Kal Wagenheim, *Clemente!* (Chicago: Olmstead, 2001; orig. published 1974), p. 71; Cope, *Sports Illustrated*, March 7, 1966.

35. Quoted in Cope, *Sports Illustrated*, March 7, 1966.

36. Campbell J. Gibson and Emily Lennon, "Historical Census Statistics on the Foreign-born Population of the United States, 1850–1990" (Washington, DC: U.S. Census Bureau, February 1999), www.census.gov/population/www/documentation/twps0029/twps0029.html.

37. Quoted in Bernardo Ruiz, *American Experience: Roberto Clemente*, DVD (PBS Home Video, 2007).

38. Howard Kohn, *Sport*, quoted in Wagenheim, *Clemente!* pp. 82–83.

39. Quoted in Ruiz, *American Experience: Roberto Clemente*.

40. Cope, *Sports Illustrated*, March 7, 1966.

41. Wagenheim, *Clemente!* pp. 135–52.

42. Ruiz, *American Experience: Roberto Clemente*; Wagenheim, *Clemente!* p. 171.

43. Rob Ruck, "Remembering Roberto Clemente," *Pittsburgh*, December 1972, pp. 40–41.

Chapter Eight: Whiteout

1. Eric Johnson, "*Nightline* Classic: Al Campanis," April 12, 2007, http://abcnews.go.com/Nightline/ESPNSports/story?id=3034914.

2. Steve Springer, "April 6, 1987: The Nightline That Rocked Baseball," *Los Angeles Times*, April 6, 1997, http://articles.latimes.com/1997-04-06/sports/sp-46070_1_league-baseball.

3. Peter Gammons, "The Campanis Affair," *Sports Illustrated*, April 20, 1987; Richard Goldstein, "Al Campanis Is Dead at 81," *New York Times*, June 22, 1998.

4. Gammons, "The Campanis Affair."

5. Reggie Jackson, "We Have a Serious Problem That Isn't Going Away," *Sports Illustrated*, May 11, 1987.

6. Jules Tygiel, *Baseball's Great Experiment: Jackie Robinson and His Legacy* (New York: Oxford University Press, 1997), p. 508.

7. Gerald W. Scully, *The Business of Major League Baseball* (Chicago: University of Chicago Press, 1989), p. 172; Michael Martinez, "Baseball's Upswing in Minority Hiring Is Followed by Clash of Interpretations," *New York Times*, April 6, 1988.

8. John Steinbreder, "Let's Make A Statement," *Sports Illustrated*, November 21, 1988.

9. Doron P. Levin, "Pittsburgh Recalls a Neglected Title," *New York Times*, September 12, 1988.

10. A disclaimer: I worked with the Pirates on the 1988 event honoring the Negro Leagues, received financial backing for a 1993 documentary film I wrote and directed, *Kings on the Hill: Baseball's Forgotten Men* (San Pedro Productions), which MLB distributed with study guides to a few thousand schools, and worked with the Pirates again on Legacy Square, their installation at PNC Park honoring the Negro Leagues.

11. Springer, "The Nightline That Rocked Baseball."

12. "Ex-Dodgers GM Campanis Dead at 81," CNN/SportsIllustrated.com, June 21, 1998, http://sports illustrated.cnn.com/baseball/mlb/news/1998/06/21/obit_campanis_lead/; Peter Schmuck, "Remembering Al Campanis," *Sporting News*, June 29, 1998.

13. Consumers, however, would pay indirectly for the bonanza of televised sport, because advertising drove up the prices. As cable television emerged, they would pay directly, too.

14. Rob Ruck, *Sandlot Seasons: Sport in Black Pittsburgh* (Champaign: University of Illinois Press, 1987), pp. 194–201. The nature of minor league ownership also changed, as local ownership faded and most surviving minor league teams became part of major league farm systems.

15. Ruck, *Sandlot Seasons*, pp. 195–99.

16. Jackson, "We Have a Serious Problem."

17. Ibid.

18. See Bret L. Billet and Lance J. Formwalt, *America's National Pastime: A Study of Race and Merit in Professional Baseball* (Westport, CT: Praeger, 1995), pp. 21–22; Rod Carew interview with John O'Dell, January 24, 2009.

19. Marvin Miller, *A Whole Different Ballgame: The Sport and Business of Baseball* (New York: Birch Lane, 1991), p. 39.

20. Ira Berkow, "Generation Gap for Blacks in Baseball," *New York Times*, February 15, 1999.

21. Scott Kendrick, "2009 Baseball Team Payrolls," December 23, 2009, About.com: Baseball, http://baseball.about.com/od/newsrumors/a/09teamsalaries.htm, accessed September 28, 2009.

22. Brent Staples, *New York Times*, May 17, 1987; Billet and Formwalt, *America's National Pastime*, discusses several of these studies, pp. 21–22, 28; Scully, *The Business of Major League Baseball*, pp. 173–78.

23. Additional choices were awarded teams that lost players to free agency.

24. Chris Isidore, "Green Behind Decline of Blacks in Baseball," April 13, 2007, http://money.cnn.com/2007/04/13/commentary/sportsbiz/index.htm.

25. Frank B. Butts, Laura M. Harfield, and Lance C. Hatfield, "African-Americans in College Baseball," *Sport Journal*, http://thesportjournal.org/article/african-americans-college-baseball, accessed September 17, 2009; John Helyar, "Robinson Would Have Mixed View of Today's Game," ESPN.com, April 9, 2007, http://sports.espn.go.com/mlb/jackie/news/story?id=28285842, accessed July 3, 2009.

26. Allan Simpson, "A Black and White Issue," Perfect Game USA (n.d. but sometime in 2009), http://www.pgcrosschecker.com/Articles/DisplayArticle.aspx?article=563.

27. Butts, Harfield, and Hatfield, "African-Americans in College Baseball"; David Ogden and Randall A. Rose, "Using Giddens's Structuration Theory to Examine the Waning Participation of African Americans in Baseball," *Journal of Black Studies* 35, no. 4 (March 2005), p. 230; Vahe Gregorian, "Blacks Are Fading from Baseball," STLtoday.com, June 19, 2006, accessed October 13, 2009, www.accessmylibrary.com/archive/5976-st-louis-postdispatch-st-louis-mo./june-2006.html.

28. Tom Verducci, "Blackout," *Sports Illustrated*, July 7, 2003.

29. Quoted in Joseph A. Reaves, "Generation Gap for Blacks in Baseball," *Arizona Republic*, April 15, 2007.

30. Quoted in Verducci, "Blackout."

31. Table CH-3, "Living Arrangements of Black Children Under 18 Years Old: 1960 to Present," U.S. Bureau of Census, Annual Social and Economic Supplement: 2003, Current Population Survey, Series P20–553, *America's Families and Living Arrangements: 2003* (Washington, DC: U.S. Census Bureau, 2003), www.census.gov/population/www.socdemo/hh-fam.html; William Darity Jr. and Samuel L. Myers Jr., "Changes in Black Family Structure: Implications for Welfare Dependency," *American Economic Review* 73, no. 2 (May 1983), pp. 59–64.

32. Marvin Miller, *A Whole Different Ball Game: The Sport and Business of Baseball* (Secaucus, NJ: Carol, 1991), pp. 82, 141.

33. Quoted in Dave Anderson, "A Flame Grew in Brooklyn," *New York Times*, December 5, 1971.

34. Brad Snyder's *A Well-Paid Slave: Curt Flood's Fight for Free Agency in Professional Sports* (New York: Penguin, 2006) is a splendid account of Flood and his struggles; see also Miller, *A Whole Different Ball Game*, pp. 185–86.

35. Bill Nunn Jr. and *Ebony* quoted in Charles Korr, *The End of Baseball As We Knew It* (Urbana: University of Illinois Press, 2002), p. 97.

36. Brent Staples, "Where Are the Black Fans?" *New York Times*, May 17, 1987.

37. These statistics were compiled by Sean Lahman, *The Pro Football Historical Abstract: A Hardcore Fan's Guide to All-Time Player Rankings* (Guilford, CT: Lyons, 2008), pp. 25–27.

38. Brad Muster, "Minority Hiring Practices in Professional Sports," *Sport Journal* 4, no. 4 (fall 2001), www.thesportjournal.org/article/minority-hiring-practices-professional-sports, accessed May 21, 2010.

39. *Bloomberg Businessweek*, "The Racial Gap in the Grandstands," October 2, 2006, www.businessweek.com/magazine/content/06_40/b4003093.htm.

40. Staples, "Where Are the Black Fans?"

41. Michael Crowley, "The Case Against Michael Jordan," *Boston Phoenix*, January 25, 1999, is one of many stories that have attributed this quote to Jordan.

42. Walter LaFeber, *Michael Jordan and the New Global Capitalism* (New York: Norton, 2002), pp. 73–74, 137.

43. William C. Rhoden, *$40 Million Slaves: The Rise, Fall, and Redemption of the New Black Athlete* (New York: Crown, 2006), p. 140.

44. Rhoden, *$40 Million Slaves*, p. 140.

45. Jeffrey M. Jones, "Football Remains Runaway Leader as Favorite Sport," December 29, 2008, www .gallup.com/poll/113503/Football-Remains-Runaway-Leader-Favorite-Sport.aspx?version=print; David W. Moore and Joseph Carroll, "Baseball Fan Numbers Steady, but Decline May Be Pending," September 5, 2002, www.gallup.com/poll/6745/baseball-fan-numbers-steady-decline-may -pending.aspx, accessed October 7, 2009; Gallup Poll, "Baseball," www.gallup.com/poll/1696/ Baseball .aspx?version=print, accessed October 7, 2009; Harris Poll, "Football Expands Lead Over Baseball as America's Favorite Sport," February 1, 2010, www.harrisinteractive.com/vault/ Harris_Interactive_Poll_Sports_Popularity_2010_02.pdf.

Chapter Nine: The Rise of the Academies

1. Steve Wulf, "Standing Tall at Short," *Sports Illustrated*, February 9, 1987.

2. Murray Chass, "A New Baseball Strategy: Latin-American Bargains," *New York Times*, March 22, 1998.

3. Roberto Caines, interviews, June and July 1987, January and June 1988, Consuelo, DR.

4. Caines interviews.

5. Rob Ruck, *The Tropic of Baseball: Baseball in the Dominican Republic*, rev. ed. (Lincoln: University of Nebraska Press, 1998), pp. 140–45.

6. Coleridge Mayers, interviews, July 1987, San Pedro de Macorís.

7. Ruck, *The Tropic of Baseball*, pp. 140–45.

8. Armando Carty, interview, July 1988, San Pedro de Macorís.

9. William Joseph, interviews, June and July 1988, Consuelo, DR.

10. Sebastián "Basilio" Ferdinand, interview, January 1988, San Pedro de Macorís.

11. Caines interviews.

12. Mayers interviews.

13. Joseph interviews; Winston Richards, interview, July 19, 1988, San Pedro de Macorís.

14. The Reverend Joseph Ainslie, interview, August 1987, Seeley's Bay, Ontario, Canada.

15. Ruck, *The Tropic of Baseball*, pp. 139 and 164.

16. Chass, "A New Baseball Strategy."

17. Kevin Barker, "Avila Led the Charge in MLB's Latin Revolution," ESPN.com, http://sports .espn.go.com/espn/hispanichistory/news/story?id=2607258, accessed July 24, 2010.

18. Juan Marichal, interview, July 4, 1987, Campos Las Palmas, DR.

19. Ruck, *The Tropic of Baseball*, p. 170.

20. Chass, "A New Baseball Strategy."

21. Alan Klein, *Growing the Game: The Globalization of Major League Baseball* (New Haven, CT: Yale University Press, 2006), pp. 96–97. Klein's *Sugarball* (New Haven, CT: Yale University Press, 1991) is an insightful portrait of Dominican baseball in the 1980s with a perceptive description and analysis of the academies. He returned to these questions in his magisterial *Growing the Game*, in which he globalizes the discussion.

22. Rob Ruck, "Japanese Turning Dominican's Beisbol into Besuboru," *Washington Post*, July 21, 1992.

23. Chass, "A New Baseball Strategy."

24. Juan Marichal, interview, January 16, 2010, Santo Domingo.

25. Ruck, *The Tropic of Baseball*, pp. 50–51.

26. Klein, *Growing the Game*, pp. 96–97.

27. Melissa Segura, "Nationals Prospect Falsified Identity," SI.com, February 17, 2009, http://sports illustrated.cnn.com/2009/baseball/mlb/02/17/nats.gonzalez/; and Melissa Segura, "When Signing a Dominican Prospect, It's Buyer Beware," SI.com, March 2, 2009, http://sportsillustrated .cnn.com/2009/writers/melissa_segura/03/02/dr.investigators/index.html.

28. Dominican Baseball Camp, "Player Development," www.dominicanbaseballcamp.com/ playerdevelopment.htm, accessed November 12, 2009; Joel Millman, "Foreign Talent Loads the Bases in Minor Leagues," WSJ.com, August 15, 2009, http://online.wsj.com/article/ SB124966930911615069.html.

29. Barry Svrluga, "Tapping In to an Economy of Sale," *Washington Post*, December 21, 2006; Melissa Segura, "When Signing a Dominican Prospect." SI.com, March 2, 2009.

30. Luke Cyphers, "Haitian Sensations: Behind the Rise of the Haitian-Dominican Player," ESPN .com, March 10, 2009, http://espn.go.com/mlb/insider/news/story?id=3974286&action= . . . 2finsider.espn.go.com%62fmlb%newsfstory%3fid%3d3974286; Patrick Clark, "The Dominican Game," Triplecanopy, www.canopycanopycanopy.com5/the_dominican_game, accessed February 25, 2008.

31. Christian Red, "Steve Swindal's Boca Chica Baseball Academy Prospects Look Strong," *New York Daily News*, October 18, 2009, www.nydailynews.com/sports/baseball/2009/10/18/2009–10–18 _steve_swindals_prospects_look_strong.html?print, accessed November 9, 2009.

32. Several individuals who worked for the Yankees, White Sox, and Red Sox lost their jobs after being implicated in the skimming. Few of those working in the island's baseball industry were surprised at the practice. Jorge L. Ortiz, "Exploitation, Steroids Hitting Home in Dominican Republic," *USA Today*, March 26, 2009.

33. Jonathan M. Katz and Dionisio Soldevila, "For Some Dominican Players, Steroids Worth the Risk," Associated Press, September 26, 2009.

34. Marichal interview.

35. Ortiz, "Exploitation, Steroids Hitting Home in the Dominican Republic."

36. Jesse Sanchez, "Game Regains Status in Puerto Rico," MLB.com, http://mlb.mlb.com/news/ article.jsp?ymd=20100629&content_id=11719758&vkey=news_mlb&fext=.jsp&c_id=mlb; Ken Belson, "Puerto Rico's Baseball Pipeline Runs Low," *New York Times*, June 28, 2010. In 2001, former major league pitcher Edwin Correa created the Puerto Rico Baseball Academy and High School. The academy, which MLB subsidizes, has seen more than seventy of its players drafted.

37. Milton H. Jamail, *Venezuelan Bust, Baseball Boom: Andres Reiner and Scouting on the New Frontier* (Lincoln: University of Nebraska Press, 2008), is a penetrating analysis of Venezuelan baseball and its connection to major league baseball and the nation's culture.

38. Ruck, *The Tropic of Baseball*, p. 186.

39. Jorge L. Ortiz, "Puerto Rican Baseball Seeks Return to Glory," USATODAY.com, January 24, 2006, www.usatoday.com/sports/baseball/2006-01-24-puerto-rico-winter-league-slump_x.htm.

40. Ibid.

Epilogue

1. Juan Marichal, interview, January 16, 2010, Santo Domingo.

2. "The Dominican Republic and Haiti: Helping a Neighbour In Need, A Break in a History of Mistrust," *Economist*, February 18, 2010.

3. Jean Damu, "Haiti: Blood, Sweat and Baseball," *San Francisco Bay View*, January 24, 2010, www.sfbayview.com/2010/haiti-blood-sweat-and-baseball/; Michel-Rolph Trouillot, *Haiti: State Against Nation: The Origins and Legacy of Duvalierism* (New York: Monthly Review Press, 1990), p. 202.

4. Karen Crouse, "In Helping Haiti, Pierre Garcon Wins Fans in Little Miami," *New York Times*, February 2, 2010.

5. Dominican Republic News and Travel Information Service, www.Dr1.com, March 12, 2010.

6. Marichal interview.

7. Junior Noboa, interview, January 15, 2010, Santo Domingo.

8. Rob Ruck, *The Tropic of Baseball: Baseball in the Dominican Republic*, rev. ed. (Lincoln: University of Nebraska Press, 1998), pp. 199–202; Milton H. Jamail, *Venezuelan Bust, Baseball Boom: Andres Reiner and Scouting on the New Frontier* (Lincoln: University of Nebraska Press, 2008), pp. 219–20.

9. Tim Wendel, *The New Face of Baseball: The 100-Year Rise and Triumph of Latinos in America's Favorite Sport* (New York: Harper Collins, 2003).

10. Bill Center, "Jones to Start Career on Suspension," *San Diego Union-Tribune*, May 22, 2010, www.signonsandiego.com/news/2010/may/22/jones-start-career-suspension/.

11. Michael Schmidt, "Five-Tool Player, One Set of Prints," *New York Times*, February 10, 2010; Michael Schmidt, "Dominican Prospects Will Face Strict Rules," *New York Times*, May 7, 2010, www.nytimes.com/2010/05/08/sports/baseball/08drugs.html.

12. Jeff Passan, "Alderson Addresses Dominican Corruption," Yahoo! Sports, April 22, 2010, http://sports.yahoo.com/mlb/news?slug=jp-dominican042210; Alden Gonzalez, "No Plans to Include Dominicans in Draft," MLB.com, April 19, 2010, http://mlb.mlb.com/news/article.jsp?ymd=20100419&content_id=9420804&vkey=news_mlb&fext=.jsp&c_id=mlb.

13. Noboa interview.

14. Schmidt, "Dominican Prospects Will Face Strict Rules."

15. Marichal interview.

16. Trevor Gooby, interview, January 17, 2010, La Gina.

17. Marichal interview.

18. Jonathan Mahler, "Building the Béisbol Brand," *New York Times*, July 31, 2005; Douglas Eikermann, "Hispanic Fans Critical to Major League Baseball," HispanicBusiness.com, July 10, 2008, http://news.newamericamedia.org/news/view_article.html?article_id=8f6c40cc51d9d391420b562189ffc007. For CFU Institute for Diversity and Ethics in Sport study, see Richard Lapchick with Alejandra Diaz-Calderon and Derek McMechan, *The 2009 Racial and Gender Report Card: Major League Baseball*, April 15, 2009, www.tidesport.org/RGRC/2009/2009_MLB_RGRC_PR_Final_rev.pdf.

19. David Waldstein, "On Robinson's Day, a Met Reflects," *New York Times*, April 16, 2010; "Mixed News in Report on Diversity," *New York Times*, April 30, 2010.

20. Ben Nicholson-Smith, "Mets Release Gary Matthews Jr.," MLB Trade Rumors, June 15, 2010, www.mlbtraderumors.com/2010/06/mets-release-gary-matthews-jr.html.

21. Richard Berlin, interview, October 15, 2009.

22. CBSSports.com, "MLB Salaries," www.cbssports.com/mlb/salaries/top50?tag=pageRow;page Container.

INDEX

Page references in italics refer to photographs.

Aaron, Henry "Hank": ability of, 106; in All-Star Game, 178; Campanis interview and, 173; Clemente and, 147; in Hall of Fame, 104; integration and, 95; Wilson, August, and, 114

ABC (TV network), 112–13, 172–73

academies: ability and, 219; in Dominican Republic, 194, 196–99, 206–17, 218–19, 225, 226–27, 230–31; education and, 208–9, 230–31; Major League Baseball and, 196–99, 206–19, 226–27, 230–31; salaries and, 209; scouting and, 208–9, 213; in Venezuela, 194, 210–12, 217–18

African Americans: ability of, generally, 24–25, 47–48, 81, 92, 98–100, 104–7, 172–74, 181, 183; in administration, 175; amateur baseball and, 20–21, 34–35, 37–39; college baseball and, 185–86; commercialization and, 180; community and, ix–x, 101, 114–15, 176–77, 187–88, 232–33, 234–35; in Cuba, 11–12; in economy, 74–75; education and, 185; fans among, 191–92, 194; free agency and, 183–84; Great Migration of, 28–30, 33–34; high school baseball and, 185–87; integration and, generally, 74–75, 88–89, 233; interracial discord and, xi, 166–67; during Jim Crow era, 20–22, 24–25, 28; in Major League Baseball, generally, viii, ix–x, xii–xiii, 177–80, 190–91, 231–32; management by, 172–77, 181, 185, 231; as mascots, 21; in National Basketball Association, x; in National Football League, x; on New York Yankees, vii–viii, ix–x, xiii; ownership by, 233; player procurement and, 183–84, 185–88; Players Association and, 188–90; population of, x, 74, 75–76, 191;

pride of, 46–48, 113; professional baseball, early, 21–22, 24–25; quotas for, 108, 109; salaries and, 183–84; segregation of, generally, 20–22, 24–25; during slavery, 19; World War II and, 74–75

age minimums, 213–14, 227–31

agents. See *buscones*; player procurement

Aguilas baseball club, 52–53, 56, 59–60

Alemán, Miguel, 67, 68, 120

Alexander, Clifford, 175, 176

Ali, Muhammad, 190, 192

All-American Girls Professional Baseball League, 74

All Nations baseball club, 30–31, 63

all-star games: East-West Classic, 26, 46, 83, 89; in Major League Baseball, 46, 106–7, 158, 167, 177–78, 196, 199

Almeida, Rafael, 16, 43, 73

Almendares baseball club, 3, 4, 12–13, 14, 137

Alou, Felipe, 161; ability of, 158, 167; in All-Star Game, 158; cricket and, 204; in Dominican Republic, 144, 160, 162, 163, 230; early career of, 149; fines against, 161, 162–63; as manager, 177; Milwaukee Braves and, 164; New York Giants and, 149–51; Peña, Orlando, and, 161; racism and, 149–51, 163–64, 167, 209; Robinson, Jackie, and, 146; San Francisco Giants and, 148, 154–57, 158, 162–64, 165

Alou, Jesús, 151, 154, 162, 165

Alou, Mateo: ability of, 167; Clemente and, 170; early career of, 152–53; New York Giants and, 153; racism and, 153–54; San Francisco Giants and, 151, 154–57, 158, 161, 165; in World Series, 158

258